Spicer and Pegler's
Book-keeping and Accounts
Workbook

To my mother and father

Spicer and Pegler's
Book-keeping and Accounts
Workbook

Paul Gee, BA, FCA
Principal Lecturer, Bristol Business
School, Bristol Polytechnic

Butterworths
London
1988

United Kingdom	Butterworth & Co (Publishers) Ltd, 88 Kingsway, LONDON WC2B 6AB and 61A North Castle Street, EDINBURGH EH2 3LJ
Australia	Butterworths Pty Ltd, SYDNEY, MELBOURNE, BRISBANE, ADELAIDE, PERTH, CANBERRA and HOBART
Canada	Butterworths. A division of Reed Inc., TORONTO and VANCOUVER
New Zealand	Butterworths of New Zealand Ltd, WELLINGTON and AUCKLAND
Singapore	Butterworth & Co (Asia) Pte Ltd, SINGAPORE
USA	Butterworths Legal Publishers, ST PAUL, Minnesota, SEATTLE, Washington, BOSTON, Massachusetts, AUSTIN, Texas and D & S Publishers, CLEARWATER, Florida

British Library Cataloguing in Publication Data

Spicer, E. E. (Ernest Evan)
  Spicer and Pegler's Book-keeping and accounts workbook.
  1. Accounting – Questions & answers
  I. Title II. Pegler, Ernest Charles
  III. Gee, Paul
  657'.076

ISBN 0 406 67813 8

Typeset by Phoenix Photosetting, Chatham
Printed and bound in Great Britain by
Billings Bookplan, Worcester

PREFACE

Spicer and Pegler's Book-keeping and Accounts has established itself over many years as one of the leading textbooks on financial accounting. In recent years it has been apparent that a demand exists for an accompanying workbook. This companion volume, together with the main textbook, provides a comprehensive learning package which it is hoped will prove invaluable to both students and lecturers.

In order to assist students and lecturers the chapters of the workbook correspond with those of the main textbook. The questions are progressive, thus helping to ensure that the learning process is as effective as possible. The workbook seeks to achieve a careful balance between essay question and computational question and between questions set in previous years by leading professional bodies and original questions. All the solutions in the workbook are my own.

I would like to pay particular thanks to Jane Leonard and Debbie Thom for all their help with the preparation of this volume and to my family for their encouragement and forebearance.

Paul Gee
Bristol Business School
March 1988

CONTENTS

Preface   v
Acknowledgments   xi
How to use the Workbook   xiii

QUESTIONS

		Grade	Marks	Source

ACKNOWLEDGMENTS

The following acknowledgments are gratefully made:

To The Institute of Chartered Accountants in England and Wales
and The Chartered Association of Certified Accountants

for permission to reproduce previous examination questions.

HOW TO USE THE WORKBOOK

Within each chapter questions are arranged in increasing order of difficulty. Questions marked basic are not generally of examination standard but are intended to help students grasp the fundamentals of the particular topic. These questions should be attempted first in order to help build up confidence!

Questions marked intermediate are of examination standard but do not include the more complex types of examination questions. Advanced questions include the more difficult type of examination question and should not be attempted until all relevant basic and intermediate questions have been completed. These advanced questions include case study questions set by the Chartered Association of Certified Accountants in the Advanced Accounting Practice Paper.

The source of each past examination question is identified by the following key. This should help students and lecturers relate questions to the current level of their studies.

Key

B = Basic
I = Intermediate
A = Advanced

ICAEW	=	Institute of Chartered Accountants in England and Wales
ACCA	=	Association of Certified Accountants
AT	=	Accounting Techniques
AAP	=	Advanced Accounting Practice
FA1	=	Financial Accounting 1
FA2	=	Financial Accounting 2
RFA	=	Regulatory Framework of Accounts
AFA	=	Advanced Financial Accounting

The solutions to computational questions generally start with workings followed by main solution as this is likely to correspond with the sequence followed in the examination room. Some solutions are presented in brief form as answer guides and aim to provide guidance as to structure of narrative-type solutions.

Whatever the temptation, please ensure that you have a proper attempt at each question before referring to the solution! An audit of the solution provided is hardly an effective way of learning and is unlikely to ensure future examination success. A careful analysis of your own solutions, strengths and weaknesses, will be far more effective!

1 INCOMPLETE RECORDS

QUESTION 1.1 (BASIC)

Patterdale

Patterdale has traded for many years as an electrical retailer. Unfortunately his accounting records leave much to be desired and his accountant valiantly attempts each year to produce a set of final accounts from incomplete records. The accountant has been able to establish the following information so far:

(1) Summary of bank account:

	£
Balance at 1.1.X3	297
Cheques and cash banked	192,495
	192,792
Payments to suppliers	(135,570)
Wages (staff)	(4,200)
Drawings	(22,200)
Sundry expenses	(340)
Rent, rates, telephone and insurance	(17,100)
Motor expenses	(7,500)
Repairs and renewals	(960)
Balance at 31.12.X3	4,922

(2) Position at 31.12.X2

	£
Stock	24,800
Debtors	19,500
Cash at bank	297
Cash at hand	530
Van – cost less depreciation	2,500
Creditors	(9,700)
Opening capital account	37,927

(3) Gross profit percentage is estimated at 30%.
(4) Depreciation is to be provided at 20% per annum on a reducing balance basis.
(5) Expenses paid out of cash takings prior to banking:

	£
Purchases	2,030
Sundry expenses	200
Motor expenses	900

(6) Balances at 31.12.X3 are calculated as follows:

	£
Stock	21,200
Debtors	21,400
Creditors	8,500
Cash in hand	405

(7) Any cash unaccounted for is to be treated as drawings.

Required

A trading and profit and loss account for the year ended 31 December 19X3 and a balance sheet as at that date.

Note: Ignore accruals and prepayments for expense and value-added tax.   (15 marks)

QUESTION 1.2 (INTERMEDIATE)

Hoffman

On 31 October 19X1 the petty cashier at Hoffman Ltd left in mysterious circumstances, taking the petty cash box and its contents with him.

The petty cash book was last written up to 30 September 19X1 at which date the balance carried down was £254. On that date the accountant had noted that there was £65 cash in the box.

You ascertain that, prior to 30 September 19X1, vouchers for £47 had not been entered and that there was a traveller's float outstanding of £32. £40 had been loaned by the cashier to wages department. The debit side of the petty cash book had been overcast by £10.

During the month ended 31 October 19X1 the following transactions took place:

(1) Cash was drawn from the bank totalling £743.
(2) The traveller claimed expenses amounting to £76 and increased his float to £40.
(3) Petty cash payments totalling £472 were made in addition to (2) above.
(4) Wages department repaid the loan.
(5) A payment entered on a voucher as £43 should have stated £34. You establish that the amount overpaid had been refunded by the claimant to the petty cashier.
(6) The sales manager took out a float of £100 in cash.
(7) A cheque was cashed for £75 by the managing director. The cheque was banked on 29 October.

Required

You are required to draft a memorandum to the managing director, incorporating your calculation of the petty cashier's defalcations.

(13 marks)

(ICAEW, AT, Nov 81)

QUESTION 1.3 (ADVANCED)

George

For many years George has been a self-employed music teacher. In his spare time, George paints water colours of local scenery. In recent years, he has been able to sell an increasing number of his paintings but has not kept any record of the income received from these sales. George is considering an additional mortgage and wants to demonstrate to the Building Society the income he has received from the sales of paintings. He has asked you to prepare a statement comparing his income and outgoings in order to arrive at an estimate of this income.

From discussions with George, and from an examination of his papers, you are able to establish the following:

(1) The profits from George's work as a music teacher, for which he is paid wholly in cash, have been as follows:

Year ended	£
30 June 19X1	5,533
30 June 19X2	6,923
30 June 19X3	7,428
30 June 19X4	7,550

(2) At 30 June:

	19X0 £	19X1 £	19X2 £	19X3 £	19X4 £
(i) Bank current account balance:					
In hand	720	140	—	—	—
Overdrawn	—	—	2,046	1,105	275
Interest debited thereon during the year	—	—	271	148	73
(ii) Bank deposit account balance	—	850	1,100	3,200	4,100
Interest credited thereon during the year	—	72	95	265	385
(iii) Building Society account balance	230	245	420	650	750
Interest credited thereon during the year	20	18	50	30	40
(iv) Premium bonds held	200	250	600	600	800
(v) National Savings Certificates held	—	500	500	1,000	1,000

(3) The normal living expenditure of George and his family is estimated at £6,000 for the year to 30 June 19X1, rising by £1,000 per year to £9,000 for the year to 30 June 19X4. This excludes holiday costs. These are approximately £1,200 each year, payable in May. In March 19X2 George and his family also had a winter holiday which cost about £1,850.

(4) In December 19X1, George bought his wife Mary a fur coat costing £1,740.

(5) In September 19X2, George's daughter married and he had additional expenditure of £975.

(6) In May 19X4 George bought a new personal car for £7,200 plus the trade-in of his old car which had been acquired in 19W8 (19W8 is 10 years before 19X8).

(7) Mary had a part time job in a restaurant throughout the period under review, earning £30 per week up to 30 June 19X1 and £40 per week thereafter. In addition to her wages it is estimated that she received tips amounting to about £15 per week. She also received a wage of £30 per week from George's music business for arranging appointments. This wage has been charged in arriving at the profits for the music business.

(8) In September 19X1, George had a premium bond win of £500.

(9) On 30 April 19X4 George received £4,700, being the proceeds of an endowment policy on which, up to one year previously, he had been paying annual premiums of £240.

(10) George's income tax payments were as follows:

| | 19X0 | 19X1 | 19X2 | 19X3 | 19X4 |
	£	£	£	£	£
1 January	850	898	1,200	1,109	983
1 July	850	898	1,200	1,109	983

(11) Total cash in hand is estimated at a constant figure of £200 throughout this period.

Required

A statement for each of the four years ended 30 June 19X1, 19X2, 19X3 and 19X4 in order to show the estimated income arising from the sales of paintings.

(18 marks)

(ICAEW, AT, Nov 84)

2 PARTNERSHIP ACCOUNTS (i)

QUESTION 2.1 (BASIC)

Turner and Bennett

Turner and Bennett were in partnership sharing profits and losses equally. Accounts are made up annually to 31 March.

On 1 October 19X6 Lloyd was admitted as a partner and it was agreed that profits and losses would be shared: Turner two-fifths, Bennett two-fifths and Lloyd one-fifth. For the purpose of this change goodwill is to be valued at £20,000.

The partners do not wish goodwill to appear in the balance sheet. Adjustments for goodwill are to be made in the partners' current accounts.

The trial balance of the partnership as at 31 March 19X7 was as follows:

	Dr	Cr
Freehold property	65,000	
Motor vehicles at cost	16,900	
Depreciation of vehicles at 1.4.X6		5,100
Fixtures at cost	12,600	
Depreciation on fixtures at 1.4.X6		2,800
Stock at 1.4.X6	5,600	
Debtors	14,800	
Creditors		15,600
Cash at bank	2,700	
Capital: Turner		15,000
Bennett		15,000
Cash introduced by Lloyd		11,000
Current account: Turner		4,800
Bennett		5,040
Drawings: Turner	15,400	
Bennett	14,900	
Lloyd	8,900	
Sales		98,500
Purchases	39,800	
Salaries and wages	16,300	
Rates, light and heat	1,900	
Telephone	1,240	
General expenses and insurance	1,450	
Bank interest	3,350	
Bank loan		48,000
	220,840	220,840

The following information is also available:

(a) Stock at 31 March 19X7 amounted to £6,000.
(b) It is estimated that one third of the sales occurred in the first 6 months and the remaining two-thirds in the second six months. The rate of gross profit remained constant.
(c) Included in general expenses is £350 relating to a sales conference attended by Turner and Bennett in July 19X6.
(d) Depreciation is to be provided on motor vehicles and fixtures at 25% on cost and 20% on cost respectively.
(e) Of the £11,000 introduced by Lloyd £7,500 is to be regarded as fixed capital.
(f) Light and heat owing at 31 March 19X7 amounted to £120.
(g) Insurance prepaid at 31 March 19X7 amounted to £110.

Required

(1) Trading and profit and loss account for the year ended 31 March 19X7.
(2) Partners current accounts.

(20 marks)

QUESTION 2.2. (INTERMEDIATE)

Kimm, Rawnsley and Flowers

Kimm, Rawnsley and Flowers are in partnership as antiquarian booksellers. Profits and losses are shared equally.

The trial balance of the partnership at 31 August 19X4 is as follows:

	£	£
Purchases	164,297	
Wages	16,240	
Sales		243,614
Stock as on 1 September 19X3	24,476	
Capital:		
Kimm		36,400
Rawnsley		27,050
Flowers		19,750
Drawings – Year ending 31 August 19X4		
Kimm	7,900	
Rawnsley	3,640	
Flowers	6,970	
Rent and Rates	22,464	
Trade expenses	1,497	
Trade creditors		26,249
Trade debtors	27,397	
Bank balance	10,483	
Telephone and postage	2,722	
Stationery and advertising	1,936	
Tenants' improvements	21,791	
Goodwill	41,250	
	353,063	353,063

Stock as on 31 August 19X4 is £27,240.

The capital accounts of Kimm, Rawnsley and Flowers are represented by goodwill, undrawn profits, and fixed capital of £6,000 per partner.

With the exception of matters referred to below, all other adjustments affecting the draft accounts have been incorporated in the trial balance.

You are provided with the following additional information relating to the partnership:

(1) Kimm commenced to trade as a sole trader on 1 September 19X1. He introduced fixed capital of £6,000.
(2) It had been agreed that on admission of partners, goodwill, which was to be shown in the accounts, would be valued at one and a half times the preceding year's profits. Surpluses arising from revaluations of goodwill were to be credited to partners' accounts. Incoming partners were to pay into the partnership for their share of goodwill.
(3) Rawnsley was admitted as an equal partner on 1 September 19X2. He introduced £6,000 capital and £6,900 for his share of goodwill.
(4) On 1 September 19X3 Flowers was admitted as an equal partner. He introduced £6,000 for capital and £13,750 for his share of goodwill.
(5) The partners are concerned at the increasing value of goodwill in the accounts and ask you to eliminate goodwill as at 31 August 19X4.
(6) Tenants' improvements, all of which relate to the year ended 31 August 19X4, are written off over three years.

Required

(a) the journal entries reflecting the transactions listed above for the three years ended 31 August 19X4 (9 marks), and
(b) a trading and profit and loss account for the year ended 31 August 19X4 and a balance sheet at 31 August 19X4, with goodwill eliminated from the accounts (5 marks).

(14 marks)

(ICAEW, AT, Nov 82)

QUESTION 2.3 (ADVANCED)

Vic

On 1 March 19X4 Vic commenced business as a wholesaler of confectionery, operating from premises rented for £2,000 per annum and using a van owned by him which had a value, at 1 March 19X4, of £6,000. He opened a business bank account into which he paid £5,000 of his own funds and £20,000 borrowed from his friend Bobby. It was agreed that Bobby would receive interest of 8% per annum on this loan, together with a commission of 6% of the net profits of the business after all charges except for this commission.

From 1 April 19X4, Vic employed an assistant, Tom, at a salary of £7,200 per annum and from 1 December 19X4 a clerk was employed at a salary of £3,600 per annum. On 1 September 19X4, Tom's employment terminated and he was taken into partnership on the basis that he would receive two fifths of the profits, after all charges, accruing from that date. Tom agreed to introduce cash of £4,000 and his estate car, which had a value of £4,200 on 1 September 19X4, into the partnership. Tom's salary ceased on 31 August 19X4 but he continued to receive the same amount each month as drawings. Vic and Tom also agreed that no interest was to be allowed or charged on capital accounts or drawings, and that the profit should be deemed to accrue evenly over the year to 28 February 19X5 for the purpose of its allocation.

Only limited records are kept from which you are able to ascertain the following:

(1) Bank statements for the year to 28 February 19X5 are available and show the following total receipts and payments:

	£
Receipts: Cash introduced	29,000
Credit customers	270,000
Cash banked	164,000
	463,000
Payments: Suppliers for purchases	470,000
Cash float	200
Insurance premiums	1,780
Bank charges	460
Rent	2,500
	474,940

(2) Payments made out of cash takings were as follows:

	£
Salaries and drawings	16,750
Motor expenses	7,410
Sundry expenses	1,740
Weighing scales (second hand)	1,600
Stationery	640

(3) After payment of the items noted above and the retention of a float of £200, all cash received has been banked, and all cheques received from credit customers have been banked.
(4) Motor vehicles are to be depreciated at the rate of 20% per annum, and the scales, which were bought on 1 December 19X4, at 25% per annum.
(5) On 28 February 19X5:
    (i) Cheques from credit customers totalling £2,140 and cash bankings of £4,260 paid into the bank had not yet appeared on the bank statement.

(ii) Stock on hand, all of which was of good saleable quality, cost £34,750.
(iii) Suppliers' unpaid invoices amounted to £7,250 and £430 was owing for sundry expenses.
(iv) Credit customers owed £11,470 of which £600 related to a customer who was bankrupt. Vic does not consider that any payment will be received from this customer.
(v) The insurance premiums paid were in respect of the year to 28 February 19X5, except for a premium of £420 which was in respect of temporary cover for frost damage for the three months to 31 March 19X5.

Required

Prepare a trading and profit and loss account for the business for the year ended 28 February 19X5 and a balance sheet as on that date.

(30 marks)

(ICAEW, AT, May 85)

3 PARTNERSHIP ACCOUNTS (ii)

QUESTION 3.1 (INTERMEDIATE)

Bruce, Henry and Malcolm

Bruce, Henry and Malcolm are in partnership as architects, sharing profits in the ratio of 5:3:2 after each partner has been credited with a salary of £6,000 per annum. The partnership agreement states that on a change of partners any excess in the value of work in progress over its book amount is to be adjusted through capital accounts between the old and new partners. On 30 June 19X4 Bruce retired and his nephew, Walter, was admitted to the partnership. Walter is entitled to 30% of the profits of the new partnership with the balance being shared equally between Henry and Malcolm. The summarised trial balance of the old partnership at 30 June 19X4 was as follows:

	£	£
Capital accounts: Bruce		4,173
Henry	21,948	
Malcolm	11,206	
Debtors	46,205	
Work in progress at 1 July 19X3	2,000	
Expenses	139,722	
Reference library	100	
Bank overdraft		11,170
Creditors for expenses		17,406
Fees rendered to clients		188,432
	221,181	221,181

You are supplied with the following additional information:

(1) The partners estimate that the realisable value of work done but not billed at 30 June 19X4 amounted to £37,000. For the purposes of the accounts, work in progress is to remain at £2,000.
(2) Full provision is required at 30 June 19X4 against a debt of £1,150 due from a client.
(3) It was agreed between the three old partners and the new partner that the following two further adjustments are to be made:
   (i) The reference library is considered to be worth £1,500 and is to be included in the books of the new partnership at that amount.
   (ii) Goodwill of the partnership, which is to be included in the books of the new partnership, is to be valued at one half of the profit of the partnership (before any charge for partners' salaries) as reflected in the accounts for the year to 30 June 19X4.
(4) On 1 July 19X4 Bruce transferred to Walter £10,000 of the amount due to him from the old partnership. The balance due to Bruce is to be repaid over three years, commencing on 1 July 19X5.
(5) On 1 July 19X4 Walter introduced cash of £7,500 to the partnership.

Required

(a) the profit and loss account of the old partnership for the year ended 30 June 19X4 and a balance sheet as on that date (9 marks);
(b) journal entries to reflect the partnership changes (detailed narrative is not required) (7 marks); and
(c) the opening balance sheet of the new partnership as on 1 July 19X4 (6 marks).

(22 marks)

(ICAEW, AT, Nov 84)

QUESTION 3.2 (INTERMEDIATE)

Martin and Norman

Martin and Norman have been partners, sharing profits equally, for many years. They manufacture office furniture. Both wish to retire and they have agreed to sell the assets and liabilities of their business, with effect from 1 April 19X5, to Oliver plc for £330,000. The draft partnership balance sheet as on 31 March 19X5 was as follows:

	Cost £	Depreciation £	£
Freehold property	173,000	37,400	135,600
Plant and equipment	214,700	107,400	107,300
Stock		132,470	
Debtors		84,330	216,800
Bank overdraft		(105,200)	
Creditors		(97,140)	(202,340)
			257,360
Partners' capital accounts: Martin			140,680
Norman			116,680
			257,360

The consideration for the sale of the business is to be discharged as follows:

– Martin to receive one half on the amount due to him in cash with the balance to be settled by the allotment to him of 70,000 ordinary shares of £1 each in Oliver plc, credited as fully paid.
– Norman to receive sufficient 8% debentures, issued at a discount of 10%, to give him an annual income of £10,200 with the balance satisfied in cash.

Oliver plc has received professional advice that the fair value of the freehold property is £210,000 and of the plant and equipment, £80,000. The book value of the other assets and liabilities of the partnership is considered to represent their fair value.

At 31 March 19X5 the summarised balance sheet of Oliver plc was as follows:

	Cost £	Depreciation £	£
Long leasehold property	875,000	121,407	753,593
Plant and equipment	1,217,400	573,208	644,192
Stock		1,407,108	
Debtors		875,906	
Cash and bank balances		147,100	2,430,114
Creditors		(1,395,400)	
8% Debenture Stock		(110,050)	(1,505,450)
			2,322,449
Share capital – shares of £1 each			
Authorised – £1,250,000			
Allotted, called up and fully paid			1,000,000
Profit and loss account			1,322,449
			2,322,449

Required

(a) Prepare the journal entry in the books of Oliver plc to record the acquisition of the partnership business.
(b) Prepare a 'proforma' balance sheet for Oliver plc as on 31 March 19X5 to show the effect of the acquisition of the partnership net assets assuming the acquisition had taken place on that date.

(17 marks)

(ICAEW, AT, May 85)

QUESTION 3.3 (ADVANCED)

Katie and Richard

Katie and Richard are in partnership running a toy shop. They share profits in the ratio 3:1. Sally is the sole proprietor of a newsagents shop which is next door to the toy shop. Katie, Richard and Sally agree to merge their businesses with effect from 1 July 19X5 with profits being shared Katie 40%, Richard 30% and Sally 30%.

The accounting records for each business were kept separately for the whole of the year ended 31 December 19X5 and no accounts were drawn up to 30 June 19X5. The trial balances for each business as on 31 December 19X5 were as follows:

	Toy shop £	Toy shop £	Newsagents £	Newsagents £
Sales		241,738		90,328
Purchases	154,208		51,443	
Stock at 31 December 19X4	17,422		1,477	
Lease premium	11,500		—	
Fixtures, net of depreciation	8,000		3,420	
Vehicles, net of depreciation	7,444		3,744	
Cash in hand	329		119	
Wages	17,942		16,257	
Rent and rates	13,720		7,720	
Repairs	1,446		811	
Bank interest to 31 December 19X5	630			197
Bank balance		7,244	3,062	
Creditors for goods		10,421		2,061
Electricity	2,241		516	
Telephones	824		227	
Current accounts: Katie	11,607			
Richard	12,090			
Sally				3,790
	259,403	259,403	92,586	92,586

You have been given the following information:

(1) For the purposes of the merger only, goodwill of the old business is to be calculated as one and a half times the average of the net profits of the respective businesses for the three years to 31 December 19X4. The profits have been as follows:

	Toy shop £	Newsagents £
Year to 31 December 19X2	20,428	8,227
Year to 31 December 19X3	32,661	12,427
Year to 31 December 19X4	36,751	18,206

No goodwill is to be carried in the books of the combined business.

(2) The lease of Katie and Richard's shop is considered to have been worth £8,000 on 1 July 19X5 and the lease of Sally's shop £3,500 on that date. These values are to be included in the accounts of the combined business and no depreciation is to be provided thereon between 1 July and 31 December 19X5.

(3) Fixtures and vehicles which have remained unchanged since 31 December 19X4 are to be introduced to the new business at their book values at that date less one half of the depreciation charge for the year to 31 December 19X5. Depreciation is to be provided on the reducing balance basis at the rates of 10% and 25% per annum on the fixtures and vehicles respectively.

(4) For the purpose of apportioning the profits for 19X5 before and after the merger it has been agreed that the gross profit of the newsagents business and the overheads of both businesses be deemed to accrue evenly over the year. The gross profit of the toy shop does not accrue evenly, and it has been agreed that two thirds of the gross profit be deemed to arise in the six months to 31 December 19X5.

(5) Stock at 31 December 19X5 amounted to £15,092 for the toy shop and £1,360 for the newsagents business.

(6) There are no accruals or prepayments required at 31 December 19X5.

(7) Katie, Richard and Sally each drew £1,000 per month from their respective businesses. Drawings by Katie and Richard were debited to their current accounts and drawings by Sally were charged to wages.

Required

(a) Prepare trading accounts for each business and a statement of the allocation of profit between Katie, Richard and Sally for the year ended 31 December 19X5 (12 marks).
(b) Prepare in columnar form the current accounts for Katie, Richard and Sally, showing the adjustments required to the figures included in the trial balances to reflect the matters referred to above (8 marks).
(c) Prepare the balance sheet of the new business as on 31 December 19X5 (3 marks).

(23 marks)

(ICAEW, AT, May 86)

4 COMPANY ACCOUNTS – BASIC CONSIDERATIONS

QUESTION 4.1 (BASIC)

Downdale

The trial balance of Downdale plc as at 31 December 19X6 is set out below:

	£'000	£'000
Freehold land and buildings		
– cost	860	
– accumulated depreciation		59
Motor vehicles		
– cost	240	
– accumulated depreciation		62
Stock at 1.1.X6	125	
Debtors	109	
Cash at bank	55	
Cash in hand	6	
Creditors		112
Sales		1,265
Purchases	703	
Wages and salaries	102	
Corporation tax		11
Directors' remuneration	38	
Rent, rates, telephone and insurance	69	
Heat, light and water	85	
Debenture interest	40	
10% debenture stock 19X23		400
Called up share capital (£1 ordinary shares)		150
Share premium account		50
Profit and loss account at 1.1.19X6		323
	2,432	2,432

The following additional information is relevant:

(1) Closing stock has been valued for accounts purposes at £141,000.
(2) The figure of £11,000 for corporation tax represents tax over-provided in 19X5. Corporation tax for the current year has been estimated at £65,000.
(3) Depreciation for 19X6 is to be charged as follows:

| Freehold buildings | £15,000 |
| Motor vehicles | £28,000 |

(4) The directors propose a dividend of £80,000 in respect of ordinary shares. Tax on dividends is to be ignored.

Required

A profit and loss account for the year ended 31 December 19X6 and a balance sheet as at that date. Ignore specific disclosure requirements of the Companies Act 1985.

(17 marks)

QUESTION 4.2 (INTERMEDIATE)

Prague

Prague Ltd manufactures and installs a range of replacement hardwood windows. The closing balances of Prague Ltd as on 31 August 19X4 were as follows:

	£	£
Plant and machinery – cost	29,427	
– depreciation		11,214
Commercial vehicles – cost	58,422	
– depreciation		47,507
Private cars – cost	19,633	
– depreciation		7,413
Stock and work in progress	186,475	
Debtors	220,980	
Cash in hand	432	
Bank overdraft		76,814
Trade creditors		137,452
Accrued commissions		33,147
Proposed dividend		5,400
Share capital – ordinary shares of £5 each		75,000
Retained profits		121,422
	515,369	515,369

You have established the following additional information relating to Prague Ltd:

(1) During the year ended 31 August 19X5:
   (i) Sales amounted to £1,731,400.
  (ii) Purchases were as follows:

Raw materials	£530,722
Manufacturing expenses	£141,677
Overheads	£ 63,849

  (iii) Wages and salaries paid to factory and installation employees were £481,441 and to administration and management employees were £187,004.
  (iv) The commercial vehicles owned at 31 August 19X4 were all traded in against a new fleet which cost £63,900. Prague Ltd received a trade-in allowance which amounted to £12,750.
  (v) Additions to plant and machinery cost £4,587.
  (vi) The dividend proposed at 31 August 19X4 was paid.
 (vii) An interim dividend of 38p per share, payable on 5 September 19X5 was declared.
(viii) £1,400 due from a customer at 31 August 19X4 was written off as irrecoverable.
  (ix) Settlement discounts of £17,411 were receivable from suppliers.
  (x) Sundry expenses paid through petty cash amounted to £4,733.
(2) At 31 August 19X5:
   (i) Trade creditors were £128,790.
  (ii) Debtors were £207,420.
 (iii) Stock and work in progress was valued at £222,666.
 (iv) Cash in hand was £327.
  (v) The directors of Prague Ltd expect to receive claims for faulty work which could cost £723 to rectify.
(3) Prague Ltd obtains its sales orders through self-employed agents who receive a commission of 15% of the sales value of each order. The commission is paid to the agent immediately the customer pays Prague Ltd.
(4) Depreciation is provided on the reducing balance basis at the following annual rates:

Plant and machinery	15%
Commercial vehicles	33⅓%
Private cars	20%

Required

(a) Write up the summary bank account for the year ended 31 August 19X5 (12 marks).
(b) Prepare a draft trading and profit and loss account for the year ended 31 August 19X5 and a draft balance sheet as on that date for consideration by the directors (12 marks).

  Ignore taxation.

(24 marks)

(ICAEW, AT, Nov 85)

QUESTION 4.3 (ADVANCED)

Scarpia

The trial balance of Scarpia Ltd as on 30 September 19X1 was as follows:

	£	£
Freehold land	1,000	
Freehold buildings	20,000	
Sales		240,900
Purchases	162,450	
Plant and machinery	22,000	
Office furniture	7,900	
Heat and light	840	
Sundry creditors		24,290
Prepayments	15,200	
Sales ledger control account	46,270	
Cash in hand	240	
Bank overdraft		72,450
Stocks – raw materials	22,400	
finished goods	8,700	
Wages and salaries	103,100	
Profit and loss account		47,110
Bank interest and charges	2,430	
Bad debts provision		700
Motor vehicles	6,400	
Insurance premiums	6,470	
Share capital		36,000
Directors' loans		6,400
Motor expenses	2,120	
Suspense account		270
Sundry expenses	100	
Commissions	230	
Trial balance difference	270	
	428,120	428,120

You are provided with the following additional information:

(1) All the office furniture was destroyed in a fire on 31 July 19X1 and is subject to an insurance claim of £1,500. Replacement furniture costing £2,000 was acquired but not paid for before 30 September 19X1. It is anticipated that the claim will be settled in December 19X1.

(2) Bad debts should be provided as to 5% of the sales ledger balances after writing off specific irrecoverable debts totalling £7,250.

(3) Motor vehicles include £1,800 which relates to a director's privately owned car and should be transferred to directors' loans.

(4) The suspense account is analysed as follows:

	£	£
Deposit on machinery to be delivered October 19X1	10,000	
Sundry income		6,270
Leasing charges received		4,000
Balance	270	
	10,270	10,270

The leasing charges received relate to an item of plant costing £12,000 included in purchases. The leasing agreement consists of 36 monthly receipts of £400.

(5) The petty cash book has not been written up since 30 June 19X1 and the cash balance included on the trial balance of £240 does not take account of the following transactions since that date:

(i) Cash drawn from the bank and correctly entered in the main cash book, totalling £1,422, has not been included in the petty cash book.

(ii) expense vouchers not entered are analysed as follows:

	£
Motor expenses	722
Sundry expenses	600
Casual labour	80

Cash in hand at 30 September 19X1 is £260.
(6) The balance on the sales ledger control account did not agree with the list of individual balances. You ascertain that the sales day book total for September 19X1 had been posted to the sales ledger control account incorrectly. The sales ledger control account balance was overstated by £1,152.
(7) Stocks were counted on 26 September 19X1 and evaluated as follows:

	£
(i) finished goods	7,200
(ii) raw materials	20,000

In the period between stocktaking and the year end, raw material deliveries totalling £6,700 were received. Invoices had not been recorded for £2,400 of this amount by 30 September 19X1. There were no other receipts or despatches of stocks between stocktaking and the year end.
(8) Depreciation should be provided as follows on fixed assets other than land:
   (i) on buildings – 4% reducing balance
   (ii) on leased plant – 2% per month on cost
   (iii) on other fixed assets – 25% reducing balance on assets in use at the year end.

Required

A draft trading account, profit and loss account and balance sheet in a form suitable to discuss with the directors.

(24 marks)

(ICAEW, AT, Nov 81)

5 COMPANY ACCOUNTS – THE REGULATORY FRAMEWORK

QUESTION 5.1 (BASIC)

Raywood

You are presented with the final trial balance of Raywood plc as at 31 December 19X3. The trial balance incorporates all the final adjustments which the directors wish to make.

	£	£
Ordinary share capital		800,000
Share premium account		1,400,000
Stocks	421,760	
Debtors	289,235	
Cash	89,640	
Land and buildings – cost	2,050,000	
– depreciation		150,000
Plant and machinery – cost	893,400	
– depreciation		221,100
Fixtures and fittings – cost	584,150	
– depreciation		95,050
Profit and loss account		615,252
8% debenture stock 19X15		200,000
Overdraft		189,650
Taxation		202,500
Creditors		387,333
Dividend		50,000
Accruals		17,300
	4,328,185	4,328,185

Required

A balance sheet as at 31 December 19X3 in a form suitable for presentation to the shareholders. Supporting notes are not required.

(10 marks)

QUESTION 5.2 (INTERMEDIATE)

Publish

The following information relates to the accounts of Publish plc for the year ended 31 December 19X4:

	£	£
Office wages and salaries		327,500
Advertising		121,400
Depreciation – office fittings	83,200	
– machinery	101,750	
– office buildings	8,570	
– delivery vans	11,460	
		204,980
Raw materials consumed		531,260
Factory overheads		137,350
Administrative overheads		85,470
Debenture interest		55,000
Bank interest		18,960
Sales		2,860,500
Preference dividends paid		75,000
Ordinary dividends proposed		250,000

	£	£
Corporation tax (19X4) profits)		335,400
Salesmens' salaries and commissions		39,630
Factory wages		138,640
Foreman's salary		12,255
Directors' remuneration		98,670
Audit fee		5,730
Balance on P/L at 1.1.X4		732,600
Discount allowed		19,850
Bad debts		38,000

Required

From the above information, present a profit account in accordance with the Companies Act 1985 using:

(a) format 1
(b) format 2.

Supporting notes are required in so far as information is available.

(16 marks)

QUESTION 5.3 (ADVANCED)

Health Sales (company accounts)

Please refer to the information contained in Annexe A.

Required

(a) Prepare a profit and loss account for the year ended 31 December 19X3 and a balance sheet as at 31 December 19X3 for Health Sales Ltd for internal use from the information provided in Appendices 1, 2, 3 and 4 (35 marks).
(b) Prepare a profit and loss account for the year ended 31 December 19X3 for Health Sales Ltd to comply as far as possible with the requirements of the Companies Act 1985 (10 marks).

(45 marks)

(ACCA, AAP, June 84)

QUESTION 5.4 (ADVANCED)

Pourwell (published accounts)

Please refer to the information in Annexe C.

Required

Prepare a draft profit and loss account for Pourwell Ltd for the year ended 31 December 19X5 and a draft balance sheet for Pourwell Ltd as at 31 December 19X5 together with supporting notes to comply as far as possible with the requirements of the Companies Act 1985.

Note: The only information available at the time is set out in Appendices 1, 2 and 3.

(36 marks)

(ACCA, AAP, June 86)

QUESTION 5.5 (INTERMEDIATE)

Stag

Stag plc is a public, unquoted company whose activities are mainly concerned with the manufacture of clothing. Although the company is not one of the largest in the industry, recent years have seen continuous expansion and the immediate prospects would appear to be good, with emphasis on the teenage fashion trade. All of the directors are members of the Roebuck family, except for Mr D. Ear, the financial director, who holds no shares in the company. T. Roebuck, who has been secretary to the company for some years and who holds 25,000 shares, joined the board on 1 August 19X5.

The following information about Stag plc may also be relevant:

(1) Summarised profit and loss account for the year ended 30 April 19X6 and the preceding year:

	19X6 £'000	19X5 £'000
Turnover	2,900	2,468
Profit before taxation	446	294
Taxation	(187)	(126)
Profit after taxation	259	168

A dividend of £150,000 has been proposed. The better results in 19X6 are attributed to a cost cutting exercise.

(2) In recent years the company has invested substantial amounts on a new synthetic fibre and other new products. To facilitate this research a new building and laboratories were purchased for £240,000 and £49,000 was spent on research during the year. The only other fixed asset acquisition during the year was a new car for the managing director costing £12,000.

(3) Land and buildings are included in the accounts at a valuation made in April 19X5 and the directors do not feel that this value has altered significantly.

(4) Share capital has been increased during the year to help finance the new building acquisition. 400,000 ordinary shares of 25p were issued by way of a rights issue of one for two for a total consideration of £128,000.

(5) The company employs a total of 260 people (prior year 283) and all may be regarded as working full time. 210 (240) are engaged in the manufacture and sale of clothing and the balance is concerned with the wholesaling of shoes. The company is generally felt to be forward thinking in its attitude to employees.

(6) The directors and their interests at the start of the financial year are as follows:

	25p ordinary shares
Mr G. Roebuck – chairman	220,000
Mrs A. Roebuck – managing director	40,500
Mr F. Roebuck	70,000
Mrs S. Fallow (resigned 1 August 19X5)	4,000

In addition, Mrs Fallow's ten-year-old son holds 6,000 shares and Mr G. Roebuck has a non-beneficial interest in 20,000 shares. Apart from taking up their rights no other changes took place in the shareholdings of the directors.

(7) Donations are made annually as follows:

	£
World Wildlife Fund	400
Social Democratic Party (SDP)	170
Liberal Party	250

Required

Making appropriate assumption, draft the directors' report for Stag plc for the year ended 30 April 19X6 in a form suitable for publication with the annual accounts. The directors will make full disclosure in the accounts and notes thereto of all items required by the Companies Act 1985 and apart from directors' interests they do not propose to repeat these items in the directors' report.

(20 marks)

(ICAEW, FA2, July 86)

QUESTION 5.6 (INTERMEDIATE)

Makewell

Makewell plc is a drug manufacturing company with a turnover of £50 million and an operating profit of £4.8 million for the year ended 31 December 19X4.

During the period of the financial statements for that year the following matters are brought to your attention:

(1) A product manufactured specifically for the North American market has recently been banned. The stock held by the company cost £750,000 but is now of no value.
(2) The 30% holding in a dormant Australian mining company purchased 52 years ago for £3,000 and written down to £1 several years ago was sold during the year for £600,000 following the discovery of gold in an adjoining mine.
(3) Production plant purchased in January 19X2 for £6 million had at that date an expected useful life of ten years. Due to major developments in micro electronics the company now believe the plant should be fully depreciated by December 19X7. They have therefore increased the depreciation charge for the year to £1.2 million.

Required

(a) Define an extraordinary item and a prior year adjustment (4 marks).
(b) Explain the distinction between an extraordinary and an exceptional item (2 marks).
(c) Discuss how the three matters above should be dealt with in the financial statements of Makewell plc (9 marks).

(15 marks)

(ICAEW, FA1, May 85)

QUESTION 5.7 (INTERMEDIATE)

Waveprocessor

Waveprocessor plc is an electronic manufacturing company with an annual turnover of £15m and trading profits of £1.5m.

In preparing the financial statements for the year ended 30 April 19X3 the following matters are brought to your attention:

(1) A factory was closed and the factory premises sold for £600,000 less than its book value.
(2) Goods exported overseas to the value of £300,000 have not been paid for due to the insolvency of the customer.
(3) Following a change in company policy all research expenditure on new technology will be written off in the year in which the expenditure arises. An amount of £425,000 has been written off in the year. This amount includes £125,000 of expenditure incurred during the year.

Required

(a) define what constitutes an extraordinary item in a company's financial statements, and indicate the distinction between extraordinary and exceptional items, and
(b) discuss the treatment of the three items referred to above in the financial statements of Waveprocessor plc.

(12 marks)

(ICAEW, PEI, May 83)

QUESTION 5.8 (INTERMEDIATE)

Fabricators

Fabricators plc, an engineering company, makes up its financial statements to 31 March in each year.

The financial statements for the year ended 31 March 19X1 showed a turnover of £3m and trading profit of £400,000.

Before approval of the financial statements by the board of directors on 30 June 19X1, the following events took place:

(1) The financial statements of Patchup Ltd for the year ended 28 February 19X1 were received which indicated a permanent decline in the company's financial position. Fabricators plc brought shares in Patchup Ltd some years ago and this purchase was included in unquoted investments at its cost of £100,000. The financial statements received indicated that this investment was now worth only £50,000.

(2) There was a fire at a company warehouse on 30 April 19X1 when stock to the value of £500,000 was destroyed. It transpired that the stock in the warehouse was under-insured by some 50%.

(3) On 31 March 19X1 a provision had been made of £60,000 in respect of any remedial work required on plant supplied and installed at a customer's premises on 26 March 19X1. No remedial work had been carried out and on 1 May 19X1 the customer had confirmed acceptance of the plant; accordingly no further liability would be involved.

(4) It was announced on 1 June 19X1 that the company's design for tank cleaning equipment had been approved by the major oil companies and this could result in an increase in the annual turnover of some £1m with a relative effect on profits.

Required

State, giving your reasons, how these events should be dealt with in the company's financial statements for the year ended 31 March 19X1, to comply with the requirements of SSAP17.

(16 marks)

(ICAEW, PEI, Nov 81)

QUESTION 5.9 (ADVANCED)

Alpha

SSAP17 and SSAP18 deal with accounting for post balance sheet events and contingencies respectively.

In eight companies whose year ends were 31 December 19X1, the financial statements were approved by their respective directors on 15 March 19X2. During 19X2, the following material events take place:

(1) Alpha Ltd sold a major property which was included in the balance sheet at £100,000 and for which contracts had been exchanged on 15 December 19X1. The sale was completed on 15 February 19X2 at a price of £250,000.

(2) On 28 January 19X2, a wholly owned subsidiary of Beta Ltd paid a dividend of £300,000 in respect of its own year ended on 31 December 19X1.

(3) On 28 February 19X2 the mail order activities of Gamma Ltd, a retail trading group, were shut down with closure costs amounting to £2.5 million.

(4) On 1 April 19X2 the discovery of sand under Delta Ltd's major civil engineering contract site causes the costs of the contract to increase by 25% for which there would be no corresponding recovery from the customer.

(5) A fire on 2 January 19X2 completely destroyed a manufacturing plant of Epsilon Ltd. It was expected that the loss of £10 million would be fully covered by insurance.

(6) A damages claim of £8 million for breach of patent had been served on Phi Ltd prior to the year end. It is the directors' opinion, backed by considered legal advice, that the claim will ultimately prove to be without foundation but that it will still involve the expenditure of considerable legal fees.

(7) The movement in a foreign exchange rate of 8% between 1 January 19X2 and 1 March 19X2 has resulted in Kappa Ltd's foreign assets being reduced by £1.3 million.

Required

State, with reasons, how each of the above items numbered (1) to (7) should be dealt with in the financial statements of the various companies for the year ended 31 December 19X1. You are not required to draft the relevant notes to the financial statements.

(14 marks)

(ICAEW, FA2, July 1982)

QUESTION 5.10 (INTERMEDIATE)

Stock Exchange

The Stock Exchange's Admission of Securities to Listing imposes upon listed companies disclosure requirements in addition to those required by statute and SSAPs.

(a) Give examples of such additional disclosure requirements from the Stock Exchange regulations (8 marks).
(b) Identify the objectives the Stock Exchange is pursuing when regulating the reporting requirements of listed companies. What means, in addition to increased disclosure, does the Stock Exchange adopt in pursuit of these objectives? (12 marks)

(20 marks)

(ACCA, RFA, Dec 82)

QUESTION 5.11 (INTERMEDIATE)

Segmental reporting

(a) What do you understand by the term 'disaggregation/segmental reporting' and to what extent do you consider that financial reporting by companies would be improved by further disclosure of disaggregated/segmental information? (12 marks)
(b) What objections and problems arise in the implementation of disaggregated/segmental reporting? (8 marks)

(20 marks)

(ACCA, RFA, June 84)

QUESTION 5.12 (ADVANCED)

Angie

The following are details of three separate companies' summarised balance sheets at 31 March 19X2:

	Angie plc £'000	Betty plc £'000	Cathy plc £'000
Fixed assets	2,500	380	500
Current assets	900	180	300
Current liabilities	(700)	(160)	(200)
	2,700	400	600
Share capital	200	300	2,000
Reserves:			
Revaluation	1,100	(200)	—
Realised capital profit	800	—	—
Bought forward realised revenue profit (loss)	400	500	(1,600)
Current year realised revenue profit (loss)	200	(200)	200
	2,700	400	600

Angie and Betty are public companies and Cathy a private company under the Companies Act 1985. Angie's property, previously included in the financial statements at original cost of £900,000 was revalued on 1 April 19X1 at £2 million. This revalued amount is included in the figures above, subject to the full amount being written off equally over the next 50 years from 1 April 19X1. Prior to this date, no depreciation had been provided on property. At 31 March 19X2, no transfer had been made between revaluation reserve and realised revenue profit.

Required

(a) compare briefly the bases for calculating the maximum distribution under the provisions of the Companies Act 1985 in respect of public, private and investment companies (8 marks);

(b) calculate the maximum distribution that Angie, Betty and Cathy could each make under the Companies Act 1985 (8 marks); and

(c) calculate the maximum distribution if Betty plc is an investment company and its dividend is to be paid from bank overdraft (3 marks).

(19 marks)

(ICAEW, FA2, July 82)

6 MODERN FINANCIAL ACCOUNTING

QUESTION 6.1 (INTERMEDIATE)

Assumptions

'It is fundamental to the understanding and interpretation of financial accounts that those who use them should be aware of the main assumptions on which they are based.'

Required

Explain how Statement of Standard Accounting Practice 2, Disclosure of accounting policies, seeks to achieve this understanding.

(15 marks)

(ICAEW, FA1, May 1987)

QUESTION 6.2 (INTERMEDIATE)

Accounting policies

(a) What do you understand by the terms accounting concepts, accounting bases and accounting policies? Explain the interrelationship between them (12 marks).
(b) Why is the disclosure of accounting policies by quoted companies considered to be desirable? (8 marks)

(20 marks)

(ACCA, RFA, Dec 84)

QUESTION 6.3 (INTERMEDIATE)

Matching

'The determination of profit for an accounting year requires the matching of costs with related revenues.'

Required

Discuss the above statement as it applies to the valuation of stocks and work in progress for accounting purposes in accordance with SSAP 9.

(12 marks)

(ICAEW, FA1, May 1985)

QUESTION 6.4 (ADVANCED)

Marvin and Welsh

Both Marvin and Welsh operate in the same industry. Their revenues, expenses and cash flows are the same. In fact they are identical in all respects except for their choice of accounting policies. The companies both adopt the historical cost convention and have produced draft accounts for their first year of trading as follows:

	Marvin		Welsh	
	£'000	£'000	£'000	£'000
Sales		20,000		20,000
Cost of sales		12,000		9,000
Gross profit		8,000		11,000
Administrative and distribution expenses	3,100		3,100	
Research and development	700		150	
Depreciation:				
plant, equipment and vehicles	2,050		640	
buildings	55		—	
Warranty costs	360		125	
Redundancy costs	285		—	
Amortisation of goodwill	65	6,615	—	4,015
Profit on ordinary activities before tax		1,385		6,985

Required

Discuss briefly the possible reasons for the differences revealed by the above figures indicating whether the policies implied are acceptable under the relevant regulations.

(25 marks)

QUESTION 6.5 (INTERMEDIATE)

Corporate report

(a) Who were considered to be the potential users of financial reports in the 'Corporate Report'? (8 marks)
(b) What do you consider to be their information needs? (8 marks)
(c) How would you expect a consideration of user needs to influence financial reporting? (9 marks)

(25 marks)

(ACCA, RFA, Dec 82)

QUESTION 6.6 (INTERMEDIATE)

True and fair

Examine the concept of a 'true and fair' view in the context of financial reporting in the UK and briefly discuss its implications in relation to accounting standards.

(20 marks)

(ACCA, RFA, Dec 85)

7 ACCOUNTING FOR FIXED ASSETS

QUESTION 7.1 (INTERMEDIATE)

Jupiter

You are the financial accountant of Jupiter Ltd, a company in the electronics industry, whose accounting reference date is 31 October and you have been provided with the following information in respect of its fixed assets:

	On 1 November 19X5 Cost £'000	Accumulated depreciation £'000	Total depreciable life (years)
Land	60	Nil	—
Freehold buildings			
Factory	150	30	50
Salesroom	180	30	45
Plant and machinery	475	365	10
Computer equipment	295	85	4
Furniture and fittings	100	40	5
Motor vehicles	50	35	4

None of these assets will be fully depreciated by 31 October 19X6.

During the year, C Star, a chartered surveyor, was engaged to value the properties at an open market value for existing use. His valuations as on 1 November 19X5 were as follows:

	£'000
Land	400
Factory	240
Salesroom	150

Additions during the year were:

Plant	100
Computer	8
Motor vehicles	28

The only disposals were cars which cost £6,000 and which had accumulated depreciation at 1 November 19X5 of £5,000.

All purchases and disposals took place on 1 May 19X6. All depreciation is charged on a straight line basis from the date of acquisition to the date of sale.

Required

(a) Present the detailed notes in relation to tangible fixed assets for the statutory accounts of Jupiter Ltd at 31 October 19X6. The accounting policy note is not required. Ignore taxation (9 marks).
(b) Discuss the arguments for and against including tangible fixed assets at revalued amounts in historical cost accounts and evaluate the alternative methods of accounting for their depreciation and sale (9 marks).

(18 marks)

(ICAEW, FA2, Dec 86)

QUESTION 7.2 (INTERMEDIATE)

Morecombe Malt

Morecombe Malt Ltd derives the major part of its income from the operation of a distillery. The company has freehold and leasehold property as follows:

(1) A factory, held freehold, in which the company operates a distillery.
(2) A village, two thirds of which is held freehold and the remainder on a 99 year lease with 15 years to run. The shops, offices and dwellings in the village are rented out on 5 and 10 year leases.
(3) A factory, held freehold, which is leased on a 35 year lease with 30 years to run, to a subsidiary company.

Required

State how each of the above items would be dealt with in the company's financial statements, having regard to the requirements of SSAP 12 and SSAP 19.

(14 marks)

(ICAEW, FA1, Nov 82)

QUESTION 7.3 (ADVANCED)

Metals

In preparing its financial statements for the year ended 30 June 19X5, Metals plc decides to adopt the requirements of SSAP 22 – Accounting for Goodwill. On 1 July 19X4, Metals plc, which had no subsidiaries previously, made the following acquisitions:

(1) The following assets were purchased for cash at the amounts shown from the Receiver of Tin Ltd:

	£'000
Freehold factory and associated plant	465
Stocks and work in progress	847
Knowhow	188

The knowhow figure related to certain patents with a fair value of £110,000. The balance represented the amount necessarily paid to secure the deal with the Receiver.
(2) The share capital of Manganese Ltd was purchased from the Ferric Group plc at a cash cost of £2,312,000. Manganese Ltd had not been profitable and the net asset acquired had a fair value of £2,460,000.
(3) The share capital of a private company, Copper Ltd, was purchased at a cash cost of £647,000. The book amounts of the assets and liabilities of that company, considered to be at a fair value, were:

	£'000
Plant and equipment	324
Current assets	512
Current liabilities	(487)

(4) The share capital of Zinc Ltd was purchased by the issue of 3 million shares of 25p each at an agreed value of 126p per share to cover the following net assets:

	£'000
Freehold factory and associated plant	1,728
Goodwill at cost	100
Current assets	3,126
Current liabilities	(1,174)

At the time of acquisition it was considered that the freehold should be revalued upwards by £80,000. Acquisition accounting was used for the consolidation.

In complying with SSAP 22, Metals plc resolves to write off goodwill immediately.
The balances at 30 June 1984 on the reserves of Metals plc were:

	£'000
Share premium	1,126
Other reserves (non-distributable)	175
Profit and loss	478

The retained profit for the year ended 30 June 19X5 was £368,000 for the group including £176,000 for the parent company.

Required

(a) Draft the accounting policy note for goodwill to be included in the group financial statements of Metals plc at 30 June 19X5.
(b) Prepare the notes to the group financial statements of Metals plc at 30 June 19X5 covering goodwill and reserves. The holding company notes are *not* required.
(c) Describe the factors which should be considered in determining the useful economic life of purchased goodwill.

(21 marks)

(ICAEW, FA2, July 85)

QUESTION 7.4 (INTERMEDIATE)

New Products

SSAP 13 'Accounting for Research and Development' became effective in respect of accounting periods commencing on or after 1 January 1978.

During the course of a year New Products Ltd incurred expenditure on many research and development activities. Details of three of them are given below.

Project 3: To develop a new compound in view of the anticipated shortage of a raw material currently being used in one of the company's processes. Sufficient progress has been made to suggest that the new compound can be produced at a cost comparable to that of the existing raw material.

Project 4: To improve the yield of an important manufacturing operation of the company. At present, material input with a cost of £100,000 p.a. becomes contaminated in the operation and half is wasted. Sufficient progress has been made for the scientists to predict an improvement so that only 20% will be wasted.

Project 5: To carry out work, as specified by a credit worthy client, in an attempt to bring a proposed aerospace product of that client into line with safety regulations.

Costs incurred during the year were:

	Project 3 £	Project 4 £	Project 5 £
Staff salaries	5,000	10,000	20,000
Overheads	6,000	12,000	24,000
Plant at cost	10,000	20,000	5,000
(life 10 years)			

Required

(a) Define the following:
   (1) pure research expenditure,
   (2) applied research expenditure, and
   (3) development expenditure (3 marks).
(b) State the circumstances in which it may be appropriate to carry forward research and development expenditure to future periods (5 marks).
(c) Show how the expenditure on projects 3, 4 and 5 would be dealt with in the balance sheet and profit and loss account in accordance with SSAP 13 (5 marks).

(13 marks)

(ICAEW, FA2, July 78)

QUESTION 7.5 (INTERMEDIATE)

R & D

'The accounting policies to be followed in respect of research and development expenditure must have regard to the fundamental accounting concepts including the "accruals" concept and the "prudence" concept.'

Required

Discuss the above statement as it applies to the different types of research and development expenditure and the accounting treatment of such expenditure in accordance with SSAP 13.

(12 marks)

(ICAEW, FA1, May 1985)

QUESTION 7.6 (INTERMEDIATE)

Capsule

Capsule Ltd is a chemical manufacturing company. The following items, in relation to the company's manufacturing processes, have been included in stocks and work in progress as on 31 July 19X3.

(1) Stocks of Banoline have been valued at £426,000 based on the following amounts:

	£
Raw materials – cost	200,000
Other direct costs	144,000
Proportion of factory overheads	38,000
Proportion of selling office expenses	44,000
	426,000

Banoline is a steady selling product which shows reasonable profit margins.

(2) Laboratory costs to 31 July 19X3 of £348,000 on research into a new tranquillizer called Calmdown. The research is being sponsored by a government agency on a one year programme. The agency has agreed to re-imburse the company on a cost plus 6% basis at the end of the programme, up to a maximum contribution of £500,000.

(3) Stocks of 1300 kg, held in bulk, of a chemical substance known as Apentone, and valued as follows:

	£
Raw materials – cost	340,000
Other direct costs	260,000
Proportion of factory overheads	47,000
Proportion of selling office expenses	59,000
	706,000

A competitor of Capsule Ltd has recently introduced to the market a similar substance, which it is selling in handy 100g packs at £35 each. To meet the competition, Capsule Ltd will also have to pack in 100g containers. The cost of packing the stock held will be £20,000 and additional advertising costs, to clear the stock are estimated at £30,000.

(4) Laboratory costs to 31 July 1983 of £365,000 on research into a new chemical substitute for Supositone, of which demand exceeds the world supply. These costs include £100,000 for special items of plant required for the research programme.

Required

State how you consider the above items should be dealt with in the company's accounts, giving your reasons in each case.

(20 marks)

(ICAEW, FA1, Nov 83)

8 STOCKS AND WORK-IN-PROGRESS

QUESTION 8.1 (BASIC)

Pamina

As cost accountant responsible for the stores ledger at Pamina Ltd you are presented with the following information relating to raw material commodity stock movements, for the three months ended 30 June 19X3:

(1) Stock at 1 April 19X3   7,240 units @ £11 per unit

(2) Purchases:

3 April 19X3	4,240 units @ £12 per unit
15 May 19X3	9,217 units @ £13 per unit
17 June 19X3	2,490 units @ £10 per unit

(3) Transferred to work-in-progress:

2 April 19X3	4,170 Units
12 April 19X3	6,716 Units
12 May 19X3	494 Units
1 June 19X3	7,460 Units

Required

(a) Prepare statements in value and quantity terms for stock movements for the three months ended 30 June 19X3 on the basis of:
  (i) weighted average price, and
  (ii) first in first out (11 marks); and
(b) suggest two other methods which could be used to record the receipt and issue of raw materials (3 marks).

(14 marks)

(ICAEW, AT, Nov 83)

QUESTION 8.2 (INTERMEDIATE)

Thornfield

Thornfield Ltd is a building contractor. During its financial year to 30 June 19X4, it commenced three major contracts. Information relating to these contracts as at 30 June 19X4 was as follows:

	Contract 1 1 July 19X3	Contract 2 1 January 19X4	Contract 3 1 April 19X4
Date contract commenced			
	£	£	£
Contract price	210,000	215,000	190,000
Expenditure to 30 June 19X4:			
Materials and subcontract work	44,000	41,000	15,000
Direct wages	80,000	74,500	12,000
General expenses	3,000	1,800	700
Position at 30 June 19X4:			
Materials on hand at cost	3,000	3,000	1,500
Accrued expenses	700	600	600
Value of work certified	150,000	110,000	20,000
Estimated cost of work completed but not certified	4,000	6,000	9,000
Plant and machinery allocated to contracts	16,000	12,000	8,000

The plant and machinery allocated to the contracts was installed on the dates the contracts commenced. The plant and machinery is expected to have a working life of four years in the case of contracts 1 and 3 and three years in the case of contract 2, and is to be depreciated on a straight line basis assuming nil residual values.

Since the last certificate of work was certified on contract number 1, faulty work has been discovered which is expected to cost £10,000 to rectify. No rectification work has been commenced prior to 30 June 19X4.

In addition to expenditure directly attributable to contracts, recoverable central overheads are estimated to amount to 2% of the cost of direct wages.

Thornfield Ltd has an accounting policy of taking two thirds of the profit attributable to the value of work certified on a contract, once the contract is one third completed. Anticipated losses on contracts are provided in full.

Progress claims equal to 80% of the value of work certified have been invoiced to customers.

Required

(a) prepare summarised contract accounts for each contract for the year to 30 June 19X4, calculating any attributable profit or loss on each contract (12 marks); and
(b) calculate the amount to be included in the balance sheet of Thornfield Ltd as on 30 June 19X4 in respect of these contracts (4 marks).

(16 marks)

(ICAEW, AT, Nov 1984)

QUESTION 8.3 (INTERMEDIATE)

Barlow

Barlow Ltd trade as building contractors. As at 30 June 19X2 there are two contracts in progress:

(1) The construction of a sewerage works and associated buildings for a local authority. The contract commenced on 1 July 19X1, is estimated to last for a period of three years and is for a total of £2,309,000.

The balances in the company's contract ledger relating to this contract are as follows:

	£	£
Plant and machinery	273,200	
Purchases	364,000	
Wages and salaries	240,000	
Sundry expenses	6,400	
Cash on account of interim certificates		620,000

As at 30 June 19X2 the value of materials on site was £12,000 and work finished but not certified was £15,000.

80% of amounts certified had been paid to Barlow Ltd, the remaining 20% being retained by the local authority until three months after completion.

(2) The construction of a new school for a local authority. The contract commenced on 1 October 19X1 and is for £475,000 and is estimated to last two years.

The balances in the company's contract ledger relating to this contract are as follows:

	£	£
Plant and machinery	24,000	
Purchases	74,000	
Wages and salaries	76,000	
Other expenses	17,200	
Cash on account of interim certificates		145,000

As at 30 June 19X2 the value of material on site was £5,000 and uncertified work was £7,000. There were retentions of £12,000 by the local authority until three months after completion.

The plant and machinery will have no material value at the end of either contract.

Required

Contract accounts in summarised form in respect of each of the above contracts indicating the basis upon which the transfers to profit and loss account are to be made.

(12 marks)

(ICAEW, FA1, Nov 82)

QUESTION 8.4 (ADVANCED)

Project X

Stock and Work-in-Progress:

'Stock and work-in-progress at 31 March 19X7 has been valued in accordance with Statement of Standard Accounting Practice No. 9. The effect of the adjustment to the basis of stock and work-in-progress valuation at 31 March 19X6 was not significant. The basis of valuation is the lower of cost and net realisable value, due allowance being made for obsolete and slow-moving items. In the case of products manufactured by companies in the Group, stock and work-in-progress consists of direct materials and labour costs and all other expenditure which has been incurred in the normal course of business and which is attributable to bringing these products to their present location and condition.'

The above extract from 'accounting policies' is typical of many that have appeared. A company adopting such an accounting policy manufactures engineering components and assembles some of these into production lines at the customers' premises.

At 31 March 19X7 there were two items of finished stock and one item of work-in-progress. The item in progress is in connection with a long-term project commenced in November 19X6 (Project X). The contracted price of Project X is £190,000. Half of the manufactured parts for Project X have been completed, delivered to the site and successfully assembled. The following information is also available:

	Manufacturing £	Assembly on location (excluding all manufacturing costs) £
Total expenditure for the year ended 31 March 19X7		
Direct material	300,000	—
Direct labour	250,000	100,000
Overheads	250,000	10,000
Direct costs of finished stock at 31 March 19X7		
Item 1 Direct material	20,000	—
Direct labour	10,000	—
Item 2 Direct material	15,000	—
Direct labour	5,000	—
Direct costs of work-in-progress to 31 March 19X7		
Direct material	25,000	—
Direct labour	20,000	15,000
Estimated total costs of Project X		
Direct material	50,000	—
Direct labour	50,000	30,000

Required

(a) show how the finished stock and work-in-progress would be included in the balance sheet at 31 March 19X7 together with any supporting notes you feel would be necessary (18 marks); and
(b) explain why SSAP 9 was required and what it seeks to achieve (7 marks).

(25 marks)

(ICAEW, FA2, Dec 77)

9 ACCOUNTING FOR TAXATION

QUESTION 9.1 (BASIC)

Pasedena

Details relating to the year ended 30 September 19X5 are as follows:

(1) The tax on 19X4 profits was previously provided for at £55,200. The tax liability has now been agreed and paid at £51,000.
(2) Dividend of £16,700 relating to a fixed asset investment was received on 4 January 19X6.
(3) No interim dividend was declared but the directors propose a final dividend of £49,000.
(4) Tax on 19X5 profits has been estimated at £73,000.

Corporation tax is to be taken at 35%, income tax at 30%.

Required

Relevant extracts from profit and loss account and balance sheet for 19X5.

(10 marks)

QUESTION 9.2 (BASIC)

Charlston

The following details relate to the accounts for the year ended 31 December 19X6:

(1) Tax liability for 19X5 of £63,050 was paid. The amount provided in last year's balance sheet was £58,240.
(2) Interim dividend of £15,230 was paid on 2 June 19X6. No other dividends were paid during the year. Assume advance corporation tax was paid by the usual date.
(3) Final dividend of £22,130 was proposed by the directors.
(4) Corporation tax on 19X6 profits was estimated at £85,072.

Corporation tax is to be taken at 35%, income tax at 30%.

Required

Relevant extracts from profit and loss account and balance sheet for 19X6.

(10 marks)

QUESTION 9.3 (INTERMEDIATE)

Hardy

Hardy is a pre-1965 company. In its previous balance sheet at 30 June 19X3 the following mainstream corporation tax balances appeared:

Re. 30.6.19X2	81,400
Re. 30.6.19X3	71,760

In addition the company had provided for deferred taxation of £21,600 in accordance with SSAP 15. No final dividend had been proposed in respect of 19X3.

The following information relates to the year ended 30 June 19X4:

(1) The 19X2 liability of £81,400 is paid.
(2) An interim dividend of £17,000 was paid on 2 March 19X4.

32

(3) The 19X3 liability was agreed by the Inland Revenue at £79,530. The provision for 19X4 has been estimated at £92,000.
(4) The directors propose a final dividend of £26,000.
(5) On the basis of capital expenditure plans the directors require a provision at 30.6.X4 in respect of deferred tax amounting to £32,070.

Corporation tax is to be taken at 35%, income tax at 30%.

Required

Relevant ledger accounts in respect of the above and extracts from profit and loss account and balance sheet for 19X4 relating to taxation matters.

(14 marks)

QUESTION 9.4 (INTERMEDIATE)

Corax

Corax has an issued capital of £330,000 in fully paid 50p ordinary shares. At 31 December 19X5 the following balances were included in the company's balance sheet:

	£
Agreed corporation tax liability on 19X3 profits	16,300
Estimated corporation tax liability on 19X4 profits	5,000
Deferred taxation account	29,400
Profit and loss account (credit)	43,000
(No dividends had been paid or proposed in respect of 19X4)	

The following information relates to the year ended 31 December 19X5:

- Corporation tax liability for 19X3 settled (January)
- Interim dividend of 2.1p per share paid (August)
- Advance corporation tax on interim dividend paid (October)
- Corporation tax liability for 19X4 agreed at £3,800 (December)
- Net profit for 19X5 before tax calculated at £88,800
- Corporation tax based on the 19X5 profits estimated at £36,000
- Directors proposed a final dividend of 4.2p per share
- A transfer to the deferred taxation account of £7,000 for 19X5 is to be made in respect of capital allowances in excess of depreciation charges.

Required

Make all relevant entries in the ledger accounts (except cash and share capital) and complete the profit and loss account for 19X5. Show how the final balances would be included in the balance sheet at 31 December 19X5. (Assume that the basic rate of income tax is 30%.)

(17 marks)

(ACCA, Accounting 3, June 1978)

QUESTION 9.5 (INTERMEDIATE)

Tax items

How should you treat the following items when preparing financial statements in accordance with statements of standard accounting practice?

(i) franked investment income (3 marks);
(ii) proposed dividends and the related advance corporation tax (2 marks);
(iii) recoverable advance corporation tax (2 marks);
(iv) irrecoverable advance corporation tax (2 marks);

(v) value added output tax on turnover for a VAT registered trader (2 marks);

(vi) irrecoverable value added input tax on a fixed asset, purchased by a VAT registered trader (2 marks);

(vii) the receipt and payment of VAT to the Customs and Excise? (2 marks)

(15 marks)

(ACCA, RFA, Dec 85)

QUESTION 9.6 (INTERMEDIATE)

Shannon

(1) Shannon's accounting policy on deferred tax has always been fully consistent with SSAP 15 (revised). At 31.12.X4, accounts net book value of fixed assets amounted to £1,600 compared with tax WDV of £400. Projections at that date showed no deferred tax provision was necessary. Consequently Shannon's balance sheet note showed:

		£
Provided	– nil	Nil
Unprovided	– 35% (1,600–400)	420

(2) During 19X5, capital allowances amounted to £410 and depreciation charges to £360.

(3) Projections at 31.12.X85 showed the following:

	Capital allowances £	Depreciation £	Net originating (reversing) £
19X6	400	380	20
19X7	425	395	30
19X8	300	380	(80)
19X9	410	370	40
19X10	430	395	35

(4) Assume that actual expenditure is as projected and that none of the above projections need to be revised for subsequent years. Corporation tax is to be taken at 35% throughout the period.

Required

Relevant extracts in summarised form from financial statements for 19X5, 19X6, 19X7, 19X8 and 19X9 indicating any memorandum disclosures required by SSAP 15.

(14 marks)

QUESTION 9.7 (ADVANCED)

Forsters

It is the accounting policy of Forsters plc to provide for deferred taxation, in accordance with SSAP 15, only where there is a probability that a liability will crystalise in the foreseeable future.

The following information is given in respect of the company's year ended on 30 June 19X12:

(1) The company has made a taxable profit for the year of £500,000.

(2) Its freehold property, which had cost £100,000 in 19X0, was revalued at £200,000. This revaluation was incorporated in the financial statements at 30 June 19X12.

(3) The other fixed assets comprised entirely plant and machinery on which 100% capital allowances had been claimed in the year of purchase. The net book value of these assets at 30 June 19X11 was £600,000.

(4) Depreciation is provided on the plant and machinery at 10% per annum on the reducing balance method and is provided for the full year in the year of purchase.

(5) During the year ended 30 June 19X12 expenditure on similar plant and machinery was £100,000.

(6) The company's forecasts show that capital expenditure on similar plant and machinery, which will attract the 100% capital allowances, will be £10,000 in each of the next three years. After that

it is anticipated that substantial replacement of scrapped plant will be required and annual expenditure of approximately £75,000 will be incurred. The scrapped plant will have no disposal value.

(7) At 30 June 19X11 a timing difference arose through the accrual of loan interest receivable at the year end of £50,000. Receipt of this interest was on 5 July 19X11. Equal amounts of interest were also received on 5 January and 5 July 19X12.

(8) On 1 April 19X12 £125,000 with interest at 15% per annum was borrowed from a finance company. Although accrued at 30 June 19X12 no payment of interest had been made. Six months interest was paid on 1 October 19X12.

(9) The company expects to be paying and receiving interest at the same time in future years.

(10) It was proposed to pay a dividend after the year end of £105,000.

Assume that the company continues to trade profitably and that there are no losses brought forward. The effective rates of corporation tax are 35% on trading profits and 30% on chargeable gains, and the rate of advance corporation tax is three-sevenths.

Required

(a) draft a suitable statement of accounting policy on deferred taxation for inclusion in the financial statements at 30 June 19X12 (2 marks); and

(b) draft the balance sheet note, omitting comparatives, on deferred taxation (14 marks).

(16 marks)

(ICAEW, FA2, Dec 82)

QUESTION 9.8 (ADVANCED)

County Manufacturing

The taxation consolidation schedules of County Manufacturing Ltd on 30 November 19X4 show the following:

	Parent county £	Essex £	Avon £	Cumbria £
			Subsidiaries	
(1) Adjusted profits (losses)	25,140	286,360	(79,290)	21,660
Depreciation	—	36,340	16,480	8,120
Capital allowances	—	70,160	56,810	9,300
(2) Corporation tax account:				
Corporation tax provisions for year to				
30 November 19X3 brought forward	(3,680)	(40,600)	—	—
Payments during year: agreed mainstream corporation				
tax liability for year to 30 November 19X3	3,700	40,500	—	—
ACT on interim dividend paid 31 July 19X4	4,650	—	—	—
Tax suffered on interest received	180	370	—	—
(3) Deferred taxation:				
Credit balance brought forward 1 December 19X3	—	(90,880)	(12,960)	—
Credit balance carried forward 30 November 19X4		(146,350)	(33,480)	—

The following information is also available:

(1) The three subsidiaries shown above are wholly owned. In addition there is another wholly owned subsidiary incorporated overseas whose charge against profits and liability to local tax for the year ended 30 November 19X4 is £26,400. No double tax relief is available. There is no deferred taxation.

(2) County has a UK associated company in which it has a 25% holding. That company's corporation tax charge for the year ended 30 November 19X4 is £37,080. There is no deferred taxation.

(3) All companies have been members of the group for many years and are trading companies. There have been no changes in their trades.

(4) Cumbria has available taxation losses of £45,600 brought forward at 1 December 19X3.

(5) The adjusted profits (losses) shown above are those for the year ended 30 November 19X4 adjusted for taxation purposes after taking account of depreciation and capital allowances.

(6) Depreciation is solely upon fixed assets which are eligible for capital allowances.
(7) It is intended to take advantage of the Group Relief provisions which are fully available.
(8) The rate of corporation tax applying for the year ended 30 November 19X4 is 35% for all group companies with no small company rate.
(9) The deferred tax balances at 30 November 19X4 have been provided at 35% and in accordance with SSAP 15. Following the March 19X4 Budget the deferred tax provision at 30 November 19X4 includes an additional amount needed to make up provisions made in previous years. As from and including the year ended 30 November 19X4 provision is to be made on the full difference between depreciation and capital allowances.
(10) A proposed final dividend will be payable on 31 March 19X5 at the same rate as the interim paid on 31 July 19X4. No change in the rate of ACT is expected and the ACT on the proposed dividend is considered to be recoverable against future liabilities.

Required

In respect of the group financial statements of County Manufacturing Ltd on 30 November 19X4 to:

(a) State, with reasons, how you would deal with the additional amount of deferred taxation in the profit and loss account and notes thereto (5 marks).
(b) Prepare the note supporting the taxation charge in the profit and loss account (12 marks).
(c) Calculate the taxation liabilities to be included in creditors (3 marks).

(20 marks)

(ICAEW, FA2, Dec 84)

10 LEASING AND HIRE PURCHASE ACCOUNTING

QUESTION 10.1 (BASIC)

Westbury

Westbury Ltd is a manufacturing company. On 2 January 19X2, the company entered into a leasing agreement the principle terms of which were as follows:

(1) Primary (non-cancellable) period of five years with an annual rental of £6,387 payable on the first day of each year. The first payment is due immediately following the signing of the lease agreement.
(2) Westbury Ltd is to be responsible for insurance and maintenance.
(3) The period of the lease may be extended on an annual basis at the option of Westbury Ltd for a further indefinite secondary period. The annual rental, should the option be exercised, would amount to £50 per annum.
(4) The fair value of the asset is £25,000.
(5) Westbury normally depreciates machinery of this category on a straight line basis at an annual rate of 10%.
(6) The company's year-end is 31 December.

Required

Assuming the lease is classified as a finance lease:

(a) Show how the finance charges would be allocated over the lease period using:
    (i) the actuarial method (using an interest rate of 14%);
    (ii) the sum of the digits method.
(b) State the minimum disclosures including accounting policy note in the financial statements of Westbury Ltd for the year ended 31 December 19X2 assuming the company adopts the actuarial method.

(14 marks)

ANSWER 10.2 (INTERMEDIATE)

Lessor and Lessee

Two companies enter into an agreement whereby the lessor (Lessor Ltd) will lease on a capital (or financial) lease to the lessee (Lessee Ltd) for a period of five years from 1 September 19X8 one item of plant, which will cost the lessor £1,000 on 1 September 19X8. The plant, to be depreciated on a straight line basis, is considered to have a nil residual value at the end of the agreement. The agreement specifies that a rental of £74 per quarter is payable in advance.

It is proposed that, in the lessor's accounts, profit should only be taken pro rata to the interest received and that the total interest element included in the rentals should be allocated over the period of the lease using the 'sum of digits' method (sometimes called the rule of 78). It is further proposed that, in the lessee's accounts, the lease should be capitalised.

Required

(a) Define a finance lease and state the criteria which distinguish it from an operating lease (4 marks).
(b) Show how these transactions would appear in the published accounts of both Lessee Ltd and Lessor Ltd for the year ending 31 August 19X9 using the respective accounting treatments proposed above (16 marks).

(c) Compare the treatment used above for reporting the lease transactions in the lessee's accounts with the minimum legal disclosure requirements (4 marks).

(24 marks)

(ICAEW, FA2, July 78)

QUESTION 10.3 (INTERMEDIATE)

Mewslade

Mewslade Ltd is a lessor company. Plant and machinery was leased to Heatherslade on the following terms:

(1) Five annual instalments paid on first day of each year of £48,000, commencing 1/1/X2.
(2) Heatherslade to be responsible for repairs, insurance etc. – the lease is classified as a finance lease.
(3) The asset would have cost £200,150 to buy outright.

Required

Relevant extracts from Mewslade's profit and loss account for the years 19X2 to 19X6 and balance sheets at 31 December 19X2 and 19X3. Assume that Mewslade uses the actuarial before tax methods of allocating finance charges and that the interest rate implicit in the lease is 10%.

(14 marks)

QUESTION 10.4 (ADVANCED)

Lessor

The Accounting Standards Committee has now issued a definitive standard on lease accounting – SSAP 21: Accounting for leases and hire purchase contracts (1984). This standard requires a lessor company to recognise annual (post-tax) income from leases and hire purchase contracts in its financial statements.

Required

(a) State clearly the principles on which the above statement is based (15 marks).
(b) The details of a finance lease made by the lessor company are given below. Using the actuarial method after tax, compute to the nearest pound the figures to be shown in the financial statements of the lessor company, for the first three years only, in relation to this finance lease (10 marks).

(25 marks)

Lessor plc leases plant (cost £50,000) to Lessee Ltd for four years from 1 January 19X7 at a rental of £8,000 per half-year, payable in advance. Corporation tax is 35%, and capital allowances on the plant are 25% per annum, reducing balance basis. The rate of return (post-tax) on the lessor's net cash investment is 5.4% per half-year. The plant is assumed to have no residual value at the end of the lease term. Corporation tax is payable 12 months after the year-end (31 December).

(ACCA, AFA, Dec 85)

11 ACCOUNTING FOR PENSION COSTS

QUESTION 11.1 (INTERMEDIATE)

Pension costs

For many years the UK–Irish Accounting Standards Committee has attempted to produce a standard on the question of accounting for pension costs in the accounts of an employer company.

Required

(a) Explain briefly why this area of accounting has caused such difficulties from the viewpoint of external financial reporting.
(b) Outline the conventional methods currently used to account for the pension costs of a company.
(c) Criticise the adequacy of such methods in the light of the accruals concept of accounting.
(d) Outline what you consider to be an acceptable treatment of accounting for pension fund contributions.

(22 marks)

QUESTION 11.2 (INTERMEDIATE)

Southgate

Accounting for pension costs has been a matter of debate for many years. In 1986, the Accounting Standards Committee published an exposure draft, ED39.

Southgate plc has recently decided to introduce a non-contributory defined benefit pension scheme to cover all of its full-time employees. A separate pension fund has now been set up.

The following information has been obtained from various sources including the results of actuarial calculations:

(1) On the recommendations of the actuary, the company intends to make payments to trustees in respect of regular pension costs. Payments to be made on 31 December 19X10 and 19X11 amount to £175,000 and £205,000 respectively.
(2) In addition the company agrees to make four annual payments of £100,000 each year (payments to be made on 31 December 19X10, 19X11, 19X12 and 19X13 respectively). These payments relate to retroactive changes in benefits (past service costs) as no pension scheme previously existed.

You ascertain that the expected average remaining service lives of employees in the scheme is ten years.

Required

(a) State the main assumptions required in order to determine an appropriate charge to profit and loss account under a defined benefit scheme (5 marks).
(b) Explain and justify the treatment proposed by ED39 in respect of the past service costs referred to in (2) above (6 marks).
(c) Provide the relevant extracts from the profit and loss accounts and balance sheets for 19X10 and 19X11 (9 marks).

(20 marks)

12 STATEMENTS OF RECOMMENDED PRACTICE

QUESTION 12.1 (INTERMEDIATE)

SORPs

The Accounting Standards Committee has recently introduced a new form of statement – a Statement of Recommended Practice (SORP).

Required

(a) State the ASC's primary aims in issuing SORPs (4 marks).
(b) Outline the main points of difference between SSAPs (Statements of Standard Accounting Practice) and SORPs (6 marks).
(c) Explain the relationship between SORPs and SSAPs (3 marks).
(d) State the two main types of SORPs (4 marks).

(17 marks)

QUESTION 12.2 (INTERMEDIATE)

Support Association

You have become honorary treasurer of a charity for handicapped children called 'The Support Association'. The full-time secretary has sent to you the following trial balance for the year ended 30 June 19X6 and has asked you to explain certain accounting aspects to him with particular reference to ED38, the proposed statement of recommended practice 'Accounting by charities'.

	£'000 Dr/(Cr)
Donations other than covenants	(147)
Covenants	(63)
Investment income received gross	(26)
Office equipment	4
Salaries and wages	24
Legacies	(465)
Sundry office expenses	6
Investments	40
Special Fund investments	96
General Fund	(810)
Special Fund	(92)
Surplus from the sale of books	(27)
Properties held for investment	106
Properties held for use of The Support Association	100
Depreciation on properties	(69)
Assets deployed for charitable purposes	470
Income from life subscriptions	(85)
Net current assets	60
Income from property occupied by beneficiaries	(6)
Grants to hospitals	178
Maintenance to families of handicapped children	147
Expenditure on schools	559

Required

Set out in the form of a letter to the secretary:

(a) an explanation of 'restricted funds' and 'designated funds' as defined in ED38 (4 marks);
(b) your suggestions as to the groupings you would consider appropriate for the revenue account and balance sheet of The Support Association (6 marks); and
(c) three reasons, in each case with an example, why accounting for commercial undertakings may be inappropriate for charities (6 marks).

(16 marks)

(ICAEW, FA2, July 86)

QUESTION 12.3 (ADVANCED)

Daffodil Bulb

Recently there has been publicity suggesting that pension fund reports should be more informative to members.

Daffodil Bulb Company plc operates a pension fund and Harold D. Quill & Co, consultant actuaries, had reported that the fund was solvent on a discontinuance basis as at 30 June 19X12. They also reported that the previous contribution rates were insufficient to meet future expected benefits to actual retirement dates. Daffodil Bulb Company plc have accepted the actuaries' comments and have increased their contributions in the year ended 30 June 19X13 to the revised rate suggested. They propose to continue this rate until the next actuarial review in 19X15.

The following balances were extracted from the books of the Pension Fund at 30 June 19X13:

	Dr £'000	Cr £'000
Capital account	—	1,696
Investments – quoted equities	861	—
– Government stocks	732	—
Daffodil Bulb Co – loan	150	—
Freehold property	500	
Cash – current account	—	1
– term deposit	149	—
– ordinary deposit	14	—
Contributions – members	—	181
– Daffodil Bulb Co	—	344
Income from investments	—	137
Interest received	—	35
Rental income	—	50
Pensions paid	21	—
Death benefits and commutation payments	167	—
Members leaving – contributions returned	5	—
Transfers to/from other schemes	4	8
Loss on investments sold	3	—
Income tax recovered	—	54
Liability for commutations	—	100
	2,606	2,606

The following information is also given:

(1) The investments are stated at cost and have the following market values at 30 June 19X13:

| Quoted equities | 1,207 |
| Government stocks | 710 |

(2) It has always been the policy of the fund to include investments at cost except where there has been a permanent diminution in value. It is not considered that any such condition exists at 30 June 19X13.

(3) The freehold property is stated at cost. A valuation at 30 June 19X13 by Hulls, Chartered Surveyors, gave an open market valuation at £1,050,000. The property is leased to Daffodil Bulb Co plc for a period of 50 years from 19X7. The current rental is £40,000 per annum with a review in 19X15.

(4) The loan to Daffodil Bulb Co plc is for 5 years at 2% above interbank rate.

(5) The investment income is the actual amount received which has suffered UK tax at 30%.
(6) The Daffodil Bulb Co plc Pension Fund is properly constituted as a contracted out scheme with full Inland Revenue approval.

Required

(a) comment on the actuaries' report dated 30 June 19X12 and the Daffodil Bulb Co plc's reaction thereto (3 marks);
(b) draft a Revenue Account and Net Asset Statement of Daffodil Bulb Co plc Pension Fund at 30 June 19X13 together with the appropriate notes thereto (12 marks);
(c) list the information you would include in a Report of the Trustees to the members of a pension fund (4 marks).

Note: Ignore comparative figures.

(19 marks)

(ICAEW, FA2, July 83)

13 GROUP ACCOUNTS (i)

QUESTION 13.1 (BASIC)

Hop and Skotch

The balance sheets of Hop Ltd and Skotch Ltd at 31.12.X8 were as follows:

	Hop Ltd £	Skotch Ltd £
Ordinary share capital – £1 ordinary shares	100,000	40,000
Reserves	75,000	25,000
Current liabilities	58,200	28,400
	233,200	93,400
Tangible fixed assets	65,000	31,700
Investment in Skotch Ltd	48,000	—
Current assets	120,200	61,700
	233,200	93,400

Required

The consolidated balance sheet at 31.12.X8 under the two following alternative assumptions:

(a) Hop Ltd acquired 100% of the share capital of Skotch Ltd when the reserves of Skotch amounted to £6,000.

(b) Hop Ltd acquired 60% of the share capital of Skotch Ltd when the reserves of Skotch amounted to £16,000.

Assume in both cases that consolidation goodwill is written off against reserves.

(12 marks)

QUESTION 13.2 (BASIC)

Helston and Sands (Part 1)

The summarised balance sheets of Helston and Sands are as follows:

	Helston £	Sands £
Fixed assets	1,900	800
Investment in Sands	630	—
Net current assets	720	100
	3,250	900
Share capital	1,000	200
Profit and loss account	2,250	700
	3,250	900

Helston acquired 90% of the share capital of Sands several years ago when the reserves of Sands amounted to £400.

Required

Consolidated balance sheet assuming goodwill on consolidation is written off against group reserves.

(12 marks)

QUESTION 13.3 (BASIC)

Helston and Sands (Part 2)

In the above example, no dividend has been paid or proposed by Sands. Assume now that Sands had proposed a dividend of £50 but Helston had not yet accrued its share of this dividend.

Required

Consolidated balance sheet assuming goodwill on consolidation is written off against group reserves.

(14 marks)

QUESTION 13.4 (BASIC)

Ainsdale and Churchtown

Ainsdale acquired 100% of the Share Capital of Churchtown several years ago when Churchtown's reserves amounted to £2,000. Summarised profit and loss accounts are as follows:

	Ainsdale £	Churchtown £
Turnover	6,000	3,000
Operating expenses	900	400
Operating profit	5,100	2,600
Taxation	2,000	1,000
Profit after tax	3,100	1,600
Balance b/f	8,000	5,000
Balance c/f	11,100	6,600

Required

(a) Consolidated profit and loss account reflecting the above information.
(b) Indicate the effect on the above if Churchtown had decided to propose a dividend of £400.

(14 marks)

QUESTION 13.5 (BASIC)

Thomas and Percy

Thomas acquired 80% of the share capital of Percy several years ago when Percy's reserves amounted to £12,000. During the current year neither company has paid or proposed a dividend. Their respective profit and loss accounts are as follows:

	Thomas £	Percy £
Turnover	96,000	25,000
Operating expenses	18,000	8,000
Operating profit	78,000	17,000
Taxation	30,000	7,000
Profit after tax	48,000	10,000
Balance b/f	120,000	35,000
Balance c/f	168,000	45,000

Required

(a) a consolidated profit and loss account reflecting the above information;

(b) a consolidated profit and loss account assuming Thomas and Percy propose dividends of £15,000 and £5,000 respectively.

(14 marks)

QUESTION 13.6 (BASIC)

James and Gordon

The summarised profit and loss accounts of James and its subsidiary Gordon were as follows:

	James £	Gordon £
Turnover	134,000	50,000
Operating expenses	31,000	12,000
Operating profit	103,000	38,000
Dividends from Gordon:		
– interim received	4,500	—
– final receivable	9,000	—
Dividends from Henry	2,100	—
Profit before tax	118,600	38,000
Taxation-corporation tax	41,000	18,000
Profit after tax	77,600	20,000
Dividends paid	(20,000)	(5,000)
Dividends proposed	(30,000)	(10,000)
Retained profit	27,600	5,000
Balance b/f	108,000	33,000
Balance c/f	135,600	38,000

The 90% holding in Gordon was acquired when Gordon's reserves were £11,000. James holds 9% of the share capital of Henry as a fixed asset investment. For the purposes of SSAP8 ('grossing up' dividends received) income tax is to be taken as 30%.

Required

A consolidated profit and loss account.

(18 marks)

14 GROUP ACCOUNTS (ii)

QUESTION 14.1 (BASICS)

Terence and Toby

The summarised balance sheets of Terence and its subsidiary Toby are as follows:

	Terence £	Toby £
Fixed assets	120,100	60,000
Investments in Toby	28,100	—
Stock	31,000	18,000
Debtors	19,700	13,000
Current account	(7,000)	7,000
Cash at bank	2,500	1,800
Creditors	(16,400)	(15,200)
Loan capital	(35,000)	(20,000)
	143,000	64,600
Ordinary share capital	50,000	20,000
Preference share capital	30,000	10,000
Profit and loss account	48,000	30,400
Revaluation reserve	15,000	4,200
	143,000	64,600

Details of shareholdings in Toby are as follows:

(1) 16,000 ordinary shares at cost of £25,000 when reserves were P/L £8,000 and revaluation reserve £1,200.
(2) 3,000 preference shares at a cost of £3,100.

Required

A consolidated balance sheet assuming that consolidation goodwill is eliminated against reserves.

(15 marks)

QUESTION 14.2 (INTERMEDIATE)

Tom and Jerry

Several years ago, Tom Ltd acquired the following shareholdings in Jerry Ltd. At the date of both acquisitions, the reserves of Jerry Ltd amounted to £20,000.

	Number of shares	Cost of investment £
£1 Ordinary shares	37,500	58,000
£1 Preference shares	16,000	15,000
		73,000

The balance sheets of the two companies at 31.12.X9 were as follows:

	Tom Ltd £	Jerry Ltd £
Ordinary share capital	200,000	50,000
7% Preference share capital	—	40,000
Profit and loss	120,000	38,000
Sundry creditors	56,100	22,100
Proposed dividends:		
Ordinary	20,000	2,500
Preference	—	1,400
	396,100	154,000
Tangible fixed assets	210,000	110,600
Current assets	113,100	43,400
Investment in Jerry Ltd	73,000	—
	396,100	154,000

You further ascertain that:

(1) Current assets of Tom Ltd includes £42,000 of goods acquired originally from Jerry Ltd. Jerry Ltd invoiced these goods at cost plus 20%.
(2) Tom Ltd has not yet accounted for dividends receivable from Jerry Ltd.
(3) Assume consolidation goodwill is written off against reserves.

Required

Consolidated balance sheet of Tom as at 31.12.X9.

(18 marks)

QUESTION 14.3 (ADVANCED)

Black Root

Please refer to the information contained in Annexe A.

Required

Prepare a summarised consolidated balance sheet as at 31 December 19X3 for Black Root Ltd and the subsidiary Confectioners Ltd.

Note: You are not required to include Health Sales Ltd in the consolidation or use the equity accounting method.

(30 marks)

(ACCA, AAP, June 84)

QUESTION 14.4 (BASIC)

Nicklaus and Palmer

Nicklaus plc has for many years held the following shareholdings in Palmer Ltd.

	Percentage held	Reserves at date of purchase £
Ordinary shares	60%	30,000
Preference shares	20%	not relevant

Summarised profit and loss accounts for the year ended 31 December 19X4 show the following:

	Nicklaus £	Palmer £
Operating profit	125,000	54,000
Dividends received and receivable		
Ordinary – received	3,000	—
– receivable	4,800	—
Preference – received	600	—
– receivable	600	—
Profit before tax	134,000	54,000
Tax	50,000	20,000
Profit after tax	84,000	34,000
Ordinary dividends – paid	(20,000)	(5,000)
– proposed	(30,000)	(8,000)
Preference dividends – paid	—	(3,000)
– proposed	—	(3,000)
Retained profit	34,000	15,000
Balance b/f	102,000	62,000
Balance c/f	136,000	77,000

Required

Prepare a consolidated profit and loss account for the year ended 31 December 19X4.

(14 marks)

QUESTION 14.5 (INTERMEDIATE)

Hydrogen

The summarised profit and loss accounts of Hydrogen, Bromine and Chlorine for the year ended 31 March 19X4 were as follows:

	Hydrogen £	Bromine £	Chlorine £
Turnover	2,000	1,750	600
Cost of sales	700	950	300
Gross profit	1,300	800	300
Distribution costs	(50)	(60)	(20)
Administrative expenses	(350)	(170)	(60)
Trading profit	900	570	220
Dividends income			
Bromine	126	—	—
Chlorine	48	—	—
Profit on ordinary activities	1,074	570	220
Corporation tax	400	200	100
Profit after tax	674	370	120
Dividends – paid 15.11.X4	(100)	—	(10)
– proposed	(300)	(140)	(60)
Retained profit	274	230	50
Balance at 1.4.X3	2,000	800	300
Balance at 31.3.X4	2,274	1,030	350

The following information is also relevant:

(1) Hydrogen acquired 90% of Bromine several years ago when Bromine's reserves were £200.
(2) Hydrogen acquired 80% of Chlorine on 1.1.X4.

Required

A consolidated profit and loss account for the year ended 31 March 19X4.

(17 Marks)

QUESTION 14.6 (INTERMEDIATE)

Holds

The summarised profit and loss accounts of Holds, Alton and Brown Ltd for the year ended 31 December 19X9 were as follows:

	Holds £	Alton £	Brown £
Turnover	500,000	200,000	100,000
Cost of sales	410,000	170,000	84,000
Gross profit	90,000	30,000	16,000
Distribution costs	(10,000)	(4,000)	(1,000)
Administrative expenses	(20,000)	(8,000)	(2,000)
Trading profit	60,000	18,000	13,000
Dividends received (receivable)			
Trade investments	1,200	—	300
Ordinary shares (Alton)	6,300	—	—
Preference shares (Alton)	200	—	—
Ordinary shares (Brown)	3,500	—	—
Profit on ordinary activities	71,200	18,000	13,300
Corporation tax	30,000	7,000	6,000
Profit after tax	41,200	11,000	7,300
Dividends:			
paid – ordinary	(12,000)	(3,000)	(2,000)
– preference	—	(500)	—
proposed – ordinary	(20,000)	(4,000)	(3,000)
– preference		(500)	
Retained profit	9,200	3,000	2,300
Balance at 1.1.X9	40,000	20,600	10,500
Balance at 31.12.X9	49,200	23,600	12,800

The following information is also relevant:

(1) Holds acquired the following shareholdings in Alton and Brown several years ago, when the profit and loss reserves were as indicated:

Alton Ltd
Ordinary shares 90% (reserves at acquisition £4,600)
Preference shares 20%

Brown Ltd
Ordinary shares 70% (reserves at acquisition £1,500)

(2) Alton Ltd sold £36,000 of goods (at selling price) to Brown. Brown holds one-sixth in stock at the year-end. Selling price is determined by adding 20% on to cost.
(3) Income tax is 30%.

Required

A consolidated profit and loss account for the year ended 31 December 19X9.

(20 marks)

QUESTION 14.7 (ADVANCED)

Redland and Kingsdown

The summarised balance sheets of Redland plc and its subsidiary Kingsdown Ltd at 31 December 19X9 were as follows:

	Redland plc £	Kingsdown Ltd £
Freehold premises, at revaluation	1,617,844	543,695
Plant, machinery and equipment – cost	892,120	693,506
– depreciation	(505,190)	(456,086)
Investment in Kingsdown Ltd at cost		
Ordinary shares	235,600	—
Preference shares	21,240	—
Stock	582,196	237,560
Debtors	367,530	196,430
Prepayments	29,240	17,233
Current account with Redland plc	—	61,320
Cash at bank and in hand	—	19,582
	3,240,580	1,313,240
Trade creditors	117,690	70,240
Accrued expenses	15,760	3,920
Corporation tax	297,380	196,730
Proposed dividends – ordinary shares	240,000	90,000
Bank overdraft	86,750	—
Current account with Kingsdown Ltd	50,320	—
8% loan stock 19X16 – 19X19	500,000	—
Share capital:		
£1 ordinary shares	800,000	300,000
£1 preference shares	—	100,000
Profit and loss account	561,230	285,000
Share premium account	175,000	80,000
Revaluation reserve	396,450	187,350
	3,240,580	1,313,240

The following additional information is provided:

(1) Investments in Kingsdown Ltd were acquired in 19X2 as follows:

			Reserves at date of purchase		
	Number acquired	Cost of investment £	Profit & loss A/C £	Share premium £	Revaluation reserve £
Ordinary shares	240,000	235,600	75,000	80,000	95,000
Preference shares	20,000	21,240	82,200	80,000	95,000

(2) There is a considerable amount of inter-company trading between Kingsdown Ltd and Redland plc. During the year, inter-company sales by Kingsdown Ltd amounted to £595,700.
   At the year end the stocks of Redland plc include £69,000 (at transfer price) of goods purchased from Kingsdown Ltd. Transfer price is determined at cost plus 25% mark-up.
   As a result of a recording error, trade creditors of Redland plc include £11,000 in respect of amounts owing to Kingsdown Ltd.

(3) During the year, Redland plc has provided management services on behalf of Kingsdown Ltd. The value of services provided amounts to £84,000. Although no accounting entries have yet been put through, both companies have agreed that this amount should be reflected in the group accounts and in the accounts of the individual companies.

Required

The consolidated balance sheet of Redland plc and its subsidiary as at 31 December 19X9.

(26 marks)

15 VERTICAL AND MIXED GROUPS

QUESTION 15.1 (INTERMEDIATE)

Greendale

Langdale acquired 90% of the share capital of Treeside on 1 July 19X2 when the profit and loss reserves of Treeside amount to £80.

On 8 August 19X4, Greendale acquired 60% of the share capital of Langdale. At that date the profit and loss reserves of Langdale and Treeside amounted to £550 and £180 respectively.

The summarised balance sheets of the three companies at 31 December 19X8 were as follows:

	Greendale £	Langdale £	Treeside £
Tangible fixed assets	800	700	400
Net current assets	340	290	170
Investment in Langdale	820	—	—
Investment in Treeside	—	242	—
	1,960	1,232	570
Ordinary share capital	1,000	500	150
Profit and loss account	960	732	420
	1,960	1,232	570

Greendale's accounting policy regarding purchased goodwill is to eliminate it by immediate write-off against reserves.

Required

Consolidated balance sheet of Greendale and its subsidiaries as at 31 December 19X8.

(15 marks)

QUESTION 15.2 (ADVANCED)

Machinery

On 1 April 19X1 Machinery Ltd bought 80% of the ordinary share capital of Components Ltd and on 1 April 19X3 Machinery Ltd was itself taken over by Sales Ltd who purchased 75% of the ordinary shares in Machinery Ltd.

The balance sheets of the three companies at 31 October 19X5 prepared for internal use showed the following positions:

	Sales Ltd £	Sales Ltd £	Machinery Ltd £	Machinery Ltd £	Components Ltd £	Components Ltd £
FIXED ASSETS						
Freehold land at cost		89,000		30,000		65,000
Buildings at cost	100,000		120,000		40,000	
Less:						
Accumulated depreciation	36,000		40,000		16,400	
		64,000		80,000		23,600
Plant and equipment at cost	102,900		170,000		92,000	
Less:						
Accumulated depreciation	69,900		86,000		48,200	
		33,000		84,000		43,800
		186,000		194,000		132,400

	Sales Ltd		Machinery Ltd		Components Ltd	
	£	£	£	£	£	£
INVESTMENTS						
Shares in Machinery at cost		135,000				
Shares in Components at cost				96,000		
CURRENT ASSETS						
Stocks	108,500		75,500		68,400	
Debtors	196,700		124,800		83,500	
Cash at bank	25,200		—		25,400	
		330,400		200,300		177,300
		651,400		490,300		309,700
CURRENT LIABILITIES						
Creditors	160,000		152,700		59,200	
Bank overdraft	—		37,400		—	
Corporation tax	57,400		47,200		24,500	
Proposed dividends	80,000		48,000		12,000	
		297,400		285,300		95,700
		354,000		205,000		214,000
Ordinary shares		200,000		120,000		100,000
10% Preference shares		—		—		40,000
Revenue reserves		154,000		85,000		74,000
		354,000		205,000		214,000

MACHINERY

Additional information:

(a) All ordinary shares are £1 each, fully paid.
(b) Preference shares in Components Ltd are 50p each fully paid.
(c) Proposed dividends in Components Ltd are:

    on ordinary shares   £10,000
    on preference shares   £2,000

(d) Proposed dividends receivable by Sales Ltd and Machinery Ltd are included in debtors.
(e) All creditors are payable within one year.
(f) Items purchased by Machinery Ltd from Components Ltd and remaining in stock at 31 October 19X5 amounted to £25,000. The profit element is 20% of selling price for Components Ltd.
(g) Depreciation policy of the group is to provide for:

    (i) buildings – at the rate of 2% on cost each year;
    (ii) plant and equipment – at the rate of 10% on cost each year including full provision in the year of acquisition.

These policies are applied by all members of the group. Included in the plant and equipment of Components Ltd is a machine purchased from the manufacturers, Machinery Ltd on 1 January 19X4 for £10,000. Machinery Ltd recorded a profit of £2,000 on the sale of the machine.

(h) Intra-group balances are included in debtors and creditors respectively and are as follows:

			£
Sales Ltd	Creditors – Machinery Ltd		45,600
	– Components Ltd		28,900
Machinery Ltd	Debtors	– Sales Ltd	56,900
Components Ltd	Debtors	– Sales Ltd	28,900

(i) A cheque drawn by Sales Ltd for £11,300 on 28 October 19X5 was received by Machinery Ltd on 3 November 19X5.
(j) At 1 April 19X1 reserves in Machinery Ltd were £28,000 and in Components Ltd £20,000. At 1 April 19X3 the figures were £40,000 and £60,000 respectively.

Required

Prepare a group balance sheet at 31 October 19X5 for Sales Ltd and its subsidiaries complying, so far as the information will allow, with the accounting requirements of the Companies Act.

(40 marks)

(ACCA, AAP, Dec 85)

16 ACQUISITIONS, MERGERS AND SSAP 14

QUESTION 16.1 (INTERMEDIATE)

Merger Corporation

The following details relate to different situations regarding the acquisition of shares by the Merger Corporation plc. You are required to indicate, giving reasons, those situations in which SSAP 23 permits the use of merger accounting for the group accounts.

In each case the total share capital of the company in which the shares are purchased is 1,000 shares of £1 nominal value.

(1) *Company A:* 50 shares in A were acquired several years ago by means of purchase on the open market at a cost of £80. 900 shares in A are now acquired by the issue of 200 shares in Merger Corporation each valued at £4.

(2) *Company B:* 150 shares in Company B acquired several years ago by means of open market purchases at a total cost of £320. Merger Corporation is now acquiring 800 shares in Company B by the issue of 500 shares in Merger Corporation valued at £4.

(3) *Company C:* Merger Corporation makes an offer to the shareholders of Company C of one £1 ordinary shares in Merger Corporation in exchange for every 2 shares in Company C, with a cash alternative of 175p per share in C.

90% of Company B's shareholders accept the share offer (the remaining 10% accepting the cash offer). Merger Corporation's shares are valued at £4 each.

(4) *Company D:* Merger Corporation acquired 240 shares in Company D by means of a cash purchase of £570 from the Loanshire Life Assurance Company. Recently 80 shares were sold for £320 to the Grenstead Trust Company (who frequently acted as financial adviser to the Merger Corporation).

Subsequently the Merger Corporation announced a bid for the shares in Company B which it did not presently hold. The terms of the bid were 3 shares in Merger Corporation (valued at £4) for every 2 shares in Company B. The offer was subsequently accepted by all the shareholders of Company D.

(5) *Company E:* Merger Corporation acquired the entire share capital of Company E by means of a share-for-share exchange. The terms of the exchange were 4 shares in Merger Corporation for every 2 shares in Company E.

Merger Corporation had entered into a vendor rights arrangement whereby the shareholders of Company E would sell their shares in Merger Corporation to the shareholders of Merger Corporation at a price of 930 pence per share.

Required

Indicate, giving reasons, in which of the above situations SSAP 23 permits the use of merger accounting for the use of the group accounts.

(15 marks)

QUESTION 16.2 (INTERMEDIATE)

Holdings

The managing director of Holdings plc is considering with his merchant bankers the mix of the consideration in formulating the proposals to make an offer for all the ordinary shares in Sitting Duck plc. He is concerned about the effect on the consolidated accounts of Holdings plc of the various offers the company could make in the light of the principles for accounting for acquisitions and mergers now embodied in SSAP 23, and the two different methods of accounting dependent upon the circumstances of the business combinations.

Required

Write a report to the managing director stating:

(a) what conditions are required to be met if merger accounting is to be used (3 marks);
(b) what the differences in principle are between acquisition accounting and merger accounting (3 marks);
(c) how the difference on consolidation is calculated under merger accounting and how it is reflected in financial statements (3 marks); and
(d) the advantages and disadvantages of using each method of accounting so that he can structure a proposed deal using the appropriate method (12 marks).

(21 marks)

(ICAEW, FA2, July 86)

QUESTION 16.3 (ADVANCED)

Hillside

On 30 September 19X4 Hillside plc issued 300,000 50p ordinary shares as consideration for the entire share capital of Birkdale plc. On 30 September 19X4, the shares at Hillside were valued at 150p.

The draft summarised financial statements of the two companies for the year ended 31 December 19X4 were as follows. No entries have yet been made in the books of Hillside as regards the investment in Birkdale.

Profit and loss account

	Hillside £'000	Birkdale £'000
Turnover	165	88
Operating expenses	65	56
Operating profit	100	32
Taxation	30	12
Profit after tax	70	20
Balance at 1.1.X4	158	65
Balance at 31.12.X4	228	85

Balance sheets at 31.12.X4

	Hillside £'000	Birkdale £'000
Tangible fixed assets	423	174
Net current assets	272	96
	695	270
Ordinary share capital (50p shares)	300	100
Share premium account	72	20
Revaluation reserve	95	65
Profit and loss account	228	85
	695	270

The following additional information may be relevant:

(1) The business combination satisfies the necessary merger conditions specified in SSAP 23 (Accounting for acquisitions and mergers).
(2) The fair value of the tangible fixed assets of Birkdale as at 30 September 19X4 has been established as £310,000.
(3) The reserves of Birkdale at 30 September 19X4 were as follows:

	£'000
(a) share premium account	20
(b) revaluation reserve	65
(c) profit and loss account	80

Required

The consolidated balance sheet at 31.12.X4 and the consolidated profit and loss account for the year ended on that date assuming the business combination is accounted for using.

(a) acquisition accounting (consolidation goodwill being written off against reserves as soon as it arises);

(b) merger accounting.

Where relevant, account should be taken of CA85, S 131.

(23 marks)

QUESTION 16.4 (ADVANCED)

Consolidated Furniture Group

Consolidated Furniture Group plc wishes to adopt the merger accounting principles in SSAP 23, *Accounting for acquisitions and mergers*, in respect of its combination with Tables & Chairs Ltd on 30 September 19X3.

On 1 August 19X3 Consolidated Furniture Group plc acquired 5% of the issued share capital of Tables and Chairs Ltd for a consideration of 80,000 shares of 25p each at an agreed value of 125p each.

The terms of the merger on 30 September 19X3, which were accepted by all shareholders and declared unconditional on the same day, were that for every 8 shares held in Tables and Chairs Ltd, a holder received 20 shares of 25p each at an agreed value of 135p each in Consolidated Furniture Group plc plus £3 nominal of 13% Unsecured Loan Stock 2002.

All the shares issued were credited as fully paid and ranked pari passu with existing shares in issue except that those issued on 30 September 19X3 were not to rank for the final dividend in respect of the year ended 30 November 19X3.

The draft summarised balance sheet and profit and loss account of the companies for the year ended 30 November 19X3, the accounting reference date for Consolidated Furniture Group plc, were:

	Consolidated Furniture Group plc £'000	Tables & Chairs Ltd £'000
Balance sheet:		
Fixed assets	4,563	3,092
Goodwill at cost	—	800
Investments	175	—
Current assets	2,369	3,626
Current liabilities	(2,286)	(4,207)
	4,821	3,311
Share capital	3,000	1,600
Reserves	1,821	1,711
	4,821	3,311
Profit and loss account:		
Turnover	36,873	25,003
Profit before tax	1,151	127
Taxation	260	—
Profit after tax	891	127
Dividends paid	288	—
Profits retained	603	127

Additional information is given as follows:

(1) The reserves of Consolidated Furniture Group plc at 30 November 19X3 consisted of a share premium account of £140,000 and revenue reserves of £1,681,000. The reserves in Tables & Chairs Ltd are undistributed revenue reserves.

(2) The issue of the shares made on 1 August 19X3 is reflected in the draft financial statements.
(3) It is the policy of Consolidated Furniture Group plc to write off goodwill in equal instalments over 5 years.
(4) It is considered that the market value of the 13% loan stock issued is par.
(5) The share capitals of the companies are:

    Consolidated Furniture Group plc – ordinary 25p each
    Tables and Chairs Ltd   – ordinary £1 each

(6) The directors of Consolidated Furniture Group plc resolve to propose a final dividend of 1p per share. This is not yet reflected in the draft financial statements.

Required

(a) prepare a consolidated balance sheet and profit and loss account in summary form, of Consolidated Furniture Group plc at 30 November 19X3 (14 marks);
(b) give the revised analysis of reserves of Consolidated Furniture Group plc at 30 November 19X3 suitable for inclusion in the published financial statements (5 marks);
(c) comment whether you consider merger accounting to be appropriate in the above example giving an indication of advantages which may arise (5 marks).

Note: Make calculations to nearest £'000 and ignore the costs of the merger and advance corporation tax.

(24 marks)

(ICAEW, FA2, Dec 83)

QUESTION 16.5 (ADVANCED)

Willow

Please refer to the information in Annexe C. This question should be completed after attempting Question 5.4.

Required

(a) Using the additional information supplied in Appendices 4 and 5, prepare a consolidated balance sheet for Willow Ltd as at 31 December 19X5 on the basis that Willow Ltd merged with Pourwell Ltd on 31 December 19X5 (18 marks).
(b) Show the capital and reserves section and the change in the composition of the assets of the consolidated balance sheet prepared on the basis that the acquisition of shares by Willow Ltd is treated as a parent acquisition (8 marks).
(c) Comment on the proposed merger from the viewpoint of a shareholder whom you may assume to currently own 100 ordinary shares in Pourwell Ltd (6 marks).

(32 marks)

(ACCA, AAP, June 86)

17 ACCOUNTING FOR FIXED ASSET INVESTMENTS

QUESTION 17.1 (BASIC)

H, S, A

Summarised balance sheets at 31.12.X4 were as follows:

	H £	S £	A £
Tangible fixed assets	6,000	12,100	6,600
Current assets	8,500	7,500	5,000
Current accounts	3,000	(2,000)	(1,000)
Dividends receivable	950	—	—
Dividends payable	(2,000)	(1,000)	(600)
Current liabilities	(5,000)	(4,000)	(2,000)
Investment in S (80%)	8,000	—	—
Investment in A (25%)	2,100	—	—
	21,550	12,600	8,000
Called up share capital – £1 ordinary shares	10,000	7,000	3,000
Profit and loss account	8,550	3,600	3,400
Revaluation reserve	3,000	2,000	1,600
	21,550	12,600	8,000

Reserves at acquisition were as follows:

P/L		1,200	700
Revaluation		400	1,200

Required

Consolidated balance sheet (in summarised form) at 31 December 19X4.

(12 marks)

QUESTION 17.2 (INTERMEDIATE)

Kettlewell

Kettlewell plc acquired 80% of the share capital of Dale Ltd several years ago when the reserves of Dale amounted to £160, and 70% of Fell Ltd when Fell's reserves amounted to £40.

The summarised balance sheets of the three companies at 31 December 19X8 are as follows:

	K £	D £	F £
Tangible fixed assets	309	230	90
Investment in D	235	—	—
Investment in F	88	—	—
Net current assets	116	100	30
	748	330	120
Called up share capital	200	100	50
Profit and loss account	548	230	70
	748	330	120

Required

Consolidated balance sheet of Kettlewell and its subsidiaries assuming:

(a) all three companies are consolidated;
(b) Dale is excluded from consolidation and accounted for by the equity method of accounting.

(15 marks)

QUESTION 17.3 (ADVANCED)

Falcondale

The summarised financial statements for 19X5 of Falcondale Ltd and its subsidiary Henleaze Ltd are as follows:

Balance sheets

	Falcondale £	Henleaze £
Fixed assets	25,180	7,260
Investment in Henleaze	6,500	—
Stock	3,100	1,900
Debtors	2,950	1,350
Cash	870	690
Dividends receivable	540	—
	39,140	11,200
Ordinary share capital	20,000	5,000
Profit and loss account	11,240	3,900
Dividends payable	3,000	600
Creditors	4,900	1,700
	39,140	11,200

Profit and loss accounts

	Falcondale £	Henleaze £
Turnover	30,000	8,000
Operating expenses	15,600	3,200
Operating profit	14,400	4,800
Dividends receivable	540	—
Profit before tax	14,940	4,800
Taxation	7,200	2,400
Profit after tax	7,740	2,400
Dividends proposed	3,000	600
	4,740	1,800
Balance B/F	6,500	2,100
Balance C/F	11,240	3,900

Falcondale acquired 90% of the ordinary share capital of Henleaze at a cost of £6,500 when the reserves of Henleaze amounted to £950.

Required

Prepare consolidated accounts under the alternative assumption that Henleaze is accounted for by:

(a) the cost method;
(b) the equity method;
(c) normal (conventional) consolidation;
(d) pro-rata (proportion equity) consolidation.

Where relevant assume goodwill arising on consolidation is to be treated as an intangible fixed asset.

(30 marks)

QUESTION 17.4 (ADVANCED)

Plural Publishers

Please refer to the information in Annexe B.

Required

Prepare a consolidated profit and loss account for the Plural Publishers Group for the year ended 30 September 19X4.

(32 marks)

(ACCA, AAP, June 85)

18 ACCOUNTING FOR OVERSEAS OPERATIONS

QUESTION 18.1 (INTERMEDIATE)

Methods

SSAP 20: Foreign currency translation (1983) constitutes the first definitive statement of practice in this area.

Required

(a) to define concisely the two methods of currency translation specified in SSAP 20 (4 marks);
(b) to explain the precise circumstances in which the use of each method is mandatory under SSAP 20 (8 marks); and
(c) to justify the treatment prescribed in SSAP 20 for overseas investment financed by overseas borrowing (3 marks).

(15 marks)

(ACCA, AFA, June 84)

QUESTION 18.2 (INTERMEDIATE)

Factors

With regard to SSAP 20 'Foreign currency translation':

(a) Explain the closing rate/net investment method (7 marks).
(b) Explain the temporal method (7 marks).
(c) What factors should be taken into account in deciding whether the temporal method should be adopted? Give *two* examples of situations where this method may be the most appropriate (11 marks).

(25 marks)

(ACCA, RFA, June 85)

QUESTION 18.3 (INTERMEDIATE)

Terrier and Spaniel

SSAP 20 deals with foreign currency translation. The overseas activities of two UK based companies are as follows:

(1) Terrier Ltd has two overseas branches as follows:
   (i) One branch in South America is concerned with buying raw materials for use in the company's UK manufacturing operation. The branch will arrange purchases from local suppliers settling the payments either on monthly accounts or on three month bills. The funds will be remitted from the UK on a monthly imprest system. The rates of exchange in the South American country have been volatile and local inflation has averaged 120% for the past three years. There are also restrictions on the export of currency. The branch's fixed assets consist of office equipment and motor vehicles and specific currency has been remitted from the UK for each item.
   (ii) The other branch is based in West Germany. It assembles local components which are shipped back to the company in the UK for inclusion in its own products. All purchases are made locally with funds remitted from the UK. The expatriate manager is paid directly from the UK. A Swiss franc loan is outstanding from a bank in Switzerland which was used to

61

purchase the factory in West Germany. The rates of exchange have been fairly constant but there has been some variation in the exchange rate between the franc and the mark.

(2) Spaniel plc has several subsidiaries. The following are its overseas subsidiaries:
  (i) Alsatian is concerned with the manufacture of chains in Italy and was purchased four years ago. It is run by local management and all transactions take place in Italy.
  (ii) Boxer is based in the Cayman Islands and is a captive insurance company for the UK parts of the group. In the UK companies' accounting records insurance premiums are credited in sterling to a current account with Boxer at the beginning of the financial year. Claims are debited to this current account as they arise and the resultant balance paid at the year end. When a premium is credited the appropriate foreign currency is bought forward at the year end rate and used to settle the balance due. Boxer, which carries on no business outside the UK group, enters each credit or debit in its accounting records in local currency translated at the daily spot rate.

Required

(a) Give the details of the two alternative treatments set out for the translation of financial statements in SSAP 20 and explain the circumstances in which they should be applied (9 marks).
(b) State briefly how you would deal with the translation of foreign currencies arising in the cases of Terrier Ltd and Spaniel plc stating specifically the accounting treatment of any profit or loss arising (9 marks).

(18 marks)

(ICAEW, FA2, July 84)

QUESTION 18.4 (INTERMEDIATE)

Overseas

Home acquired 80% of the share capital of Overseas several years ago when the reserves of Overseas amounted to $200 and the exchange rate was 3$ = £1.
  The summarised financial statements of the two companies for the year ended 31 December 19X4 are as follows:

Balance sheets

	Home (£) £	Overseas ($) £
Fixed assets	7,350	2,400
Investment in Overseas	650	—
Net current assets	1,500	1,200
	9,500	3,600
Loans	1,000	600
Ordinary share capital	2,000	1,300
Profit and loss account	6,500	1,700
	9,500	3,600

Profit and loss account

Sales	2,000	800
Operating expenses	500	500
Operating profit	1,500	300
Balance b/f	5,000	1,400
Balance c/f	6,500	1,700

Exchange rates:

1.1.X4	2.6$ = £1
Average X4	2.3$ = £1
31.12.X4	2.0$ = £1

Required

Summarised consolidated balance sheet and profit and loss account assuming the subsidiary is translated using the closing rate/net investment method, profit and loss account being translated at average rate (16 marks).

QUESTION 18.5 (ADVANCED)

Basil's Hotels plc – closing rate

Basil's Hotels plc acquired 90% of the equity share capital of Manuel SA when Manuel's reserves amounted to 225 pesetas.

The summarised financial statements of the two companies for the year ended 31 December 19X9 were as follows:

(a) Profit and loss account

	Basil's Hotels £	Manuel P
Turnover	1,500	900
Operating expenses	(630)	(240)
Operating profit	870	660
Dividends from Manuel	52	—
Loan interest paid	(10)	(20)
Profit before tax	912	640
Taxation	(405)	(300)
Profit after tax	507	340
Dividends:		
interim (paid)	(50)	(80)
final (proposed)	(90)	(120)
Retained profit	367	140
Balance at 1.1.X9	725	610
Balance at 31.12.X9	1,092	750

(b) Balance sheets

	Basil's Hotels £	Manuel P
Tangible fixed assets		
– cost	3,076	2,650
– accumulated depreciation	1,322	1,447
	1,754	1,203
Investment in Manuel	84	—
Stock	737	309
Debtors	698	234
Cash at bank	211	96
Dividends receivable	32	—
Long-term loans	(900)	(200)
Creditors	(229)	(172)
Taxation	(405)	(300)
Proposed dividends	(90)	(120)
	1,892	1,050
Called up share capital		
– ordinary shares	800	300
Profit and loss account	1,092	750
	1,892	1,050

(c) Exchange rates

Acquisition of Manuel	7.1p = £1
1.1.X9	4.0p = £1
Average X9	3.7p = £1
Payment of dividend	3.5p = £1
31.12.X9	3.4p = £1

Required

Consolidated balance sheet at 31.12.X9 and a consolidated profit and loss account for the year ended on that date using the closing rate/net investment method.

Assume that profit and loss items are to be translated at an average for the year exchange rate and that goodwill on consolidation was written off against reserves in the year of acquisition.

(25 marks)

QUESTION 18.6 (ADVANCED)

Basil's Hotels plc – temporal method

Using the information in Basil's Hotels – closing rate, prepare a consolidated balance sheet and consolidated profit and loss account assuming the subsidiary is translated into sterling using the temporal method. The following additional information regarding exchange rates is provided:

At acquisition of fixed assets 6.9 = £1

Assume that operating expenses include 152 pesetas in respect of depreciation and that the tax charge is to be translated at average rate.

(25 marks)

QUESTION 18.7 (ADVANCED)

Basil's cover

The basic information is as provided in Basil's Hotels plc – closing rate. Assume in addition that Basil's Hotels took out a foreign currency loan in order to help finance the investment in Manuel. The company wishes to compare the implications of the relief offered by SSAP 20 in respect of equity interests financed by foreign borrowings both as regards the separate accounts of Basil's Hotels and as regards the consolidated accounts.

Required

Compare the situations both with and without relief for holding company and consolidated accounts respectively, assuming the loan was

(a) 320 pesetas
(b) 1,060 pesetas.

(20 marks)

19 ACCOUNTING FOR PRICE CHANGES (i)

QUESTION 19.1 (INTERMEDIATE)

Sandilands

Several years ago, accountants were attempting to deal with the controversy over the preparation and presentation of annual accounts. The debate at that time was between historical cost (HC), current purchasing power (CPP) and replacement cost (RC).

The CPP technique is based on the same conventions as the HC technique; the only difference between them is the adjustment for general inflation.

Replacement cost has several varieties. The one you are asked to consider in part (a) of this question is that which requires adjustment to an RC basis of fixed asset values in the balance sheet, and of annual depreciation in the profit and loss account plus an adjustment to an RC basis of stock values in the balance sheet and of the cost of stocks used in the profit and loss account. In addition 'holding gains' (excess of RC over HC cost) are credited to replacement reserve and are not transferred to profit and loss account as the asset is realised (i.e. stock sold or asset depreciated). Assume the depreciation charge is based on year-end replacement costs.

Consider the following data:

All transactions are cash transactions. No credit is given or received.

1 Jan	Company formed with issued share capital of £1,500
	Raises loan of £500
	Buys goods £1,000
	Buys an accounting machine £1,000
	General price index = 100
30 June	Sells goods for £1,200
	Replaces goods for £1,100
	General price index = 108
31 Dec	Sells goods for £1,320
	Replaces goods for £1,200
	Pays loan interest £50
	General price index = 116

To replace the accounting machine would cost £1,300.
Depreciation 10% per annum straight line.

The summarised cash account is provided to show (a) the balance at 31 December, and (b) the adjustments made under the customary working schedule to reflect the change in purchasing power between the date of transaction and 31 December.

Summarised cash account

	£H		X	÷	£ December	
CASH RECEIPTS						
1 Jan	1,500		116	100	1,740	
1 Jan	500		116	100	580	
30 June	1,200		116	108	1,289	
31 Dec	1,320	4,520	116	116	1,320	4,929
CASH PAYMENTS						
1 Jan	1,000		116	100	1,160	
1 Jan	1,000		116	100	1,160	
30 June	1,100		116	108	1,181	
31 Dec	1,200		116	116	1,200	
	50	4,350	116	116	50	4,751
net balance		170				178

Required

(a) prepare the profit and loss account for the year ended 31 December and balance sheet at this date using the three different techniques, and
(b) comment upon the differences.

Ignore taxation.

(25 marks)

(ICAEW, FA2, July 76)

QUESTION 19.2 (ADVANCED)

Martin (CPP)

The following information relates to the historical cost accounts of Martin plc:

(a) Profit and loss account for the year ended 31 December 19X5

	£	£
Sales		900
Opening stock	100	
Purchases	690	
	790	
Closing stock	150	
Cost of sales		640
Gross profit		260
Sundry expenses (excl. depreciation)	126	
Depreciation	42	
Interest paid (on last day of year)	24	192
Profit before tax		68
Tax		20
Profit after tax		48
Dividends proposed		25
Retained profit		23
Balance at 1.1.X5		104
Balance at 31.12.X5		127

(b) Balance sheets at 31 December

	19×5 £	19×5 £	19×4 £	19×4 £
Tangible fixed assets		318		280
Current assets				
Stock	150		100	
Debtors	160		140	
Cash at bank	124		191	
	434		431	
Creditors – payable within one year				
Creditors	80		70	
Dividends	25		20	
Taxation	20		17	
	125		107	
Net current assets		309		324
		627		604

Creditors payable in more than one year		
8% debenture stock	(300)	(300)
	327	304
Called up share capital	200	200
Profit and loss account	127	104
	327	304

ADDITIONAL INFORMATION

(1) *Tangible fixed assets*

	19X5	19X4
	£	£
Cost	480	400
Accumulated depreciation	162	120
	318	280

There were no disposals during the year. Depreciation is provided on a straight-line basis at the rate of 10%. Additions to fixed assets took place on 30 September 19X5. Fixed assets held at 31.12.X4 were acquired on 1.1.X2.

(2) *Profit and loss account items*
Sales, purchases and sundry expenses occurred at an even rate during the year.

(3) *Stock ageings*
For both 19X5 and 19X4, it is assumed that balance sheet stock was acquired evenly over the last two months of the year.

(4) *RPI information*

1. 1.X1	100
31.12.X1	106.5
30.11.X4	121.9
31.12.X4	122.5
Average for 19X5	126.7
30. 9.X5	128.5
30.11.X5	129.6
30.12.X5	130.4

Required

Constant purchasing power (CPP) accounts for 19X5, drawn up on the basis of purchasing power at the balance sheet date.

(25 marks)

20 ACCOUNTING FOR PRICE CHANGES (ii)

QUESTION 20.1 (INTERMEDIATE)

Golding

(a) The draft historical cost balance sheets of Golding plc at 31 December 19X2 and 31 December 19X3 are as follows:

	19X2 £	19X3 £
Plant	6,000	5,400
Stock	2,500	3,000
Cash	1,500	12,600
	10,000	21,000
Creditors	2,000	1,000
Shareholder equity	8,000	20,000

The draft historical cost profit and loss account of Golding plc for the year ended 31 December 19X3 is as follows:

		19X3 £
Sales		30,000
Stock at 1 January 19X3	2,500	
Purchases	15,500	
	18,000	
Stock at 1 January 19X3	3,000	
Cost of goods sold		15,000
Gross profit		15,000
Depreciation of plant	600	
Other expenses	2,400	3,000
Profit		12,000

Notes:
 (i) The stock at 31 December 19X3 comprised 300 units acquired at a cost of £10 per unit. The replacement cost of the stock on that date was £11 per unit. The replacement cost of the goods sold on the dates the sales were made was £17,500.
(ii) The gross replacement cost of the plant at 31 December 19X3 was £7,000. There were no additions or disposals of plant during the year. The plant was purchased on the 31 December 19X2, and is depreciated at 10% per annum using the straight line method.

Required

(a) Prepare a replacement cost balance sheet at 31 December 19X3 and a profit and loss account for the year ended on that date, distinguishing between operating gains, and realised and unrealised holding gains (10 marks).
(b) Outline the main arguments for current entry value accounting. (Note: this is also referred to as replacement cost/business income accounting) (10 marks).

(20 marks)

(ACCA, RFA, June 85)

QUESTION 20.2 (ADVANCED)

Martin (CCA)

In 1986, the Accounting Standards Committee published a handbook on accounting for the effects of changing prices. The handbook referred to several capital maintenance concepts including the operating capital maintenance concept.

You are provided with the data contained in Martin plc (CPP) except that the following indices are relevant to the above concept, being based on specific indices for fixed assets and stock:

Fixed assets
1.1.X2	170
1.1.X5	236
30.9.X5	258
31.12.X5	266
Average X5	251

Stocks
30.11.X4	127
31.12.X4	129
Average X5	135
30.11.X5	140
31.12.X5	142

Required

A profit and loss account, incorporating operating capital maintenance concept adjustments, for the year ended 31 December 19X5. Depreciation charge is to be based on year-end replacement costs. Your answer should refer to the two measures of gearing adjustment in the handbook.

(25 marks)

21 ANALYSIS OF ACCOUNTS (i): FUNDS FLOW AND VALUE ADDED

QUESTION 21.1 (BASIC)

Fozzie

You are provided with the following summarised balance sheets of Fozzie Ltd:

	31.12.X2	31.12.X1
Plant and machinery – cost	560,000	500,000
– depreciation	236,000	190,000
– NBV	324,000	310,000
Stock	189,000	142,000
Debtors	99,400	96,300
Cash at bank	—	5,200
Creditors	(86,700)	(88,200)
Overdraft	(18,100)	—
Proposed dividends	(55,000)	(48,000)
Corporation tax	(110,500)	(96,200)
Loans	—	(109,500)
	342,100	211,600
Ordinary share capital	150,000	100,000
Share premium ac.	50,000	—
Profit and loss account	142,100	111,600
	342,100	211,600

Profit and loss account for the year ended 31.12.X2 is as follows:

	£	£
Profit before tax (after depreciation of £46,000)		231,000
Corporation tax		110,500
Profit after tax		120,500
Dividends		
– ordinary (paid)	35,000	
– ordinary (prop)	55,000	90,000
Retained profit		30,500
Balance at 1.1.X1		111,600
Balance at 31.12.X1		142,100

Required

A source and application of funds statement for the year ended 31 December 19X2.

(12 marks)

QUESTION 21.2 (INTERMEDIATE)

Bamford

The balance sheets of Bamford plc at 31.12.X3 and 31.12.X2 were as follows:

	31.12.X3 £	31.12.X2 £
Tangible fixed assets – freehold property	301,000	391,000
Tangible fixed assets – plant and machinery	225,600	160,200

	31.12.X3	31.12.X2
	£	£
Stock	520,000	440,000
Debtors	83,100	53,100
Cash	70,300	1,700
Investment in Upton Ltd	200,000	—
	1,400,000	1,046,000
Called up share capital	150,000	100,000
Profit and loss account	615,000	405,000
Share premium account	100,000	—
Long term loans	—	170,000
Creditors	65,000	51,000
Corporation tax	350,000	230,000
Proposed dividends	120,000	90,000
	1,400,000	1,046,000

ADDITIONAL INFORMATION

(1) Extracts from profit and loss account for year ended 31 December 19X3:

	£	£
Profit on ordinary activities before tax		760,000
Corporation tax		350,000
Profit on ordinary activities after tax		410,000
Dividends on ordinary shares		
Interim (paid)	80,000	
Final (proposed)	120,000	200,000
Retained profit		210,000
Balance at 1.1.X3		405,000
Balance at 31.12.X3		615,000

(2) During the year, depreciation charged on plant and machinery amounted to £16,400. There were no disposals of plant and machinery.
(3) Freehold property with a net book value at sale of £90,000 was sold for proceeds of £125,000. No depreciation had been provided on this asset and the profit on sale was included in profit on ordinary activities before tax.
(4) The investment in Upton Ltd is held as a fixed asset investment.

Required

A source and application of funds statement for the year ended 31.12.X3 in accordance with SSAP 10. Advance corporation tax is to be ignored.

(17 marks)

QUESTION 21.3 (ADVANCED)

Oxenholme

(1) The summarised consolidated balance sheets of Oxenholme at 31 December were as follows:

	19X2	19X1
	£	£
Ordinary share capital (£1 shares)	140,000	100,000
Reserves	609,920	450,400
Minority interest – share capital & reserves	231,475	192,730
– dividends	18,940	12,120
Investment grant suspense account	5,489	4,065
Creditors	196,530	126,490
Taxation	146,300	98,250
Dividends	60,000	35,000
	1,408,654	1,019,055

	19X2 £	19X1 £
Fixed assets	528,090	410,940
Associated company	91,600	71,250
Debtors	156,940	101,253
Cash	21,299	12,672
Quoted investment	13,160	—
Stock	597,565	422,940
	1,408,654	1,019,055

(2) Fixed asset details are as follows:

	Freehold property £	Plant and machinery £	Goodwill £	Development expenditure £	Total £
COST OR REVALUATION					
Balance at 1.1.X2	206,000	183,500	55,000	40,000	484,500
Revaluation	72,000	—	—	—	72,000
Additions	90,000	106,020	20,000	30,000	246,020
Disposals	(120,000)	(67,200)	—	—	(187,200)
Balance	248,000	222,320	75,000	70,000	615,320
DEPRECIATION AND AMORTISATION					
Balance at 1.1.X2	4,600	45,960	11,000	12,000	73,560
Provided during year	1,250	18,020	7,500	14,000	40,770
Eliminated on disposal	(2,020)	(25,080)	—	—	(27,100)
Balance at 31.12.X2	3,830	38,900	18,500	26,000	87,230

(3) Reserves are as follows:

	Retained profits £	Revaluation reserve £	Share premium £	Total £
Balance at 1.1.X2	235,400	130,000	85,000	450,400
Issue of shares	—	—	20,000	20,000
Retained profit	81,920	—	—	81,920
Revaluation	—	57,600	—	57,600
Balance at 31.12.X2	317,320	187,600	105,000	609,920

During the year, the freehold property of an 80% subsidiary was revalued to give a surplus of £72,000 compared with book value. No depreciation had been provided on the freehold buildings.

(4) During the year a subsidiary was acquired for consideration of £83,225 made up as follows:

	£
40,000 £1 shares at 150p	60,000
Cash	23,225
	83,225

The net assets acquired were as follows:

	£
Fixed assets	50,000
Stock	22,100
Debtors	13,600
Creditors	(15,450)
	70,250

Group share 90% (i.e. £63,225) giving rise to goodwill of £20,000.

(5) Details of associated company:

	19X2 £	19X1 £
Premium	2,400	2,400
Net assets	29,200	23,850
	31,600	26,250
Loans	60,000	45,000
	91,600	71,250

(6) Summarised consolidated profit and loss account:

	£	£
Group profit		375,345
Associated company profit		11,075
Profit on ordinary activities before tax		386,420
Corporation tax		
Group	168,915	
Associate	4,225	173,140
Profit on ordinary activities after tax		213,280
Minority interest		49,760
		163,520
Extraordinary loss	(45,000)	
Tax on extraordinary loss	23,400	(21,600)
		141,920
Proposed ordinary dividends		60,000
		81,920

Group profit is arrived at after crediting:

	£
Investment grant credits	596
Profit on sale of freehold	17,880
Profit on sale of plant and after charging:	4,020
Amortisation of goodwill	7,500
Amortisation of development costs	14,000
Depreciation provided	19,270

Required

A source and application of funds statement for the year ended 31 December 19X2. Prepare in accordance with SSAP 10 using both the detailed breakdown and net outlay methods.

(30 marks)

QUESTION 21.4 (ADVANCED)

Plural Publishers – funds flow

Please refer to the information contained in Annexe B.

Required

Prepare a Statement of Source and Application of Funds for the Plural Publishers Group for the year ended 30 September 19X3 in accordance with the principles set out in the relevant Statement of Standard Accounting Practice.

(36 marks)

(ACCA, AAP, June 85)

QUESTION 21.5 (ADVANCED)

Plural Publishers – value added

Please refer to the information contained in Annexe B.

Required

(a) Prepare a Value Added Statement for the Plural Publishers Group for the year ended 30 September 19X4 (16 marks).
(b) Discuss the use of such a statement to an existing shareholder of Plural Publishers Ltd (10 marks).
(c) Discuss alternative treatments for:
   (i) minority interest
   (ii) depreciation (6 marks).

(32 marks)

(ACCA, AAP, June 85)

QUESTION 21.6 (ADVANCED)

Confectioners – valued added

Please refer to the information contained in Annex A.

Required

(a) Prepare a Value Added Statement for Confectioners Ltd for the year ended 31 December 19X3 with comparative figures (15 marks).
(b) Provide five ratios from the Value Added Statement that you consider would be of interest to employees of the firm with a brief note on the information shown by each (10 marks).

(25 marks)

(ACCA, AAP, June 84)

QUESTION 21.7 (INTERMEDIATE)

Additional statements

There has been increasing concern in recent years that successive Accounting Standards and statutory requirements have made published financial statements understandable only by accountants and investment analysts and not by one of the groups most concerned, a company's employees.

Required

(a) outline the content (without figures) of two additional statements, not at present required by either Company Law or Accounting Standard, which would be helpful to a company's employees as distinct from its shareholders (9 marks), and
(b) appraise the usefulness of your chosen statements for their intended purposes (5 marks).

(14 marks)

(ICAEW, FA2, Dec 83)

22 ANALYSIS OF ACCOUNTS (ii): EARNINGS PER SHARE

QUESTION 22.1 (BASIC)

Portishead

The following extract is taken from the group accounts of Portishead for the year ended 31 December 19X7:

	£
Turnover	3,760,000
Operating expenses	1,890,000
Operating profit	1,870,000
Interest receivable	120,000
Profit on ordinary activities before tax	1,990,000
Taxation	635,000
Profit after tax	1,355,000
Minority interest	460,000
	895,000
Extraordinary items	210,000
	1,105,000
Dividends	550,000
Retained profit	555,000

The number of 25p ordinary shares in issue throughout the year was 4 million. The company also had 500,000 £1 6% preference shares.

Required

Calculate the earnings per share for 19X7.

(4 marks)

QUESTION 22.2 (INTERMEDIATE)

Orbison

The following extract relates to the profit and loss account of Orbison plc for the year ended 31 December 19X4.

	£
Operating profit	230,000
Interest payable	16,000
Profit before tax	214,000
Corporation tax (assumed 50%)	107,000
Profit after tax	107,000
Dividends on ordinary shares	50,000
Retained profit	57,000

(1) The company has 400,000 ordinary shares in issue.
(2) The interest above relates to £200,000 of 8% convertible loan stock. Conversion terms are as follows:

19X6	100 shares for £200 loan stock
19X7	97 shares for £200 loan stock
19X8	95 shares for £200 loan stock

Required

The basic earnings per share and the fully diluted earnings per share statistics in relation to the year ended 31 December 19X4.

(12 marks)

QUESTION 22.3 (INTERMEDIATE)

Earnings per share

Answer the following questions in accordance with SSAP 3 'Earnings per Share' (EPS).

(a) Why is it considered important to measure EPS and what figure for earnings should you use when calculating EPS for a group of companies with ordinary and preference shares? (8 marks)
(b) Explain the difference between the nil distribution basis and the net basis for calculating EPS and give the advantage of each method (7 marks).
(c) How should you deal with the following situations when calculating EPS?
   (i) the issue of a separate class of equity shares which do not rank for any dividend in the period under review, but which will do so in the future (2 marks);
   (ii) a scrip (or bonus) issue of shares during the year (2 marks);
   (iii) shares issued during the period as consideration for shares in a new subsidiary (2 marks).
(d) On 1 January 19X3 a company had 3 million ordinary shares of £1 each in issue. On 1 July 19X3 the company made a rights issue of 1 for 2 at a price of £1.50. The market price of the existing shares immediately before the rights issue was £2.00. The earnings of the company for the year ended 31 December 19X3 were £750,000.
   Calculate the EPS for the year ended 31 December 19X3 (4 marks).

(25 marks)

(ACCA, RFA, Dec 1984)

QUESTION 22.4 (ADVANCED)

Sandgrit

The consolidated profit and loss account of Sandgrit plc for the year ended 31 December 19X1 showed the following:

	£	£
Trading profit before interest		2,498,151
Interest payable		1,948,268
		549,883
Share of profits less losses of associated companies		277,085
Group trading profit before taxation and extraordinary items		826,968
Taxation		110,648
Group profit after taxation and before extraordinary items		716,320
Extraordinary items		188,320
Group profit after taxation and extraordinary items		904,640
Dividends – preference	119,000	
– ordinary	386,403	
		505,403
Retained earnings transferred to reserves		399,237

The relevant note in the financial statements on share capital contained the following extract:

	7% Preference shares of £1 each	Ordinary shares of 25p each
Issued and fully paid:		
At 31 December 19X0	1,700,000	11,534,000
Issued in connection with the rights issue on 31 May 19X1	—	4,943,000
Issued in connection with conversion of loan stock on 30 June 19X1	—	20,000
At 31 December 19X1	1,700,000	16,497,000

The middle market price of the company's ordinary shares immediately prior to and after the rights issue on 31 May 19X1 was 33p cum rights and 30.6p ex rights respectively.

Required

(a) Calculate the earnings per share of Sandgrit plc on the net basis for the year ended 31 December 19X1 together with a suitable note for inclusion in the financial statements (10 marks).
(b) State what you understand by the 'nil distribution basis' of calculating earnings per share (3 marks).
(c) Explain why earnings per share is often not a meaningful figure in the context of smaller unquoted companies (3 marks).

(16 marks)

(ICAEW, FA2, Dec 82)

QUESTION 22.5 (ADVANCED)

Toff

The following details have been extracted from the accounts of Toff plc for the year ended 30 June 19X5:

	£'000
Profit before taxation	5,089
Taxation (50%)	2,280
Profit after taxation	2,809
Extraordinary items	156
	2,965
Preference dividend paid	(100)
Ordinary dividends paid and proposed	(1,600)
	1,265

Paid up share capital has been as follows:

1 July 19X3	Ordinary shares — 2 million of 25p each 10% Preference shares — 1 million of £1 each
1 February 19X4	Share options issued to directors. The terms of options were 1 million shares at 40p each subject to the number and price of shares being adjusted for any scrip or rights issue. The option may be exercised in whole or in part on the first day of May 19X5 to 19X7 inclusive.
1 August 19X4	Scrip issue of one ordinary share for every 2 ordinary shares then held.
31 March 19X5	Rights issue made to ordinary shareholders. Terms were one for four already held at a price of 40p payable 31 March 19X5. The cum rights price just prior to the issue was 50p and the ex rights price just after the issue was 46p. The issue was fully taken up.
1 May 19X5	The directors exercised their options in respect of 400,000 shares.

The relevant yields on 2½ per cent Consolidated Stock were as follows:

	Yield
	%
I February 19X4	9.8
30 June 19X4	10.6
1 February 19X5	10.1
30 June 19X5	10.4

Required

Calculate, with detailed workings, the amounts to be disclosed in the accounts in respect of earnings per share for the year ended 30 June 19X5 (17 marks).

Note: You are not required to draft the notes for inclusion in the statutory accounts or to provide corresponding figures.

(17 marks)

(ICAEW, FA2, Dec 85)

23 ANALYSIS OF ACCOUNTS (iii): INTERPRETATION

QUESTION 23.1 (INTERMEDIATE)

Hendale Contractors

The summarised balance sheets and profit and loss accounts of Hendale Contractors plc for the year ended 30 September 19X6 were as follows:

Balance sheets as at 30 September 19X6

	19X6 £	19X6 £	19X5 £	19X5 £
Tangible fixed assets				
Property (at revaluation)		225,000		100,000
Plant (at cost less depreciation)		301,000		295,000
		526,000		395,000
Current assets				
Stock	407,000		221,000	
Debtors	283,000		267,000	
Cash	8,000		310,000	
	698,000		798,000	
Current liabilities				
Creditors	201,000		196,000	
Tax	90,000		120,000	
Dividends	100,000		90,000	
	391,000		406,000	
Net current assets		307,000		392,000
Total assets less current liabilities		833,000		787,000
10% secured debenture stock 19X8		(150,000)		(150,000)
		683,000		637,000
Called up share capital (50p ordinary shares)		100,000		100,000
Profit and loss account		388,000		467,000
Share premium account		60,000		60,000
Revaluation reserve		135,000		10,000
		683,000		637,000

Note: Act is to be ignored.

Profit and loss accounts for the year ended 30 September

	19X6 £	19X5 £
Turnover (credit sales)	1,800,000	1,670,000
Cost of sales	(1,436,000)	(1,169,000)
Gross profit	364,000	501,000
Overhead expenses	(143,000)	(140,000)
Operating profit	221,000	361,000
Interest paid	(20,000)	(18,000)
Profit before tax	201,000	343,000
Taxation	(90,000)	(120,000)
Profit after tax	111,000	223,000
Extraordinary items	(45,000)	—

	19X6	19X5
	£	£
	66,000	223,000
Dividends – paid	(45,000)	(40,000)
– proposed	(100,000)	(90,000)
Retained profit	(79,000)	93,000
Balance b/f	467,000	374,000
Balance c/f	388,000	467,000

Required

You have been approached by Jones, a wealthy individual and prospective purchaser of the business, who has given you a copy of the above financial statements. You have been asked to advise Jones as to the position and prospects of the company. Jones wishes to use any information you may provide in his forthcoming negotiations with the board of directors. The members of the board hold the majority of the shares in the company and have indicated their desire to sell at 'the right price'. In giving your advice you should indicate any additional information which you consider Jones should obtain from the directors prior to making a final decision.

Note: A funds flow statement is *not* required.

(25 marks)

QUESTION 23.2 (INTERMEDIATE)

Financial terms

You act in the capacity of financial adviser to a number of companies. One of them, Fig plc, whose managing director is not familiar with finance, has asked you to explain some financial terms which he does not understand and has also asked you to assist him in obtaining certain information. An extract of the letter received from the managing director of Fig plc is as follows:

'I should be grateful if you would briefly explain the following matters:

(1) For ordinary shares quoted in the *Financial Times*, the following particulars:

Company	Price	+ or –	Dividend net	Cover	Yield gross	P/E
x	x	x	x	x	x	x

(2) This extract from the quotations page of the *Financial Times:*

"Price/earnings ratios are calculated on 'net' distribution basis . . .; bracketed figures indicate 10 per cent or more difference if calculated on 'nil' distribution. Covers are based on 'maximum' distribution."

In addition could you please inform me where I might obtain the following information:

(a) daily share prices for any share quoted on the Stock Exchange, London;
(b) recent dividends and rights issues of UK listed companies;
(c) copies of the financial statements of my competitors, which include both public and private companies in the UK.'

Required

Draft a letter in reply.

(17 marks)

(ICAEW, FA2, Dec 85)

QUESTION 23.3 (ADVANCED)

Hopeful Booksellers

Please refer to the information in Annexe B.

Required

(a) Draft a report interpreting the interfirm comparison data available for Hopeful Booksellers Ltd (20 marks).
(b) State the questions you would put to the directors when attempting to establish how the rate of return on capital employed might be improved (12 marks).

(32 marks)

(ACCA, AAP, June 85)

QUESTION 23.4 (ADVANCED)

Olympic Group Ltd

The new managing director of Olympic Group Ltd, a company in the sports goods industry, has asked you, as auditor and financial adviser, to analyse and give your views on the relative profitability and liquidity of its two wholly-owned subsidiaries Walkers Ltd and Runners Ltd, whose activities are the manufacture and sale of sports equipment and sports clothing, respectively. There were no intercompany transactions.

The following information has been extracted from the summarised financial statements of each company for the two years ended 31 March 19X6.

	Walkers Ltd		Runners Ltd	
	19X6	19X5	19X6	19X5
	£'000	£'000	£'000	£'000
Profit before tax	2.1	1.4	1.9	2.3
Turnover	45.2	38.1	17.0	14.0
Depreciation	.5	.4	.5	.3
Cost of sales	38.4	30.5	11.2	9.4
Other costs	4.2	5.8	3.4	2.0
Tangible fixed assets	8.3	9.2	3.5	2.5
Stock	9.3	10.2	1.8	2.3
Trade debtors	6.9	7.2	10.2	6.3
Trade creditors	8.5	8.2	3.2	2.2
Borrowings				
Overdraft	3.4	6.7	4.6	2.1
Long term	2.1	1.8	.2	—
Capital and reserves	10.5	9.9	7.5	6.8

Required

Write a report to the managing director analysing the results of each company and commenting on any significant trends, using not more than four relevant ratios as illustrations (18 marks).

(ICAEW, FA2, July 86)

24 INTERNATIONAL ACCOUNTING STANDARDS

QUESTION 24.1 (INTERMEDIATE)

International Standards

The need to conform to two sets of Accounting Standards – International and UK-Irish – may create problems for accountants.

Required

(a) set out the objectives of the International Accounting Standards Committee in preparing International Accounting Standards, and the obligations of the Members in support of those objectives (6 marks);
(b) explain the difficulties that arise from the existence of two sets of Standards (3 marks); and
(c) explain what has been done to reconcile the demands of the two sets of Standards (6 marks).

(15 marks)

(ACCA, AFA, Dec 82)

25 CAPITAL REORGANISATIONS AND RECONSTRUCTIONS

QUESTION 25.1 (INTERMEDIATE)

Ender

The summarised balance sheet of Ender plc on 31 March 19X6 showed the following position:

	£
Authorised share capital	1,750,000
Called up share capital, fully paid:	
1,500,000 ordinary shares of 50p	750,000
200,000 11% preference shares of £1	200,000
	950,000
Profit and loss account	135,000
	1,085,000
Convertible unsecured loan stock	230,000
	1,315,000
Investments	47,000
Cash at bank	74,800
Other assets, less liabilities	1,193,200
	1,315,000

(1) Holders of the unsecured loan stock have the right to convert their holdings into ordinary shares on 1 April in any year. The conversion rights are 150 ordinary shares for each £100 of loan stock. On 1 April 19X6 holders of £60,000 loan stock exercised their rights to convert into ordinary shares.

(2) The preference shares, which were originally issued at par, are redeemable on 1 April 19X6 at a premium of 15p per share. To finance the redemption the company decided:
  (a) to realise the investments for £51,000;
  (b) to have a rights issue of ordinary shares, at a price of 65p per share, the terms of the rights issue being one new share for every ten existing ordinary shares held, or for every ten ordinary shares to which holders of loan stock are entitled as a result of their conversion rights exercised at the date of the rights issue.
  (c) to charge the premium on the redemption of the preference shares to the profit and loss account.

The expenses of the rights issue which were paid on 1 April 19X6 amounted to £8,000.

Required

(a) Prepare the necessary journal entries (including cash) to record the matters referred to above.
(b) Prepare a summarised balance sheet for Enders plc incorporating the above matters.

(13 marks)

(ICAEW, AT, May 86)

QUESTION 25.2 (ADVANCED)

Strawberry

The following companies wish to purchase their own shares in accordance with the provisions of the Companies Act 1985.

(1) Strawberry plc, whose shares are dealt in on the U.S.M., has the following shareholders' funds:

	£'000
Called up share capital	500
Reserves – Revaluation	100
– Profit and loss account	300
	900

The company intends to purchase 20,000 shares of £1 each at a price of 90p per share on the market. At the same time it is issuing to a merchant bank 13,000 shares at a price of £1 each payable in cash.

(2) Greengage plc has the following shareholders' funds:

	£'000
Called up share capital	200
Share premium account	20
Profit and loss account	50
	270

All the shares, of £1 each, were originally issued at a price of £1.10 each. 100,000 shares are now to be purchased at a price of £1.50 each which will be financed by a new issue to a merchant bank of 100,000 shares at £1.30 per share.

(3) Peach Ltd is a private company with shareholders' funds as follows:

	£
Called up share capital	5,000
Share premium account	500
Profit and loss account	50
	5,550

It is intended to purchase 10,000 shares of £1 each, originally issued at par, at a price of £1.10 per share. A fresh issue of 850 shares will be made at par.

(4) Plum Ltd is a private company and has the following shareholders' funds:

	£
Called up share capital	2,000
Share premium account	500
Profit and loss account	5,000
	7,500

It is intended to purchase 1,000 shares of £1 each, which were originally issued at £1.50 per share, for £1.60 per share. Simultaneously a fresh issue will be made of 500 shares of £1 each at £1.70 per share.

(5) Raspberry plc, a listed company, has the following shareholders' funds:

	£'000
Called up share capital	400
Reserves – Revaluation	120
– Profit and loss account	40
	560

It is proposed to purchase 200,000 50p shares from a venture capital trust at a 5% discount on the current market price of £2 per share. The shares purchased will then be issued to the company's founders at 75p each.

Required

In each of the above five examples comment, with reasons, on whether the transactions are permitted under the Companies Act 1985 and if so to give the revised shareholders' funds after the share transactions, the necessary journal entries and where appropriate, the permissible capital payment.

Note: Ignore all taxation and duties.

(18 marks)

(ICAEW, FA2, July 84)

QUESTION 25.3 (INTERMEDIATE)

Popular Furnishings

Popular Furnishings manufactures and retails low-price furniture and household equipment. Business has declined over recent years as the company has failed to introduce new product-ranges.

Trading losses have gradually increased and the results of the last two years have been disastrous. There have been far-reaching changes in the management of the company and the recently-appointed board of directors know that drastic action is required if liquidation is to be avoided. Consequently a scheme of reconstruction has been drawn up, and it is hoped that this will be acceptable to all parties.

You are provided with the following information:

(1) Summarised audited balance sheet at 31 December 19X1:

	£'000	£'000	£'000
FIXED ASSETS – (net book value			
Offices and showroom			280
Factory and warehouse			222
Plant and machinery			290
Motor vehicles			155
			947
CURRENT ASSETS			
Stock		250	
Debtors		180	
		430	
CURRENT LIABILITIES			
Creditors	310		
Overdraft	520		
Arrears of interest	40	870	(440)
			507
LONG-TERM LIABILITIES			
10% unsecured loan stock 19X16			(400)
			107
Ordinary share capital (£1 shares)			300
8% preference share capital (£1 shares)			100
Profit and loss account			(293)
			107

(2) The bank overdraft is secured by a floating charge. No other liabilities are secured.
(3) Preference dividends are 2 years in arrears.
(4) On a liquidation, realisable values of assets would be:

	£'000
Offices and showrooms	350
Factory and warehouse	230
Plant and machinery	125

	£'000
Motor vehicles	120
Stock	150
Debtors	128

Liquidation costs would amount to £90,000.

(5) On a going concern basis, provided a suitable reconstruction scheme is accepted and approved and provided adequate finance is obtained, the following asset values would be appropriate:

	£'000
Offices and showrooms	380
Factory and warehouse	260
Plant and machinery	207
Motor vehicles	145
Stock	225
Debtors	165

(6) The reconstruction proposals are as follows:
   (a) The 300,000 £1 ordinary shares are to be redesignated as 10p ordinary shares.
   (b) The preference shares and arrears of dividends are to be cancelled. In return former preference shareholders would receive 200,000 10p ordinary shares.
   (c) The bank overdraft would be converted to a fluctuating-rate loan repayable in 19X2 and secured by a fixed charge on the property assets. Overdraft facilities of £100,000 would be provided secured by a floating charge.
   (d) Unsecured loan stock would be converted to 14% secured loan stock 19X16. Security would be by means of a floating charge.
      Loan stock holders would also receive £30,000 cash and the balance in 10p ordinary shares issued at par in satisfaction of their arrears of interest.
   (e) The company would make a rights issue of 10 for 1 at par. The proceeds of the rights issue would be applied in paying off creditors, reconstruction costs and in providing working capital.
   (f) The directors have produced figures which indicate that profit before interest but after all other expenses should amount in 19X4 to £500,000. 19X2 would be expected to break-even and 19X3 to show a small profit.
   (g) Reconstruction scheme costs would amount to £50,000.

Required

(a) state what considerations the loan stock holders should take into account in deciding whether to accept the reconstruction scheme;
(b) show the journal entries required, and resulting balance sheet, assuming the scheme is implemented in full;
(c) comment briefly on the scheme.

(25 marks)

QUESTION 25.4 (ADVANCED)

Pourwell (reconstruction)

Please refer to the information contained in Annexe C.

Required

(a) Prepare the reduction and reconstruction account to give effect to the proposed reorganisation described in Appendix 6 (19 marks).
(b) Prepare the draft balance sheet of Pourwell Ltd as at 31 December 19X5 after the reorganisation has been effected (13 marks).

(32 marks)

(ACCA, AAP, June 86)

QUESTION 25.5 (ADVANCED)

Combined Engineering

Combined Engineering plc, a holding company, makes up financial statements to 31 July. During 19X1 the group experienced difficult trading conditions which have strained its finances and its bankers have applied pressure on the directors for a substantial reduction in borrowings. Trading has been particularly bad in the wholly owned subsidiary, Rex Garages Ltd, engaged in the motor trade. The directors therefore resolved early in 19X2 to dispose of Rex Garages Ltd.

Management accounts drawn up at 30 April 19X2 showed the following:

	Parent £'000		Rex £'000
Fixed assets:			
Properties		3,646	1,352
Plant and machinery		4,201	462
Vehicles		2,948	437
		10,795	2,251
Shares in subsidiaries at cost (includes £500,000 re Rex)		1,550	—
Loans to subsidiaries (includes £1,000,000 re Rex)		2,000	—
Current assets:			
Stocks	12,529		3,368
Debtors and prepayments	11,620		1,675
Cash	25		8
	24,174		5,051
Current liabilities:			
Trade creditors and accruals	11,206		1,486
Bank overdrafts	17,483		1,817
	28,689		3,303
Net current (liabilities)/assets		(4,515)	1,748
		9,830	3,999
Share capital		2,000	500
Reserves		2,830	499
Loan capital		5,000	3,000
		9,830	3,999

In early May 19X2 the following plan of action, relating to Rex, was agreed:

(1) Certain properties with a book value of £950,000 will be sold to a third party for £1.2m. The sale proceeds will be used to repay the loans of £750,000 secured on these properties and the balance used to reduce the loan of £1m from the holding company (included in Rex's loan capital).
(2) The three group executives concerned with the management of Rex will be declared redundant. Under their contracts of employment they will be entitled to £150,000 each which will be paid to them in cash and borne by Combined Engineering plc.
(3) The same three will purchase Rex at net asset value as shown in the 30 April 19X2 management accounts after the adjustments for the properties to be sold and after further adjustments referred to below.
(4) The remaining property is to be written down by £100,000. This will necessitate a repayment of £150,000 of the third party loan secured thereon. This sum will be advanced temporarily by combined Engineering plc.
(5) Subsequently the loan from Combined Engineering plc, including the temporary advance, will be repaid. To raise the necessary finance for this, sufficient new car stocks will be sold off to the trade at a discount of 30% on the cost price used in 30 April 19X2 management figures.
(6) The three executives will acquire Rex's shares using their compensation for redundancy augmented by personal borrowing.
(7) Management Venture Capital Ltd, an independent company, will advance £600,000 loan capital which will be used to reduce Rex's bank overdraft.

(8) The consideration for the Rex shares will be paid in cash by 31 July 19X2.

Required

Produce the pro forma balance sheets of Combined Engineering plc and Rex Garages Ltd at 31 July 19X2 assuming that the above transactions duly take place and that both companies break even in trading between 30 April 19X2 and that date.
  Ignore taxation.

(18 marks)

(ICAEW, FA2, July 82)

QUESTION 26.1 (ADVANCED)

Norfolk

Norfolk plc has recently acquired the whole of the ordinary share capital of Suffolk Ltd, an unlisted company. The regulations of the Stock Exchange require a circular to be sent to Norfolk plc's shareholders, and this circular must include an accountants' report on Suffolk Ltd's results for the five years ended 31 December 19X5 (its latest year-end). Your firm of Certified Accountants has been asked by Norfolk plc's directors to prepare such a report on the basis of Suffolk's consolidated profit and loss accounts, of which the most significant items are tabulated below.

Required

(a) Explain why you would, or would not, make adjustments in respect of each of the items mentioned in the notes below (15 marks).
(b) Tabulate the Suffolk Group's results for the five years ended 31 December 19X5, in respect only of the items in the table below, after making such adjustments as you have judged necessary in (a) above (10 marks).

(25 marks)

(ACCA, AFA, June 1986)

SUFFOLK LTD AND ITS SUBSIDIARIES

Consolidated profit and loss accounts (extracts) for the years ended 31 December

	19X1 £'000	19X2 £'000	19X3 £'000	19X4 £'000	19X5 £'000
Turnover	3,000	4,500	5,800	7,200	8,000
Exceptional items	—	(200)	—	—	—
Share of profits (losses) of related companies	70	(20)	—	210	228
Profit on ordinary activities before taxation	253	352	450	600	650
Profit on ordinary activities after taxation	128	172	225	290	320
Extraordinary items	(400)	120	(290)	25	90
Taxation attributable thereto	200	(60)	145	—	(45)
	(200)	60	(145)	25	45

Notes:
(1) All subsidiaries were consolidated by the acquisition method, and all related (associated) companies were accounted for by the equity method. Corporation tax is assumed to have been 50% throughout.
(2) Suffolk Ltd, as at 1 January 19X3, acquired Essex Ltd's entire ordinary share capital by means of an issue of ordinary shares. For the years ended 31 December 19X2 and 19X2, Essex's results were as follows:

	19X1 £'000	19X2 £'000
Turnover	800	1,000
Profit on ordinary activities before taxation	40	50
Profit on ordinary activities after taxation	20	25
Extraordinary item (no tax attributable)	—	15

(3) Suffolk Ltd, as at 1 January 19X4, purchased for cash 35% of the equity of Kent plc, and obtained a seat on its board of directors. Kent's results were as follows (for years ended 30 September):

	Pre-tax profit £'000	Post-tax profit £'000	Extraordinary items (pre-tax) £'000	Extraordinary items (post-tax) £'000	
19X1	400	200	40	20	Gain on disposal of subsidiary
19X2	420	220	—	—	
19X3	500	240	(50)	(50)	Costs in unsuccessful lawsuit
19X4	600	300	—	—	
19X5	650	320	(600)	(300)	Loss on disposal of unlisted investments

(4) Up to 31 December 19X2, Suffolk Group's accounting policies included capitalisation of all purchased goodwill arising on acquisition of subsidiaries, and its amortisation over not more than five years. Goodwill arising on acquisition of related (associated) companies was not amortised. The relevant charges in the consolidated profit and loss account were: 19X1, £12,000; 19X2, £10,000 (not tax deductible). As from 1 January 19X3, the policy was changed to immediate write-off of all purchased goodwill of subsidiaries and related companies. All unamortised goodwill (totalling £60,000) was written off against reserves as at 1 January 19X3.

(5) During the year ended 31 December 19X2, Suffolk Group's consolidated accounts showed an exceptional charge of £200,000 in respect of bad debts arising from the failure of a major customer of a group company. In the year ended 31 December 19X4, a final dividend of £50,000 was obtained from the failed company's liquidator.

(6) The Suffolk Group's extraordinary items were as follows:

	Before taxation £'000	After taxation £'000
19X1: Expropriation of assets of a subsidiary by a foreign government	(400)	(200)
19X2: Gain on disposal of a subsidiary (see Note 7)	120	60
19X3: Loss on liquidation of a related company (see Note 8)	(290)	(145)
19X4: Damages obtained in a lawsuit for infringement of a patent	25	25
19X5: Compensation obtained from a foreign government for expropriation of assets in 19X1 (see above)	300	150
Share of Kent plc's extraordinary item (see Note 3)	(210)	(105)

(7) The subsidiary referred to in Note 6 was disposed of for cash on 30 June 19X2. During the year ended 31 December 19X1, and the six months ended 30 June 19X2, its results were as follows:

	12 months ended 31 December 19X1 £'000	6 months ended 30 June 19X2 £'000
Turnover	250	160
Profit on ordinary activities before taxation	24	16
Profit on ordinary activities after taxation	12	8

There were no extraordinary items.

(8) The related company referred to in Note 6 went into liquidation on 1 January 19X3. During 19X1 it contributed £70,000 to the Suffolk Group's pre-tax profits, and £35,000 to its post-tax profits. The corresponding figures for 19X2 were losses of £20,000 pre-tax, and £10,000 post-tax. There were no extraordinary items in either year.

QUESTION 26.2 (ADVANCED)

Avaricious

It has been announced that Avaricious plc, a quoted company, has undertaken to purchase the whole of the issued share capital of Parochial Ltd, a private company carrying on business as wholesalers and retailers of wines and spirits.

The following are extracts from the accountants' report on Parochial Ltd.

Profit and loss accounts

			YEARS ENDED 31 MARCH			
		19X4	*19X5*	*19X6*	*19X7*	*19X8*
	Note	*£'000*	*£'000*	*£'000*	*£'000*	*£'000*
Sales		5,157	6,489	8,651	13,026	18,042
Cost of sales	1	5,013	6,299	8,375	12,647	17,520
		144	190	276	379	522
Interest on bank deposits		—	11	6	29	78
Profit before taxation		144	201	282	408	600
Taxation		55	106	125	223	306
Profit after tax		89	95	157	185	294
Dividends – ordinary		27	17	22	15	20
Retained profits for year		62	78	135	170	274

Note:
(1) Cost of sales is stated after charging:

Depreciation	11	13	23	25	29
Directors' remuneration	57	52	59	77	80
Finance charges	5	6	17	3	4

Statement of net assets at 31 March 19X8

	Note	*£'000*	*£'000*
Tangible fixed assets	1		1,430
Investments			18
Current assets			
Stock		3,256	
Debtors		348	
Cash		4	
		3,608	
Creditors payable within one year			
Creditors		2,378	
Loans		68	
Bank overdraft		617	
		3,063	
Net current assets		545	
		1,993	
Deferred tax		(696)	
Net assets at 31 March 19X8		1,297	

Note:
(1) Fixed assets

	At cost *£'000*	*Aggregate depreciation* *£'000*	*Net book value* *£'000*
Freehold land and buildings			
Warehouses etc.	241	—	241
Retail outlets	1,032	—	1,032
	1,273	—	1,273
Short leasehold property	58	14	44
Plant and motor vehicles	200	87	113
	1,531	101	1,430

Two companies which are considered to be in the same line of business as Parochial Ltd are quoted and the most recent data from the *Financial Times* relating to them is shown below:

19X8 High	Low	Stock		Price	+ or –	Div net	Cover	Yield gross	P/E
117½	87	Company K	50p	103	+2	4.25	3.5	6.3	6.9
390	225	Company L	10p	340	–1	4.4	4.8	2.0	16.2

Required

(a) to calculate for Parochial Ltd the dividend per share and cover, assuming that there are 400,000 shares of £1 each in issue (4 marks);

(b) with the disclosed information to estimate, and justify, a value for Parochial Ltd (15 marks);

(c) state and explain the necessity for three additional topics you would expect to find dealt with in the accountant's report (6 marks).

(25 marks)

(ICAEW, FA2, Dec 1978)

ANNEXE A: BLACK ROOT LTD

Information for the questions

There are six appendices which contain the following information.

APPENDIX
1 Information about group structure
2 Summarised profit and loss accounts for the year ended 31 December 19X3 and summarised balance sheets as at 31 December 19X3 of Black Root Ltd and Confectioners Ltd
3 Draft balance sheet of Pharar, Khadir and Benson as at 31 December 19X2
4 Transaction by Health Sales Ltd during the year ended 31 December 19X3
5 Additional information relating to the partnership
6 Employee productivity statistics

APPENDIX 1

Information about group structure

Black Root Ltd is a company that imports liquorice into the United Kingdom and sells to pharmaceutical companies and confectionery manufacturers. After a period of falling sales the company decided to acquire shares in a confectionery manufacturer and to acquire retail outlets in the health food market.

Accordingly on 1 January 19X3 it paid £3,205,000 in cash to acquire 1,209,600 shares in Confectioners Ltd. On 31 December 19X3 Confectioners Ltd made a rights issue for cash of 1 ordinary £1 share for every 6 shares held at 250p per share, payable immediately. Black Root took up its full entitlement.

Also on 1 January 19X3 Black Root Ltd subscribed for 1,190,000 ordinary shares of £1 each, at par, in a newly formed company, Health Sales Ltd.

Health Sales Ltd entered into an agreement on 1 January 19X3 to acquire the retail business carried on by the partnership of Pharar, Khadir and Benson. The purchase consideration was 510,000 ordinary shares of £1 each issued at a premium of 50p per share and a cash payment of £714,000. Health Sales Ltd acquired all of the assets of the partnership and all of the liabilities, with the exception of the bank account. The freehold land was revalued at £1,020,000 otherwise the closing balance sheet values were accepted as those shown in Appendix 3.

APPENDIX 2

Summarised profit and loss accounts for the year ended 31 December 19X3 and summarised balance sheets as at 31 December 19X3 of Black Root Ltd and Confectioners Ltd

	Black Root Ltd		Confectioners Ltd	
	19X2	19X3	19X2	19X3
	£'000s	£'000s	£'000s	£'000s
Turnover	27,968	34,523	2,492	3,536
Trading profit	6,992	8,740	608	868
Depreciation	1,472	1,840	128	192
Debenture interest	736	920	64	96
	4,784	5,980	416	580
Taxation	2,208	2,346	240	224
Profit after tax	2,576	3,634	176	356

	Black Root Ltd 19X2 £'000s	Black Root Ltd 19X3 £'000s	Confectioners Ltd 19X2 £'000s	Confectioners Ltd 19X3 £'000s
Dividends paid:				
Ordinary	402.5	483	—	—
Preference	322	322	22	22
Dividends proposed	805	1,041	100	235
Issued ordinary shares	8,050	10,410	2,016	2,352
Issued 7% preference shares	4,600	4,600	320	320
Share premium	—	2,110	—	504
Retained profits	3,680	5,468	300	399
10% Debentures	7,360	9,200	640	960
Creditors	736	1,044	320	384
Current account with Black Root Ltd				57
Tax	1,897	2,070	230	257
ACT payable	345	446	43	101
Proposed dividend	805	1,041	100	235
	27,473	36,389	3,969	5,569
Fixed assets	18,400	22,080	1,792	2,176
Investments in Confectioners Ltd		3,709		
Investment in Health Sales Ltd		1,190		
Stock	1,104	1,397	512	640
Current account with Confectioners Ltd		70		
Current account with Health Sales Ltd		140		
Debtors	2,530	5,060	1,404	1,600
ACT recoverable	345	446	43	101
Cash at bank	5,094	2,297	218	1,052
	27,473	36,389	3,969	5,569

Additional information

(1) Black Root Ltd's investment in Confectioners Ltd consisted of 1,209,600 ordinary shares of £1 each acquired on 1 January 19X3 and 201,600 ordinary shares of £1 each acquired under the rights issue on 31 December 19X3.

(2) During the year ended 31 December 19X3 Black Root Ltd purchased from Confectioners Ltd one of its fixed assets, a machine, for £126,000. Confectioners Ltd had invoiced the machine at book value plus 40%. Black Root Ltd has depreciated the machine at 20% of the invoiced price.

(3) Black Root Ltd supplied goods to Confectioners Ltd at cost plus 25%. During the year ended 31 December 19X3 Black Root Ltd despatched goods with an invoiced value of £485,000 and received cash of £415,000 from Confectioners Ltd.

   During the year Confectioners Ltd received goods from Black Root Ltd with an invoiced value of £475,000 and made payments to them totalling £418,000. At 31 December 19X3 the stock of Confectioners Ltd included goods supplied by Black Root Ltd with an invoiced value of £50,000.

(4) During the year ended 31 December 19X3 Black Root Ltd sold fixed assets for £575,000 (net book value £460,000) and Confectioners Ltd sold fixed assets of £32,000 (net book value £48,000). The respective profit and loss have been included in the respective trading profit.

(5) The proposed dividends from Confectioners Ltd have been included in the Black Root Ltd debtors in the Balance Sheet as at 31 December 19X3.

(6) It is group policy to disclose Goodwill on Consolidation in the Consolidated Balance Sheet.

APPENDIX 3

Draft balance sheet of Pharar, Khadir and Benson as at 31 December 19X2

	£	£	£	£
Capital accounts				
Pharar		368,000		
Khadir		552,000		
Benson		100,000	1,020,000	

	£	£	£	£
Current accounts				
Pharar		(120,800)		
Khadir		(56,000)		
Benson		(170,000)	(346,800)	673,200
				£673,200

	Cost	Depreciation	Net book value	
	£	£	£	£
FIXED ASSETS				
Freehold	617,000	—	617,000	
Shop fittings	602,000	301,000	301,000	
Total fixed assets				918,000
Current assets				
Stock		212,400		
Debtors		265,200	477,600	
Current liabilities				
Creditors		112,200		
Bank		610,200	722,400	
				(244,800)
				£673,200

APPENDIX 4

Transactions by Health Sales Ltd during the year ended 31 December 19X3

(a) During 19X3 the following transactions took place:
  (i) Sales amounted to £1,254,000 and £500,400 for credit and cash respectively.
  (ii) Purchases from Black Root Ltd totalled £816,000. This was the invoiced value to Health Sales Ltd.
  (iii) Purchases from non-group suppliers were all acquired on credit. The credit terms were that Health Sales Ltd should receive 2% discount for payment within 1 month, 1% discount for payment within 2 months and no discount for payment in the third month.
  (iv) The position in respect of non-group purchases from 1 January 19X3 to 30 September 19X3 was that purchase invoices totalled £155,500, cheque payments totalled £140,856 and discounts received totalled £1,628.

   The records for payments in the period 1 October to 31 December 19X3 showed as follows:

	August £	September £	October £	November £	December £
Invoiced	17,200	16,100	15,095	18,300	25,305
Payments for:					
August supplies	3,000	12,000	Balance		
September supplies		5,000	8,000	Balance	
October supplies			4,000	9,800	Balance
November supplies				3,300	14,100
December supplies					15,200

   Cheques had been drawn, awaiting signature, for payment of December supplies £8,000 and the balance of the November supplies. The cheques were dated 15 January 19X4.
  (v) The company paid the creditors taken over from the partnership in full in January 19X3. It collected all of the debtors taken over subject to a special discount of 10%. All debtors of the partnership, subject to the discount, had been collected by 30 June 19X3.
  (vi) Fixed assets were acquired as follows:

Freehold land	£306,000
Shop fittings	£765,000

   The directors have produced a five year plan which shows that there will be a regular programme of expansion at the same level each year.

(vii) Shop fittings were disposed of for £105,000. Their book value at 1 January 19X3 was £97,280 and their original cost to the partnership in 19X7 had been £183,000.

(viii) The expenses for the year were:

	Paid by cheque £	Invoiced £
Administration	150,000	161,853
Establishment	81,060	83,695
Selling	72,416	79,850
Distribution	27,148	28,960
Miscellaneous	16,193	17,500

(ix) The administration expense includes £25,000 for auditors remuneration and £42,000 for directors' remuneration for services as a director and £8,000 for directors' pension contributions. The miscellaneous expense includes interest on the bank overdraft of £13,000.

(x) An interim dividend of 5% was paid in July 19X3. The Advanced Corporation Tax was paid in November 19X3. Assume an Advanced Corporation Tax rate of 30%.

(b) At 31 December 19X3 the following information was available:

(i) The stock turnover for goods supplied by Black Root Ltd was ten to one, calculated on the invoiced price. The stock turnover for goods supplied by non-group suppliers was four to one, calculated on invoiced price.

(ii) The debtor turnover rate was twelve to one.

(iii) Depreciation of shop fittings was to be made at 12½% of cost to the group.

(iv) The Black Root Ltd Current Account was £100,000.

(v) A final dividend of 2½% was proposed.

APPENDIX 5

Additional information relating to the partnership

(1) Pharar, Khadir and Benson share profits and losses in the proportion 3:2:1 respectively.

(2) The partnership agreement allowed 15% interest on their capital accounts.

(3) The draft profit for the year ended 31 December 19X2 was £346,800.

(4) Before finalising the balance sheet as at 31 December 19X2 the following errors were discovered:

(a) Interest had been calculated at 10% on the partners' capital accounts.

(b) Stock valued at £5,100 withdrawn by Khadir had been recorded in Benson's current account.

(c) The depreciation on the shop fittings for the year had been calculated at 10% of the original cost instead of 15% of the net book value.

(d) No record had been made of the stopping of a cheque for £2,550. The cheque, payable to a creditor for goods, had been duplicated by mistake.

(5) The agreement entered into with Health Sales Ltd provided that the purchase consideration should be paid in three instalments as follows:

1 January 19X3 – Cash payment of £707,650
1 February 19X3 – Issue of shares
1 March 19X3   – Balance of cash

(6) Benson was adjudicated bankrupt on 31 December 19X2 and will be unable to make any contribution to the partnership.

APPENDIX 6

Employee productivity statistics

The following information has been prepared by the management accountant of Black Root Ltd.

	Gross wages		Sales/Wages		No of employees	
	19X2 £'000s	19X3 £'000s	19X2	19X3	19X2	19X3
Black Root Ltd	6,400	8,950	4.37	3.86	1164	1492
Confectioners Ltd	628	891	3.97	3.97	143	197
Health Sales Ltd	—	223	—	7.87	—	72

Note 1: No adjustment has yet been made to show the effect of the change in the Retail Price Index. The index was:

1 January 19X2	120
31 December 19X2	140
31 December 19X3	154

Note 2: The summary appears to show that productivity of staff in Black Root Ltd is falling and that productivity in Health Sales Ltd is substantially better than in Black Root Ltd and in Confectioners Ltd.

Note 3: The employees are categorised as follows:

	Selling	Distribution	Administration
Black Root Ltd	837	452	203
Confectioners Ltd	93	44	60
Health Sales Ltd	22	20	30

ANNEXE B: PLURAL PUBLISHERS LTD

Information for the questions

APPENDIX
1 Notes on the group structure
2 Draft consolidated profit and loss account for the year ended 30 September 19X13
3 Draft consolidated balance sheets as at 30 September 19X12 and 19X13 respectively
4 Information relating to the profit and loss accounts of Plural Publishers Ltd, Video Hire Ltd, and Computer Software Texts Ltd for the year ended 30 September 19X14
5 Interfirm comparison data for the year ended 30 September 19X14 for Hopeful Booksellers Ltd

APPENDIX 1

Notes on the group structure

Plural Publishers Ltd was incorporated on 1 October 19X2 to publish computer magazines. In 19X9 it acquired a 40% interest in Computer Software Texts Ltd, a company which specialised in publishing self instruction texts on computer programming.

On 1 April 19X13 Plural Publishers Ltd acquired a majority holding in Video Hire Ltd by purchasing 80% of the issued share capital. The purchase consideration was £625,000. The purchase consideration was settled in full by the payment of Plural Publishers Ltd of £250,000 in cash and the issue of 250,000 £1 ordinary shares.

At the date of acquisition Video Hire Ltd had net assets of £575,000.

Video Hire Ltd had a financial year ending on 30 September. The draft profit and loss account of Video Hire Ltd for the year ended 30 September 19X13 disclosed a loss of £300,000. Enquiries indicated that profits and losses accrued evenly throughout the year.

APPENDIX 2

PLURAL PUBLISHERS GROUP

Draft consolidated profit and loss account for the year ended 30 September 19X13

	£'000s	£'000s
Operating profit (after charging depreciation of £700,000)		3,300
Share of profits in Computer Software Texts Ltd		400
		3,700
Less taxation		
Plural Publishers Ltd & Video Hire Ltd	1,800	
Computer Software Texts Ltd	150	1,950
		1,750
Extraordinary items less tax		45
		1,705
Minority interest		30
		1,735
Less dividends		
Interim paid	450	
Final proposed	800	1,250
		485

	£'000s	£'000s
Retained profit held in:		
Plural Publishers Ltd	555	
Video Hire Ltd	(120)	
Computer Software Texts Ltd	50	
	485	

APPENDIX 3

Draft consolidated balance sheets for the Plural Publishing Group as at 30 September 19X12 and 19X13

19X12 £'000s		19X13 £'000s
	Capital and Reserves	
3,450	Share capital	3,700
2,375	Share premium	2,500
7,615	Retained earnings	8,100
	Minority interest	85
13,440		14,385
	Fixed assets	
—	Intangible asset	165
5,685	Tangible assets (Note 1)	6,400
490	Investment in Computer Software Texts Ltd	540
	Current assets	
7,305	Stocks	8,135
4,150	Debtors	3,600
390	ACT recoverable	470
1,200	Cash	1,015
	Creditors (due within 1 year)	
2,010	Creditors	2,150
1,700	Taxation	1,640
745	Proposed dividends	800
	Creditors (due after more than 1 year)	
515	Debentures	500
810	Deferred Taxation Account	850
13,440		14,385

Note 1: Fixed assets with a book value of £75,000 were sold for £100,000 during the year.

APPENDIX 4

Information relating to the profit and loss account of Plural Publishers Ltd, Video Hire Ltd and Computer Software Texts Ltd for the year ended 30 September 19X14

	Plural Publishers Ltd £'000s	Video Hire Ltd £'000s	Computer Software Texts Ltd £'000s
Balance brought forward at 1 October 19X13	8,080	(120)	350
Sales	17,280	7,560	3,825
Purchases of materials	10,368	4,158	2,056
Purchases of services	3,430	936	431
Salaries and wages	1,322	1,386	573
Profit on trading	2,160	1,080	765

	Plural Publishers Ltd £'000s	Video Hire Ltd £'000s	Computer Software Texts Ltd £'000s
The profit on trading was before taking the following information into account:			
Directors' emoluments	225	78	68
Auditors' fees	58	7	4
Depreciation	360	180	93
Debenture interest	60	5	
Tax on trading profit	630	360	315
Proposed dividends on ordinary shares	900	300	150

APPENDIX 5

Interfirm comparison data for the year ended 30 September 19X14 for Hopeful Booksellers Ltd

Plural Publishers Ltd has been approached by the directors of Hopeful Booksellers Ltd to initiate discussions for a possible takeover by Plural Publishers Ltd. The directors of Hopeful Booksellers Ltd produced copies of the accounts for the five years 19X10–19X14 together with copies of the Interfirm Comparison Report comparing their company with a group of similar companies.
   The comparative data is set out below:

		19X13	19X14	Group average
1 Net profit/Operating assets	%	5	5	10
2 Net profit/Sales	%	5	5	3½
3 Sales/Operating assets	No. of times	1	1	3
4 Gross profit/Sales	%	40	40	27
5 Total costs/Sales	%	35	35	23⅔
6 Sales/Current assets	No. of times	1.5	1.5	3.5
7 Sales/Fixed assets	No. of times	2.5	2.5	15
8 Sales/Other stock	No. of times	—	—	5
9 Sales/Retail books stock	No. of times	1.5	1.5	4
10 Sales/Debtors	No. of times	50	50	20
11 Retail sales/Sales	%	100	100	75
12 Retail gross profit/Retail sales	%	40	40	27
13 Library sales/Sales	%	0	0	2
14 Library gross profit/Sales	%	N/A	N/A	10
15 Agent sales/Sales	%	0	0	5
16 Agent gross profit/Agent sales	%	N/A	N/A	8
17 School sales/Sales	%	0	0	5
18 School gross profit/School sales	%	N/A	N/A	15
19 Other sales/Sales	%	0	0	13
20 Other sales gross profit/Other sales	%	N/A	N/A	12
21 Fixed assets/Area in sq ft	£000s	30	30	4
22 Sales/Area in sq ft	£	79	80	71
23 Labour costs/Sales	%	10	10	15
24 Overheads/Sales	%	25	25	8⅔
25 Interest/Sales	%	0	0	2
26 Rent & rates/Sales	%	18	18	4
27 Other overheads/Sales	%	7	7	6
28 Power/Sales	%	1	1.5	1
29 Phone/Sales	%	0.7	0.7	0.7
30 Postage/Sales	%	0.03	0.03	0.03
31 Printing/Sales	%	0.3	0.35	0.35
32 Advertising/Sales	%	0.75	0.8	0.75
33 Repairs/Sales	%	0.9	0.6	0.9
34 Travel/Sales	%	1.2	0.7	1.2
35 Depreciation/Sales	%	1.8	1.9	0.75
36 Other expenses/Sales	%	0.32	0.42	0.32
37 Sales/Wages	No. of times	11	11	9
38 Sales/Staff	£000	19	19	14
39 Wages/Staff	£000	3.5	3.5	3.1

ANNEXE C: POURWELL LTD

Information for the questions

The following appendices are attached:

APPENDIX
1 General introduction to Pourwell Ltd
2 List of balances extracted from the books of Pourwell Ltd as at 31 December 19X5
3 Further information available when drafting the profit and loss account of Pourwell Ltd for the year ended 31 December 19X5 and the balance sheet as at that date
4 Draft balance sheet of Willow Ltd as at 31 December 19X5
5 Proposed terms of the merger with Willow Ltd
6 Proposed terms of the reorganisation of Pourwell Ltd
7 Further information available after the preparation of Appendix 2 to be used for Question 4 (not reproduced here)

APPENDIX 1

General introduction to Pourwell Ltd

(i) Pourwell Ltd is a company that manufactures plastic decanters.
(ii) It was incorporated in 19W4 with an authorised share capital of £500,000 consisting of 300,000 £1 ordinary shares and £200,000 7% cumulative preference shares of £1 each.
(iii) The issued share capital is £300,000 consisting of 200,000 £1 ordinary shares and £100,000 7% cumulative preference shares. The preference shares are all held by an insurance company. The ordinary shares are held as follows:

75,000	Mr Albert (who is also managing director and chairman)
25,000	Mr Bryant (who is also a director)
12,500	Mr Chad (who is also a director)
87,500	held by 7 other shareholders, each with 12,500 shares
200,000	

(iv) The company has incurred significant trading losses over the past five years.
(v) The directors have been discussing with the company's accountants the advisability of either (a) arranging a merger with Willow Ltd or (b) carrying out a scheme or reorganisation.
(vi) The directors estimate that the company will make profits in future years. The profits are estimated to be:

19X6	£10,000
19X7	£15,000
19X8	£20,000

APPENDIX 2

List of balances extracted from the books of Pourwell Ltd as at 31 December 19X5

	£
Accrued interest on debentures	10,500
Administrative expenses	105,113
Audit fee accrual	2,850
Bank overdraft	38,022
Debenture interest	5,250
Bank interest	7,100
Cost of sales	410,778

	£
Creditors (trade) (control account total)	258,550
7% debentures (redeemable 19X22)	75,000
Debtors (trade) (control account total)	89,505
Deferred development expenditure	87,500
Directors' loans	125,000
Dividend received (cash)	3,500
Expense accrual	1,900
Fixtures and fittings	9,900
Goodwill	150,000
Insurance prepayment	4,000
Investment (at cost)	42,500
Land and buildings	100,000
Ordinary shares of £1 each	200,000
Plant	90,800
Preference shares (7% cumulative)	100,000
Profit and loss account (debit balance)	97,160
Profit on sale of land	15,000
Provision for depreciation of buildings	19,200
Provision for depreciation of plant	47,880
Provision for depreciation of fixtures	4,620
Sales	696,000
Selling and distribution expenses	200,101
Stock of raw material	20,210
Stock of work in progress	10,103
Stock of finished goods	170,102
Wages accrual	2,100

(Modified)

APPENDIX 3

Further information available when drafting the profit and loss account of Pourwell Ltd for the year ended 31 December 19X5 and a balance sheet as at that date

(i) Directors received the following remuneration:

Albert	£31,000
Bryant	£22,000
Chad	£15,000

In addition, fees of £2,000 per annum were paid to each director.

(ii) Depreciation has been provided for in the appropriate expenses accounts for the year on the following basis:

	£	Estimated useful life
Land	Nil	
Buildings	1,600	50 years
Plant	4,540	20 years
Fixtures and fittings	660	15 years

(iii) During the year the company sold land with a book value of £10,000 and purchased plant for £12,000.

(iv) The goodwill arose on the purchase of the assets and liabilities of Mr Chad's business in 19X0. The company are proposing to write off over 10 years commencing in 19X5.

(v) The preference dividend has not been paid for 19X4 or 19X5.

(vi) The directors estimate that the company will return to profits in 19X6 and given that they estimate profits will be £10,000 in 19X6 rising to £20,000 in 19X8 they proposed to leave the development costs as an asset for the purpose of the 19X5 accounts

(vii) The trade creditors aged analysis shows:

	£
Payable before 1 July 19X5	93,490
Payable before 1 October 19X5	50,060
Payable before 1 December 19X5	30,000
Current	35,000
Payable in 19X7	50,000

(viii) Tax at 30% had been deducted from the dividend received.

APPENDIX 4

Draft balance sheet of Willow Ltd as at 31 December 19X5

FIXED ASSETS	Cost £	Aggregate depreciation £	£
Tangible assets			
Freehold land and buildings	360,000	120,000	240,000
Plant and machinery	348,000	240,000	108,000
	708,000	360,000	348,000
Current assets:			
Stocks of raw materials		56,200	
Stock – work in progress		63,000	
Stock – finished goods		97,360	
Debtors		168,760	
Cash		45,636	
		430,956	
Creditors: amounts due in less than one year			
Creditors	137,148		
Corporation tax	97,600		
Proposed dividends	40,000	274,748	
Net current assets			156,208
			504,208
Share capital and reserves			
Share capital			
Ordinary shares of £1 each			250,000
Retained earnings			254,208
			504,208

APPENDIX 5

Proposed terms of the merger with Willow Ltd

(1) The estimated market value of a £1 ordinary share in Pourwell Ltd is 50p.
(2) The estimated market value of a £1 ordinary share in Willow Ltd is £2.50.
(3) The merger is to be effected by the offer of ordinary shares to be issued by Willow Ltd to all of the ordinary shareholders of Pourwell Ltd in exchange for their shares.
(4) The shares are to be exchanged in proportion to their estimated market values.
(5) It is anticipated that there would be a 100% acceptance.
(6) The authorised share capital of Willow Ltd is sufficient to accommodate the transaction.

APPENDIX 6

Proposed terms of reorganisation

The directors have produced the following information relating to the proposed reorganisation:

(1) *Assets*

(a) The land and buildings have been professionally valued. The valuer has quoted the following values:

	£
Open market in existing use	120,000
Existing user	62,000
Net replacement cost	179,000
Open market alternative use	156,000

(b) The goodwill is thought to have no realisable value.
(c) The deferred development expenditure was incurred in producing a collapsible decanter. The directors forecast that the project will produce sales as follows:

	£
19X6	75,000
19X7	125,000
19X8	150,000
19X9	150,000

and that the contribution margin will be 15%.
(d) The valuation of stock of finished goods is to be reduced to a level which shows a stock turnover (based on sales) of 6 times per year.
(e) Plant and machinery was revalued at £58,824.
(f) A reduction of £19,200 was to be made to take account of irrecoverable trade debts.

(2) *Liabilities*

(g) The trade creditors payable prior to 1 July 19X5 will require immediate payment.
(h) The directors have agreed to waive £100,000 of their loans and to accept an issue of ordinary shares of 10p each to satisfy the balance.
(i) The bank overdraft is to be repaid in full.
(j) The preference shareholder is to be offered the right to convert the holding into a new issue of 10% cumulative preference shares, or, alternatively, to accept ordinary shares of 10p each on a 6 for 1 (ordinary: preference) basis. The initial response indicates that 50% of the holding will be converted into 10% cumulative preference shares and 50% into ordinary shares.
(k) The cumulative unpaid dividend for 19X4 and 19X5 is to be paid immediately. (The accountant advised that legal advice would be required to ascertain whether it was legal to pay a dividend other than out of profits. For the immediate exercise it has been decided to treat the dividends as paid in cash but to take advice before making the final decision.)
(l) The debenture holder has agreed to convert the existing issue of debentures into a new issue carrying interest at 15% per annum. The accrued interest is to be paid immediately.

(3) *Equity*

(m) The ordinary shares are to be written down to 10p each.
(n) The profit and loss account debit balance is to be eliminated.
(o) A rights issue is to be made to raise sufficient cash to give the company a current ratio of 2:1. The shares are to be issued at 18p each.

ANSWERS

ANSWER 1.1 (BASIC)

Patterdale

WORKINGS

(1) Calculation of purchases:

Bank	135,570	Bal B/D	9,700
Cash	2,030	Purchases (balancing	
Bal C/D	8,500	figure)	136,400
	146,100		146,100

(2) Calculation of sales:

Opening stock	24,800
Purchases	136,400
Closing stock	(21,200)
Cost of sales	140,000

$$\therefore \text{Sales} = \frac{100}{70} \times £140,000 = £200,000$$

(3) Construct sales account:

Bal B/D	19,500	Total receipts	
Sales	200,000	(balancing figure)	198,100
		Bal C/D	21,400
	219,500		219,500

(4) Construct cash account:

Bal B/D	530	Bankings	192,495
Receipts (sales ac)	198,100	Purchases	2,030
		Sundry expenses	200
		Motor expenses	900
		Drawings (balancing	
		figure)	2,600
		Bal C/D	405
	198,630		198,630

SOLUTION

Trading and profit and loss account for the year ended 31 December 19X3

	£	£
Sales		200,000
Opening stock	24,800	
Purchases	136,400	
Closing stock	(21,200)	140,000
Gross profit		60,000
Depreciation	500	
Wages	4,200	
Sundry expenses (340 + 200)	540	
Rent, rates, telephone and insurance	17,100	
Motor expenses	8,400	
Repairs and renewals	960	31,700
Net profit		28,300

Balance sheet as at 31 December 19X3

Fixed assets	£	£
Van (2,500 − 500)		2,000
Current assets		
Stock	21,200	
Debtors	21,400	
Bank	4,922	
Cash	405	
	47,927	
Less current liabilities		
Creditors	8,500	39,427
		41,427
Capital account		
Balance at 1.1.X3		37,927
Net profit		28,300
		66,227
Less drawings (22,200 + 2,600)		24,800
		41,427

ANSWER 1.2 (INTERMEDIATE)

Hoffman

ANSWER GUIDE

(a) Calculation of shortage at 30.9.X1:

	£	£
Balance per book		254
Less expenses not entered	47	
casting error	10	57
Adjusted balance		197
Cash in box		65

(Assumptions: loan to wages and travellers floats recorded as payments in petty cash book)
∴ Apparent shortage was (197–65) i.e. £132 at 30.9.X1.

(b) Further discrepancy during October:

Balance at 30.9 (adjusted)		65
Bank		743
Loan repaid		40
Overpayment (43 − 34)		9
		857
Expenses	76	
Increase in float	8	
Sundry payments	472	
Sales manager	100	
Cheque cashed	75	731
Balance at 31.10 – misappropriated		126
Total misappropriated		258
As at 30.9		132
During October		126
		258

ANSWER 1.3 (ADVANCED)

George

SOLUTION

Statement of income and expenditure for years ended 30 June

	19X1 £	19X2 £	19X3 £	19X4 £
Balances B/D				
Current account	720	140	(2,046)	(1,105)
Deposit account	—	850	1,100	3,200
Building Society	230	245	420	650
Interest charged	—	(271)	(148)	(73)
Interest on deposit	72	95	265	385
Interest on Building Society	18	50	30	40
Income from music teaching	5,533	6,923	7,428	7,550
Premium bonds acquired	(50)	(350)	—	(200)
National Savings Certificates acquired	(500)	—	(500)	—
Living expenses	(6,000)	(7,000)	(8,000)	(9,000)
Holiday costs	(1,200)	(1,200)	(1,200)	(1,200)
Winter holiday	—	(1,850)	—	—
Fur coat	—	(1,740)	—	—
Wedding expenses	—	—	(975)	—
New car	—	—	—	(7,200)
From George (assumed 52 weeks)	1,560	1,560	1,560	1,560
Part-time job (assumed 52 weeks)	1,560	2,080	2,080	2,080
Tips (assumed 52 weeks)	780	780	780	780
Premium bond win	—	500	—	—
Endowment policy (premiums for full year)	(240)	(240)	(240)	4,700
Tax payments	(1,748)	(2,098)	(2,309)	(2,092)
Subtotal (1)	735	(1,526)	(1,755)	75
Balances C/D				
Current account	140	(2,046)	(1,105)	(275)
Deposit account	850	1,100	3,200	4,100
Building Society	245	420	650	750
Subtotal (2)	1,235	(526)	2,745	4,575
Income from painting (2)–(1)	500	1,000	4,500	4,500

ANSWER 2.1 (BASIC)

Turner and Bennett

SOLUTION

1 Trading and profit and loss account for the year ended 31 March 19X7

	Total £	To 30 Sept £	To 31 March £
Sales	98,500		
Cost of sales			
Opening stock	5,600		
Purchases	39,800		
Closing stock	(6,000)		
	39,400		
Gross profit	59,100	19,700	39,400
Expenses:			
Salaries and wages	16,300		
Rates, light and heat (1,900 + 120)	2,020		
Telephone	1,240		
General expenses, insurance (1,450 − 350 − 110)	990		
Bank interest	3,350		
	23,900	11,950	11,950

	Total £	To 30 Sept £	To 31 March £
Depreciation – vehicles	4,225		
– fixtures	2,520		
	6,745	3,372	3,373
Conference fee	350	350	—
Total expenses	30,995	15,672	15,823
Net profit	28,105	4,028	24,077

2 Current accounts

	Turner £	Bennett £	Lloyd £
Per trial balance	4,800	5,040	—
Cash introduced (11,000– 7,500)	—	—	3,500
Profit to 30 Sept (1:1)	2,014	2,014	
Profit to 31 Mar (2:2:1)	9,631	9,631	4,815
Goodwill in OPSR	10,000	10,000	—
Goodwill in NPSR	(8,000)	(8,000)	(4,000)
Drawings	(15,400)	(14,900)	(8,900)
Per balance sheet	3,045	3,785	4,585

ANSWER 2.2 (INTERMEDIATE)

Kimm, Rawnsley and Flowers

SOLUTION

a Journal entries

		Dr £	Cr £
(1) 1/9/X1			
Bank		6,000	
Capital ac. of Kimm			6,000
Introduction of fixed capital by Kimm			
(2) 1/9/X2			
Bank		12,900	
Capital ac. of Rawnsley			12,900
Introduction of fixed capital and goodwill share by Rawnsley			
(3) 1/9/X2			
Goodwill (2 × £6,900)		13,800	
Capital ac. of Kimm			13,800
Revaluation of goodwill on introduction of new partner Rawnsley			
(4) 1/9/X3			
Bank		19,750	
Capital ac. of Flowers			19,750
Introduction of fixed capital and goodwill share by Flowers			
(5) 1/9/X3			
Goodwill (3 × 13,750 − 13,800)		27,450	
Capital ac. of Kimm			13,725
Capital ac. of Rawnsley			13,725
Revaluation of goodwill on introduction of a new partner Flowers			

	Dr £	Cr £
(6) Capital account of:		
Kimm	13,750	
Rawnsley	13,750	
Flowers	13,750	
Goodwill		41,250

Write off of goodwill between the three partners

	Dr £	Cr £
(7) Depreciation charge (21,791 ÷ 3)	7,264	
Accumulated depreciation		7,764

Depreciation charge on tenants' improvements

b Trading and profit and loss account for the year ended 31 August 19X4

	£	£
Sales		243,614
Opening stock	24,476	
Purchases	164,297	
	188,773	
Less closing stock	27,240	
Cost of sales		161,533
Gross profit		82,081
Less wages	16,240	
rent and rates	22,464	
trade expenses	1,497	
telephone and postage	2,722	
stationery and advertising	1,936	
depreciation	7,264	52,123
Net profit		29,958

Balance sheet as at 31 August 19X4

Fixed assets

	£	£
Tenants' improvements – cost		21,791
– accumulated depreciation		7,264
		14,527
Current assets		
Stock	27,240	
Debtors	27,397	
Bank	10,483	
	65,120	
Less current liabilities		
Creditors	26,249	38,871
		53,398
Capital accounts		
Kimm		24,736
Rawnsley		19,646
Flowers		9,016
		53,398

Workings – capital accounts

	Kimm £	Rawnsley £	Flowers £
Per trial balance	36,400	27,050	19,750
Profit shares (29,958 ÷ 3)	9,986	9,986	9,986
Drawings	(7,900)	(3,640)	(6,970)
Goodwill w/o	(13,750)	(13,750)	(13,750)
Adjusted totals	24,736	19,646	9,016

ANSWER 2.3 (ADVANCED)

Vic

WORKINGS

(1) Read thoroughly through the question, making brief notes of key points from the first two paragraphs. The instruction that 'profit should be deemed to accrue evenly . . .' should be interpreted as relating to net profit.

(2) The first main task is to complete the trading account, the sales figure requiring particular care.

   (a) Adjust bank account balance:

	£
Balance per statements (474,940 − 463,000)	(11,940)
Outstanding bankings (2,140 + 4,260)	6,400
Adjusted balance (overdrawn)	(5,540)

   (b) Construct total cash account:

	£		£
Takings		Salaries and drawings	16,750
(sales ac)	196,400	Motor expenses	7,410
Bank	200	Sundry expenses	1,740
		Weighing scales	1,600
		Stationery	640
		Bankings	
		(164,000 + 4,260)	168,260
		Balance C/D	200
	196,600		196,600

   (c) Construct total sales account:

	£		£
Sales		Bank – credit	
(balancing figure)	480,010	customers	
		(270 + 2,140)	272,140
		Cash ac	196,400
		Bad debt	600
		Balance C/D	10,870
	480,010		480,010

   (d) Purchase is (470,000 + 7,250) i.e. £477,250 and closing stock is £34,750. The trading account may now be completed.

	£	£
(3) Salaries and drawings amount to		16,750

This figure may be broken down as follows:

	£
Tom – wages (1.4.X4 – 1.9.X4)	
5 × £600	3,000
Clerk – wages (1.12.X4 – 28.2.X5)	
3 × £300	900
∴ Total wages	3,900

	£	£
Tom – drawings (1.9.X4 – 28.2.X5)		
6 × £600	3,600	7,500
∴ Vic's drawings		9,250

(4) Remaining expenses items may be easily calculated and profit and loss account and balance sheet completed.

SOLUTION

Trading and profit and loss account for the year ended 28 February 19X5

	£	£
Sales		480,010
Purchases	477,250	
Less: closing stock	34,750	
Cost of sales		442,500
Gross profit		37,510
Wages	3,900	
Insurance (1,780 − 140)	1,640	
Bank charges	460	
Rent (2,500 − 500)	2,000	
Motor expenses	7,410	
Sundry expenses (1,740 + 430)	2,170	
Stationery	640	
Depreciation – van	1,200	
– car (6/12 × 840)	420	
– scales (3/12 × 400)	100	
Loan interest	1,600	
Bad debts	600	
	22,140	
Commission (6% × 37,510 − 22,140)	922	23,062
Net profit		14,448

Allocation of profit

	Total £	Vic £	Tom £
1.3.X4 – 31.8.X4 (6/12 × 14,448)	7,224	7,224	—
1.9.X4 – 28.2.X5 (6/12 × 14,448)	7,224	4,334 (3)	2,890 (2)
	14,448	11,558	2,890

Capital accounts

	Vic £	Tom £
Cash introduced	5,000	4,000
Vehicles introduced	6,000	4,200
Profit shares	11,558	2,890
Drawings	(9,250)	(3,600)
Per B/S	13,308	7,490

Balance sheet as at 28.2.X5

Fixed assets

	Cost £	Accumulated depreciation £	£
Van	6,000	1,200	4,800
Car	4,200	420	3,780
Scales	1,600	100	1,500
			10,080

Fixed assets	Cost £	Accumulated depreciation £	£
Current assets			
Stock		34,750	
Debtors		10,870	
Prepayments (500 + 140)		640	
Cash in hand		200	
		46,460	
Less creditors due within one year			
Creditors	7,680		
Commission	922		
Loan interest	1,600		
Overdraft	5,540		
		15,742	
Net current assets		30,718	
		40,798	
Loans payable . . .		(20,000)	
		20,798	
Capital accounts			
Vic		13,308	
Tom		7,490	
		20,798	

ANSWER 3.1 (INTERMEDIATE)

Bruce, Henry and Malcolm

SOLUTION

a(1) **Profit and loss account of the old partnership for the year ended 30 June 19X4**

	£	£
Fees rendered to clients		188,432
Expenses	139,722	
Bad debts	1,150	
		140,872
Net profit		47,560

Allocation of profit

	Salary £	Profit share	Total
Bruce	6,000	14,780	20,780
Henry	6,000	8,868	14,868
Malcolm	6,000	5,912	11,912
	18,000	29,560	47,560

(2) *Capital accounts*

	Bruce £	Henry £	Malcolm £
Per trial balance	4,173	(21,948)	(11,206)
Profit shares	20,780	14,868	11,912
	24,953	(7,080)	706

(3) *Balance sheet as at 30 June 19X4*

	£	£	£
Fixed assets – reference library			100
Current assets			
Work in progress		2,000	
debtors (46,205 – 1,150)		45,055	
		47,055	

	£	£	£
Less creditors due within one year			
Bank overdraft	11,170		
Creditors	17,406	28,576	18,479
			18.579
Capital accounts			
Bruce			24,953
Henry			(7,080)
Malcolm			706
			18,579

b Journal entries to reflect the partnership changes

	Dr £	Cr £
(1) Work in progress (37,000 − 2,000)	35,000	
Bruce's capital account (50%)		17,500
Henry's capital account (30%)		10,500
Malcolm's capital account (20%)		7,000
(2) Henry's capital account (35%)	12,250	
Malcolm's capital account (35%)	12,250	
Walter's capital account (30%)	10,500	
Work in progress		35,000
(3) Reference library	1,400	
Bruce's capital account (50%)		700
Henry's capital account (30%)		420
Malcolm's capital accouant (20%)		280
Goodwill (0.5 × £47,560)	23,780	
Bruce's capital account (50%)		11,890
Henry's capital account (30%)		7,134
Malcolm's capital account (20%)		4,756
(4) Bruce's capital account	10,000	
Walter's capital account		10,000
(5) Bruce's capital account	45,043	
Loan account		45,043
(6) Cash	7,500	
Walter's capital account		7,500

c Balance sheet as at 1 July 19X4

	£	£	£
Fixed assets – reference library			1,500
– goodwill			23,780
			25,280
Current assets			
work in progress		2,000	
Debtors		45,055	
		47,055	
Less creditors due within one year			
Bank overdraft			
(11,170 − 7,500)	3,670		
Creditors	17,406	21,076	
Net current assets			25,979
			51,259
Loan account – Bruce			(45,043)
			6,216

	£	£	£
Capital accounts			
Henry		(1,276)	
Malcolm		492	
Walter		7,000	6,216

WORKINGS

Capital accounts	*Bruce*	*Henry*	*Malcolm*	*Walter*
	£	*£*	*£*	*£*
Per balance sheet of old partnership	24,953	(7,080)	706	—
W-I-P	17,500	10,500	7,000	
W-I-P	—	(12,250)	(12,250)	(10,500)
Reference library	700	420	280	—
Goodwill	11,890	7,134	4,756	—
Transfer of capital	(10,000)			10,000
Loan account	(45,043)	—	—	—
Cash introduced				7,500
Balances C/D	—	(1,276)	492	7,000

ANSWER 3.2 (INTERMEDIATE)

Martin and Norman

WORKINGS

(1) Calculation of purchased goodwill:

Assuming that the overdraft is taken over, goodwill on purchase by Oliver may be calculated:

	£
Freehold	210,000
Plant and machinery	80,000
Stock and debtors	216,800
Overdraft and creditors	(202,340)
	304,460
Purchase consideration	330,000
∴ Purchased goodwill	25,540

(2) Profit on realisation shared equally between partners = (330,000 − 257,360) = £72,640.

(3) Settlement to partners:

	Martin	*Norman*
	£	*£*
Capital acs	140,680	116,680
Profit on realisation	36,320	36,320
Final entitlement	177,000	153,000
Issue of shares		
(NV = 70,000)	88,500	
Issue of debs		
(NV = $\frac{10,200}{0.8}$ = 127,500)		
Issue price = 0.9 × 127,500		114,750
Cash (to balance)	88,500	38,250
	177,000	153,000

SOLUTION

a Journal entries in books of Oliver plc

		£	
(1) *Dr*	freehold property	210,000	
	plant and equipment	80,000	
	goodwill	25,540	
	stock	132,470	
	debtors	84,330	
Cr	cash at bank		105,200
	creditors		97,140
	purchase of business account		330,000
		532,340	532,340
(2) *Dr*	purchase of business account	330,000	
	share premium account		
	(deb. discount w/o)	12,750	
Cr	ordinary share capital		70,000
	share premium account		18,500
	8% debentures		127,500
	cash (88,500 + 38,250)		126,750
		342,750	342,750

b Pro forma balance sheet at 31.3.X5

	£	£	£
Fixed assets			
Intangible – goodwill			25,540
Tangible			
– freehold			210,000
– leasehold (875,000 – 121,407)			753,593
– plant and equipment (1,297,400 – 573,208)			724,192
			1,713,325
Current assets			
Stocks (1,407,108 + 132,470)		1,539,578	
Debtors (875,906 + 84,330)		960,236	
		2,499,814	
less creditors due within one year			
creditors (1,395,400 + 97,140)	1,492,540		
bank overdraft			
(147,100 – 105, 200 – 88, 500 – 38, 250)	84,850	1,577,390	
			922,424
			2,635,749
less creditors due in more than one year			
8% debenture stock (110,050 + 127,500)			(237,550)
			2,398,199
Called up share capital (1,000,000 + 70,000)			1,070,000
Share premium (18,500 – 12,750)			5,750
Profit and loss account			1,322,449
			2,398,199

Note:
For the purposes of this solution, the requirement to write off purchased goodwill in accordance with SSAP 22 has been ignored.

ANSWER 3.3 (ADVANCED)

Katie and Richard

SOLUTION

a Trading accounts for the year ended 31 December 19X5

	Toy shop £	Toy shop £	Newsagents £	Newsagents £
Sales		241,738		90,328
Opening stock	17,422		1,477	
Purchases	154,208		51,443	
Closing stock	(15,092)		(1,360)	
		156,538		51,560
Gross profit		85,200		38,768
Depreciation				
– fixtures	800		342	
– vehicles	1,861		936	
Wages (excl Sally)	17,942		4,257	
Rent and rates	13,720		7,720	
Repairs	1,446		811	
Interest	630		(197)	
Electricity	2,241		516	
Telephones	824		227	
		39,464		14,612
Net profit		45,736		24,156

Allocation of net profit

		Toy shop 1.1.x5– 30.6.x5 £	Toy shop 1.7.x5– 31.12.x5 £	Newsagents 1.1.x5– 30.6.x5 £	Newsagents 1.7.x5– 31.12.x5 £
Gross profit					
	1 : 2	28,400	56,800		
	1 : 1			19,384	19,384
Expenses	1 : 1	(19,732)	(19,732)	(7,306)	(7,306)
Net profit		8,668	37,068	12,078	12,078
Katie		6,501	14,828		4,832
Richard		2,167	11,120		3,623
Sally			11,120	12,078	3,623
Totals		8,668	37,068	12,078	12,078

b   Current accounts in column form

	Katie £	Richard £	Sally £		Katie £	Richard £	Sally £
Bal B/D	11,607	12,090	3,790	Profit			
Drawings			12,000	Shares			
Goodwill				1.1. – 30.6	6,501	2,167	12,078
(£64,350, 4:3:3)	25,740	19,305	19,305	1.7 – 31.12	19,660	14,743	14,743
				Goodwill (3:1)	33,690	11,230	
Revaluation							
(£3,500, 3:1)	2,625	875		Goodwill			19,430
				Revaluation			3,500
Bal C/D	19,879	—	14,656	Bal C/D	—	4,130	—
	59,851	32,270	49,751		59,851	32,270	49,751

Goodwill working	Toy shop £	Newsagents £
Total 3 year profits	89,840	38,860
Average	29,947	12,953
1½ times (= goodwill)	44,920	19,430
Combined total	64,350	

c **Balance sheet of new business as at 31 December 19X5**

	£	£	£
Fixed assets			
Lease premiums			11,500
Fixtures (net depreciation)			10,278
Motor vehicles (net of depreciation)			8,391
			30,169
Current assets			
Stock		16,452	
Cash at bank		3,062	
Cash in hand		448	
		19,962	
Current liabilities			
Creditors	12,482		
Bank overdraft	7,244	19,726	
			236
			30,405
Current accounts			
Katie			19,879
Richard			(4,130)
Sally			14,656
			30,405

ANSWER 4.1 (BASIC)

Downdale

SOLUTION

Profit and loss account for the year ended 31 December 19X6

	£'000	£'000
Sales		1,265
Opening stock	125	
Purchases	703	
	828	
Less closing stock	141	
Cost of sales		687
Gross profit		578
Depreciation (15 + 28)	43	
Wages and salaries	102	
Directors remuneration	38	
Rent, rates, telephone and insurance	69	
Heat, light and water	85	
Debenture interest	40	377
Profit before tax		201
Corporation tax		
charged this year	65	
over-provided last year	(11)	54

	£'000	£'000
Profit after tax		147
Proposed dividends		80
Retained profit		67
Balance brought forward		323
Balance carried forward		390

Balance sheet as at 31 December 19X6

	£'000 Cost	£'000 Accumulated depreciation	£'000 Net book value
Tangible fixed assets			
Freehold land and buildings	860	74	786
Motor vehicles	240	90	150
	1,100	164	936
Current assets			
Stock		141	
Debtors		109	
Cash at bank		55	
Cash in hand		6	
		311	
Current liabilities			
Creditors		112	
Taxation		65	
Dividend		80	
		257	
Net current assets			54
10% debenture stock 19X23			990
			(400)
			590
Called up share capital (£1 ordinary shares)			150
Share premium account			50
Profit and loss account			390
			590

ANSWER 4.2 (INTERMEDIATE)

Prague

WORKINGS

(1) Workings for bank account entries are as follows:

Total debtors

	£		£
B/D	220,980	*Bank	1,743,560
Sales	1,731,400	Bad debts	1,400
		C/D	207,420
	1,952,380		1,952,380

Total creditors

	£		£
Discounts	17,411	B/D	137,452
*Bank	727,499	Purchases	736,248
C/D	128,790		
	873,700		873,700

Commissions

	£		£
Bank (15% × 1,743,560)	261,534	B/D (15% × 220,980)	33,147
C/D (15% × 207,420)	31,113	P/L (15% × 1,730,000)	259,500
	292,647		292,647

Cash

	£		£
B/D	432	Sundry expenses	4,733
*Bank	4,628	C/D	327
	5,060		5,060

* denotes balancing figures

(2) The bank account may be now be constructed:

	£
Balance B/D	76,814 (O/D)
Wages and salaries (481,441 + 187,004)	668,445
Motor vehicles (63,900 − 12,750)	51,150
Plant and machinery	4,587
Dividends	5,400
Petty cash	4,628
Commissions	261,534
Purchases	727,499
	1,800,057
less receipts from sales	1,743,560
Balance C/D (overdrawn)	56,497

SOLUTION

Draft trading profit and loss account for the year ended 31 August 19X5

	£	£
Sales		1,731,400
Opening stock	186,475	
Purchases		
Raw materials	530,722	
Manufacturing expenses	141,677	
Overheads	63,849	
Factory wages and salaries	481,441	
Closing stock	(222,666)	
Cost of sales		1,181,498
Gross profit		549,902
Discounts received		17,411
		567,313

	£	£
Administration wages and salaries	187,004	
Sundry expenses	4,733	
Commissions	259,500	
Depreciation		
– commercial vehicles (33⅓% × 63,900)	21,300	
– plant and machinery (15% × 29,427) – 11,214 + 4,587)	3,420	
– private cars (20% × 19,633 – 7,413)	2,444	
– over-provided on vehicles disposal (12,750 – 58,422 + 47,507)	(1,835)	
Bad debts	1,400	
Rectification costs	723	
		478,689
Profit available for appropriation		88,624
Interim dividend (proposed) (15,000 × 38p)		5,700
Retained profit for the year		82,924
Balance at 1.9.X4		121,422
Balance at 31.8.X5		204,346

(*Note:* it would be acceptable to include depreciation of plant and machinery and rectification costs within the cost of sales calculation.)

Draft balance sheet as at 31 August 19X5

Fixed assets	Cost	Accumulated depreciation	Net book value
	£	£	£
Plant and machinery	34,014	14,634	19,380
Commercial vehicles	63,900	21,300	42,600
Private cars	19,633	9,857	9,776
			71,756

Current assets			
Stock		222,666	
Debtors		207,420	
Cash in hand		327	
		430,413	

Creditors due within one year			
Trade creditors	128,790		
Rectification provision	723		
Commissions owing	31,113		
Proposed dividends	5,700		
Bank overdraft	56,497	222,823	207,590
			279,346

Called up share capital		75,000
Profit and loss account		204,346
		279,346

ANSWER 4.3 (ADVANCED)

Scarpia

WORKINGS

Points to note:

(1) The loss on office furniture (7900 – 1500 = 6400) should be charged to P/L.

(2) Be careful with the bad debt charge calculation – notes (2) and (6) should be considered together.
   (a) Adjusted debtor balance after writing off specific bad debts and correcting for error in note (6) is

$$(46270 - 1152 - 7250) = \underline{\underline{37868}}$$

(b) Bad debt charge is:

	£	£
Specific		7,250
Increase in provision		
Existing	700	
Required 5% × 37868	1,893	1,193
		8,443

(3) Cash account adjustment:

	£	£
Per trial balance		240
From main cash book (double entry not previously completed contributing to difference on trial balance)		1,422
		1,662
Less motor expenses	722	
sundry expenses	600	
casual labour	80	1,402
Balance C/D		260

(4) Difference on trial balance of £270 consists of:

	£
Error re sale ledger control	1,152
Error re posting of cash book	1,422
	270

(5) Depreciation calculations:

		£
Building	4% × £20,000	800
Plant	25% × £22,000	5,500
Vehicles	25% × (6400 − 1800)	1,150
Furniture	25% × £2000	500
Leased equipment	2% × 10 months × £12,000	2,400

SOLUTION

Draft trading and profit and loss account for the year ended 30 September 19X1

	£	£
Sales		240,900
Opening stocks (22,400 + 8,700)	31,100	
Purchases (162,450 + 2,400 − 12,000)	152,850	
Closing stocks (7,200 + 20,000 + 6,700)	(33,900)	
Cost of sales		150,050
Gross profit		90,850
Sundry income		6,270
Leasing income		4,000
		101,120
Depreciation of buildings	800	
Depreciation of plant	5,500	
Depreciation of vehicles	1,150	
Depreciation of furniture	500	
Loss on furniture destroyed in fire	6,400	
Depreciation of leased equipment	2,400	
Wages and salaries (103,100 + 80)	103,180	
Heat and light	840	
Bank interest and charges	2,430	
Bad debts	8,443	

	£	£
Insurance	6,470	
Motor expenses (2,120 + 722)	2,842	
Sundry expenses (100 + 600)	700	
Commissions	230	
		141,885
Loss for the year		(40,765)
Balance brought forward		47,110
Balance carried forward		6,345

Draft balance sheet as at 30 September 19X1

Fixed assets	£	£	£
Freehold land			1,000
Freehold buildings			19,200
Plant and machinery			16,500
Leased plant (12,000 − 2,400)			9,600
Office furniture (2,000 − 500)			1,500
Motor vehicles (6,400 − 1,800 − 1,150)			3,450
			51,250
Current assets			
Stocks		33,900	
Trade debtors	37,868		
Less provision for doubtful debts	1,893		
		35,975	
Other debtor – insurance claim		1,500	
Prepayments and deposits		25,200	
Cash in hand		260	
		96,835	
Less			
Current liabilities			
Trade creditors (24,290 + 2,400)	26,690		
Other creditors	2,000		
Directors' loans	4,600		
Bank overdraft	72,450		
		105,740	(8,905)
			42,345
Called up share capital			36,000
Profit and loss account			6,345
			42,345

ANSWER 5.1 (BASIC)

Raywood

SOLUTION

Balance sheet of Raywood plc as at 31 December 19X3

	Cost £	Accumulated depreciation £	Net book value £
Fixed assets – tangible			
Land and buildings	2,050,000	150,000	1,900,000
Plant and machinery	893,400	221,100	672,300
Fixtures and fittings	584,150	95,050	489,100
	3,527,550	466,150	3,061,400

	Cost £	Accumulated depreciation £	Net book value £
Current assets			
Stocks		421,760	
Debtors		289,235	
Cash at bank and in hand		89,640	
		800,635	
Creditors: amounts falling due within one year			
Bank overdraft		189,650	
Trade creditors		387,333	
Current corporation tax		202,500	
Accruals		17,300	
Proposed dividend		50,000	
		846,783	
Net current liabilities			(46,148)
Total assets less current liabilities			3,015,252
Creditors: amounts falling due after more than one year			
8% debenture stock 19X15			(200,000)
			2,815,252
Capital and reserves			
Called up share capital			800,000
Share premium account			1,400,000
Profit and loss account			615,252
			2,815,252

ANSWER 5.2 (INTERMEDIATE)

Publish

WORKINGS PART (A)

(i)

	Cost of sales £	Distribution costs £	Administrative expenses £
Office wages and salaries			327,500
Advertising		121,400	
Depreciation	101,750	11,460	83,200⎱ 8,570⎰
Raw materials	531,260		
Factory overheads	137,350		
Admin overheads			85,470
Salesmens' Salaries		39,630	
Factory wages	138,640		
Foreman's salary	12,255		
Directors' remuneration (assumed admin as no other information available)			98,670
Audit fee			5,730
Discount allowed		19,850	
Bad debts			38,000
Totals	921,255	192,340	647,140

(ii) *Staff costs*

	£
Office	327,500
Salesmen	39,630
Factory	138,640
Foreman	12,255
Directors	98,670
	616,695

124   *Answer 5.2 (intermediate)*

SOLUTION PART (A)

Profit and loss account for the year ended 31 December 19X4 (format 1)

	£	£
Turnover		2,860,500
Cost of sales		921,255
Gross profit		1,939,245
Distribution costs	192,340	
Administrative expenses	647,140	839,480
Operating profit (note 1)		1,099,765
Interest payable (note 3)		73,960
Profit on ordinary activities before tax		1,025,805
Tax on profit on ordinary activities		335,400
Profit on ordinary activities after tax		690,405
Dividends (note 4)		325,000
Retained profit		365,405
Retained profit brought forward		732,600
Retained profit carried forward		1,098,005

Notes to the accounts

		£
(1)	Operating profit is arrived at after charging	
	Directors' remuneration	98,670
	Auditors' remuneration	5,730
(2)	Staff costs amounted to	616,695
(3)	Interest payable	
	Bank loans and overdrafts	18,960
	Other loans not wholly repayable within 5 years	55,000
		73,960
(4)	Dividends	
	Preference – paid	75,000
	Ordinary – proposed	250,000
		325,000

WORKINGS PART (B)

(i) Staff costs – see part (a).
(ii) Other operating charges

Advertising	121,400
Factory	137,350
Admin	85,470
Audit	5,730
Discount	19,850
Bad debts	38,000
	407,800

SOLUTION PART (B)

Profit and loss account for the year ended 31 December 19X4 (format 2)

	£	£
Turnover		2,860,500
Change in stocks of finished goods and work in progress		—
		2,860,500
Raw materials and consumables		531,260
		2,329,240

	£	£
Staff costs	616,695	
Depreciation	204,980	
Other operating charges	407,800	1,229,475
Operating profit		1,099,765

Note: The remainder of the profit and loss account is as for format 1. All notes relevant to format 1 are also relevant.

ANSWER 5.3 (ADVANCED)

Health Sales (company accounts)

WORKINGS PART (A)

(1) *Purchase of partnership*

	£
1.1.X3 H.S. Ltd acquires partnership PKB	
Purchase consideration 510,000 shares at 150p	765,000
Cash	714,000
	1,479,000

All assets (at book except freehold at £1,020,000)
All liabilities NOT bank

Freehold	1,020,000	
Shop fittings	301,000	
Stock	212,400	
Debtors	265,200	
Creditors	(112,200)	
		1,686,400
Capital reserve		207,400

(2) *Calculation of payments and discounts on non-group purchases*

	Aug	Sept	Oct	Nov	Dec	Jan	Feb	Discounts re payments Oct onwards
	17,200							
C	3,000	12,000	2,018					—
I	3,061	12,121	2,018					
		16,100						
C		5,000	8,000	2,917				81
I		5,102	8,081	2,917				
			15,095					
C			4,000	9,800	1,114			82⎫
I			4,082	9,899	1,114			99⎭
				18,300				
C				3,300	14,100	691		67⎫
I				3,367	14,242	691		142⎭
					25,305			
C					15,200	8,000	1,714	310⎫
I					15,510	8,081	1,714	81⎭
								862

Explanation of table
(1) Consider August sales.
    (i) Cash (C) of £3,000 is after discount of 2% so invoice (I) was
    $\dfrac{£3,000}{0.98}$ = £3,061 and discount received £61 (included in Jan–Sept total of £1,628).

(ii) Cash of £12,000 is after discount of 1% so invoice was

$\dfrac{£12,000}{0.99}$ = £12,121 and discount received £121 (also part of £1,628).

(iii) Final payment in October (no discount) = £17,200 − 3,061 − 12,121 = 2,018.

(2) Discounts of £862 include provision for discount receivable £81 on December purchases as regards part paid in January.

Summary

(i) Invoices for the year (155,500 + 15,095 + 18,300 + 25,305)	= £214,200
(ii) Payments for the year (140,856 + 2,018 + 8,000 + 2,917 + 4,000 + 9,800 + 1,114 + 3,300 + 14,100 + 15,200)	= £201,305
(iii) Discounts received and receivable = (1,628 + 862)	= £2,490

(iv) Calculation of creditor balance at 31 December:

Purchases	214,200
Cash	(201,305)
Discounts	(2,490)
Balance	10,405

Note: This reflects amount owing taking account of discount receivable on December purchases of £81 (cheque sent off in January).

(3) *Debtors ex partnership*

Book value	265,200
Discount allowed (10%)	26,520
∴ cash received	238,680

(4) *Disposal of shop fittings*

Profit on disposal (105,000 − 97,280)	= £7,720
Book value remaining (before charging annual depreciation) (301,000 − 97,280 + 765,000)	= £968,720
Depreciation charge 12½% × £968,720	= £121,090

(5) *Creditors for expense payments*

	Cheque £	Invoice £
Admin	150,000	161,853
Estab	81,060	83,695
Selling	72,416	79,850
Distrib	27,148	28,960
Misc	16,193	17,500
	346,817	371,858

∴ Creditor (371,858 − 346,817) = £25,041.

(6) *Dividends*

		Div	ACT (3/7)
Paid	5% × (1,190 + 510) =	85,000	36,429
Proposed	2½% × (1,190 + 510) =	42,500	18,214

(7) *Stock turnover information*

	£
Ex Black Root $\dfrac{816,000}{10}$	81,600
Ex non group suppliers $\dfrac{214,200}{4}$	53,550
Closing stock	135,150

(8) *Debtor turnover information*

Credit sales	£1,254,000
∴ Closing debtors $\dfrac{1,254}{12}$	£104,500
∴ Calculate cash received 1,254 − 104.5	£1,149,500

(9) *Current account information*

	£
Purchases ex Black Root	816,000
Closing balance	100,000
∴ Cash paid	716,000

(10) *Summary of bank account*

	Dr £	Cr £
Issue of shares	1,190,000	
Purchase of business		714,000
Cash sales	500,400	
Non-group purchases		201,305
Creditors ex partnership		112,200
Debtors ex partnership	238,680	
Fixed assets acquired		
– land		306,000
– fittings		765,000
Fixed asset disposals	105,000	
Expense payments		346,817
Dividend paid		85,000
ACT paid		36,429
Cash received from credit sales	1,149,500	
Current account		716,000
Balance (o/d)	99,171	
	3,282,751	3,282,751

SOLUTION PART (A)

Profit and loss account of Health Sales Ltd for the year ended 31 December 19X3 – for internal use

	£	£
Sales – credit		1,254,000
– cash		500,400
		1,754,400
Opening stock	212,400	
Purchases – group	816,000	
– external	214,200	
	1,242,600	
Closing stock	135,150	
Cost of sales		1,107,450
Gross profit		646,950
Discounts received		2,490
Profit on sale of assets		7,720
		657,160
Expenses		
Administration	161,853	
Establishment	83,695	
Selling	79,850	
Distribution	28,960	
Miscellaneous	17,500	
Depreciation on fittings	121,090	
Discounts allowed	26,520	
		519,468
Profit before tax		137,692
Tax		—
Profit after tax		137,692
Dividends – interim (paid)	85,000	
– final (proposed)	42,500	
		127,500
Retained profit		10,192

Balance sheet of Health Sales Ltd as at 31 December 19X3 – for internal use

	£	£
Tangible fixed assets		
Freehold land (1,020,000 + 306,000)		1,326,000
Shop fittings (968,720 − 121,090)		847,630
		2,173,630
Current assets		
Stock	135,150	
Debtors	104,500	
ACT recoverable (36,429 + 18,214)	54,643	
	294,293	
Creditors due within one year		
Trade creditors	10,405	
Expense creditors	25,041	
Current account (Black Root)	100,000	
ACT payable	18,214	
Proposed dividend	42,500	
Bank overdraft	99,171	
	295,331	
		(1,038)
Net current liabilities		2,172,592
Capital and reserves		
Share capital		1,700,000
Share premium		255,000
Capital reserve		207,400
Profit and loss account		10,192
		2,172,592

WORKINGS PART (B)

	Cost of sales	*Distribution costs*	*Administrative expenses*
	£	*£*	*£*
Cost of sales per internal accounts	1,107,450		
Depreciation of fittings	121,090		
Profit on disposal of fittings	(7,720)		
Discounts received	(2,490)		
Admin expenses			161,853
Establishment expenses			83,695
Selling expenses		79,850	
Distribution expenses		28,960	
Misc. excl. interest (17,500 − 13,000)			4,500
Discounts allowed		26,520	
Adjusted totals	1,218,330	135,330	250,048

SOLUTION PART (B)

Profit and loss account of Health Sales Ltd for the year ended 31 December 19X3 – in a form suitable for presentation to the shareholders

	£	£
Turnover		1,754,400
Cost of sales		1,218,330
Gross profit		536,070
Distribution costs	135,330	
Administrative expenses	250,048	385,378

	£	£
Operating profit (note 1)		150,692
Interest payable (note 2)		13,000
Profit on ordinary activities before tax		137,692
Tax on profit on ordinary activities		—
Profit on ordinary activities after tax		137,692
Dividends on ordinary shares (note 3)		127,500
Retained profit transferred to reserves		10,192

Notes to the accounts

(1) Operating profit is after charging:	£
Depreciation	121,090
Auditors' remuneration	25,000
Directors' remuneration	
Fees	—
Management remuneration	50,000
Staff costs	223,000
Average number of employees	

Selling	22
Distribution	20
Administration	30
	72

(2) Interest payable on bank overdraft	131,000
(3) Dividends on ordinary shares	
Interim (paid) at 5p per share	85,000
Final (proposed) at 2.5p per share	42,500
	127,500

ANSWER 5.4 (ADVANCED)

Pourwell (published accounts)

Profit and loss account of Pourwell Limited for the year ended 31 December 19X5

	Notes	£	£
Turnover			696,000
Cost of sales			410,778
Gross profit			285,222
Distribution costs		200,101	
Administrative expenses (105,113 + 15,000)		120,113	320,214
Operating loss	1		(34,992)
Income from fixed asset investment	2	5,000	
Interest payable	3	(12,350)	(7,350)
Loss on ordinary activities before tax			(42,342)
Extraordinary gain – profit on sale of land			15,000
			(27,342)
Balance brought forward			(97,160)
Balance carried forward			(124,502)

Balance sheet of Pourwell Limited as at 31 December 19X5

Fixed assets	Notes	£	£
Intangible assets	4		222,500
Tangible assets	5		129,000
Investments			42,500
			394,000

	Notes	£	£
Current assets			
Stocks	6	200,415	
Debtors	7	95,005	
		295,420	
Creditors: amounts falling due within one year	8	263,922	
Net current assets			31,498
Total assets less current liabilities			425,498
Creditors: amounts falling due after more than one year	9		250,000
			175,498
Capital and reserves			
Called up share capital	10		300,000
Profit and loss account			(124,502)
			175,498

(5) Tangible assets

	Land and buildings £	Plant £	Fixtures £	Total £
Cost at 1 Jan	110,000	78,800	9,900	198,700
Additions		12,000		12,000
Disposals	(10,000)			(10,000)
Cost at 31 Dec	100,000	90,800	9,900	200,700
Depreciation at 1 Jan	17,600	43,340	3,960	64,900
Provided	1,600	4,540	660	6,800
Depreciation at 31 Dec	19,200	47,880	4,620	71,700
Net book value at 31 Dec	80,800	42,920	5,280	129,000

(6) Stocks

	£
Raw materials	20,210
Work in progress	10,103
Finished goods	170,102
	200,415

(7) Debtors

	£
Trade debtors	89,505
Prepayments and accrued income	4,000
Tax recoverable	1,500
	95,005

(8) Creditors – falling due within one year

	£
Trade creditors (258,550 − 50,000)	208,550
Accruals (10,500 + 2,100 + 2,850 + 1,900)	17,350
Bank overdraft	38,022
	263,922

(9) Creditors – falling due after more than one year

	£
7% debenture stock 19X22	75,000
Directors' loans	125,000
Deferred creditors	50,000
	250,000

(10) Called up share capital

	£
200,000 ordinary shares of £1	200,000
100,000 7% preference shares of £1	100,000
	300,000

Note: Preference dividends arrears – no dividend has been paid in respect of 19X4 and 19X5.

ANSWER 5.5 (INTERMEDIATE)

Stag
ANSWER GUIDE

Report of directors ......

Directors present ......

Profit for year after tax was .... The directors recommend a dividend of £150,000 which leaves a retained profit for the year of £109,000.

Principal activities and business review
There have been no significant changes during the year of the principal activities which consist of ...... Profit has improved as a result of the cost cutting exercise ...

Share capital
...... increased during the year by 400,000 shares rights issue ...... to finance the new building acquisition.

Directors
Directors at 31.12.X6 ....

Directors' interests
Interests .... in shares of the company ....

	30.4.X6		30.4.X6	
Name	Number	Amount	Number	Amount
G. Roebuck				
A. Roebuck				
F. Roebuck				
D. Ear				
T. Roebuck				

(No need to disclose Mrs Fallow since not director at year-end).

Market value of land and buildings
...... valuation 19X5. No significant change since that date.

Significant changes in fixed assets
...... new building and laboratories £240,000.

Research and development
...... new synthetic fibre ...... etc.

Political and charitable contributions
...... charitable   £400
...... political £420 including £250 to Liberal Party

Employees
...... disabled persons
...... information

Events since year end

Auditors
...... resolution to re-appoint P. Ranger & Co.

ANSWER 5.6 (INTERMEDIATE)

Makewell
SOLUTION

(a)(1) Extraordinary items are defined by SSAP 6 as material items which derive from events or transactions that fall outside the ordinary activities of the company and which are therefore expected not to recur frequently or regularly.

(2) Prior year adjustments are defined as those material adjustments applicable to prior years arising from changes in accounting policies or from the correction of fundamental errors.

(b) The essential difference between extraordinary items and exceptional items is that the latter derive from events or transactions that fall within the ordinary activities of the company. In other words exceptional items are routine in nature but separate disclosure is required on account of their abnormal size or incidence if financial statements are to give a true and fair view.

(c)(1) The possibility of a ban on a particular product would appear to derive from the ordinary activities of a company such as this one. The loss of £750,000 which is material in amount therefore derives from an event or transaction that falls within the ordinary activities of the company. The loss should be treated as an exceptional item and separately disclosed.

(2) The original holding was acquired as a fixed asset investment. The gain now recorded of £599,000 which is material to the company derives from an event outside the ordinary activities of the company. It is not expected to recur. The gain should therefore be recorded as an extraordinary item.

(3) SSAP 12, Accounting for depreciation, requires companies to keep expected remaining asset lives under regular review. Where the estimated remaining useful life is subsequently revised, the net book amount should be written off over the revised remaining useful economic life. The company appear to have followed SSAP 12. The depreciation charge for 19X8 is correctly recorded at £1.2 million. As the charge of £1.2 million is double what it would have been had no change in useful life taken place some disclosure of the effect on the financial statements might be desirable.

ANSWER 5.7 (INTERMEDIATE)

Waveprocessor

SOLUTION

(a) SSAP 6 defines extraordinary items as material items which derive from events or transactions that fall outside the ordinary activities of the company and which are therefore expected not to recur frequently or regularly.

By contrast exceptional items, although material, are items which derive from events or transactions that fall within the ordinary activities of the company. It is the size or incidence of such items which requires separate disclosure if financial statements are to give a true and fair view.

In order to assist with interpretation of these definitions SSAP 6 provides non-mandatory guidance by way of actual examples of such items.

(b)(1) The loss on sale of the factory results from the discontinuance of a business segment. The loss derives from an event that falls outside the ordinary activities of the company, the event is material and it is not expected to recur frequently or regularly. The loss should therefore be treated as an extraordinary item.

(2) The customer's insolvency is an event which falls within the ordinary activities of the company. In this particular situation the bad debt is abnormally large and so should be treated as an exceptional item, thus affecting the profit on ordinary activities before taxation. The item will be separately disclosed either on the face of the profit and loss account or in a memorandum note.

(3) The change from the previous policy of capitalisation of research and development expenditure to one of immediate write-off constitutes a change in accounting policy. This gives rise to a prior year adjustment. £125,000 of expenditure relating to the current year should be charged to profit and loss account. The balance of £300,000 relating to previous years should be charged against opening reserves as a prior year adjustment.

ANSWER 5.8 (INTERMEDIATE)

Fabricators

SOLUTION

SSAP 17, Accounting for post balance sheet events, defines such events as those which occur between the balance sheet date and the date of approval of the financial statements by the board of directors.

Post balance sheet events fall essentially into two groups:

(a) adjusting events which are reflected in the current year financial statements either because they provide additional evidence of conditions existing at the balance sheet date or because of statutory or conventional requirements;

(b) non-adjusting events which although they do not relate to conditions existing at the balance sheet date are disclosed in a memorandum note because failure to disclose would otherwise affect the ability of users of accounts to reach a proper understanding of the financial position.

Dealing with each matter in turn:

(1) The event in question appears to provide evidence of a condition which existed at the balance sheet date, namely impairment in value of the investment. It appears that the investment was not held for the purpose of resale at a profit. As the amount involved is material to the company, the decline in value of £50,000 should be recognised in the financial statements – the balance sheet value should be adjusted and the diminution charged to P/L as an extraordinary item.

(2) The event is a non-adjusting event and does not affect conditions existing at the balance sheet date. Details of the event and the uninsured loss would normally be disclosed by way of memorandum note. This assumes that the fire does not have such a drastic affect on the business that it can no longer be viewed as a going concern (in which event the balance sheet would have to be drawn up on an alternative basis).

(3) This is clearly an adjusting event as it provides 'additional evidence of conditions . . .' and the balance sheet should reflect a reduction in provision of £60,000 i.e. the earlier entry should be reversed.

(4) The announcement clearly constitutes a non-adjusting event. It could be argued that some form of disclosure is necessary for a 'proper understanding . . .' However, it would not be appropriate to refer to the possible effect on turnover and profits. Also it may be advisable to provide the information in some other part of the annual report such as the Chairman's statement.

ANSWER 5.9 (ADVANCED)

Alpha

SOLUTION

(1) In the case of Alpha the critical date is the date of exchange of contracts when the sale became binding on both parties. As this took place before the year-end the event should be regarded as adjusting and the sale should be reflected in the financial statements. In the absence of further information it is not possible to say whether the profit of £150,000 is to be regarded as an exceptional or extraordinary item.

(2) The dividend from the subsidiary should be regarded as an adjusting event. Beta should set up a debtor for dividend receivable, crediting its own profit and loss account.

(3) Gamma's mail order activities would be classified as a business segment under SSAP 6.

It would be important to establish when the closure decision was made. If the decision was effectively made prior to the year-end then the financial consequences should be reflected in the financial statements for 19X1. Closure costs relating to the discontinuance of a business segment would usually be treated as an extraordinary item.

It would also be necessary to consider whether the going concern assumption is valid for the whole of the business (SSAP 2 refers to 'no intention or necessity to . . . curtail significantly the scale of operation'). It may be necessary to restate the carrying amounts of certain fixed and current assets for balance sheet purposes, any profits or losses should be treated as extraordinary.

Alternatively it may be argued that if the closure was not anticipated at the year-end, the event should be treated as non-adjusting requiring only memorandum disclosure. Against this it could be argued that on prudence grounds, having regard to the dates and other factors, that the event should be regarded as adjusting.

(4) This is not a post balance sheet event as defined since it took place after the approval of the financial statements. However SSAP 17 indicates that in material cases such as this the directors should consider publishing the relevant information so that users of financial statements are not misled.

(5) The event is a non-adjusting event since the fire took place after the year-end. Although it is expected that the loss of plant of £10 million is covered by insurance, it is important to establish that disruption of business etc. does not prevent the business being regarded as a going concern. Subject to this, memorandum disclosure in a note would be necessary to enable users to assess the financial position.

(6) The damages claim represents a contingent liability since the outcome of the claim will be confirmed only on the occurrence or non-occurrence of an uncertain future event. As loss is only possible rather than probable it would be sufficient to refer to it in the notes to the accounts. The note should indicate the nature of the contingency, the uncertainties expected to affect the ultimate outcome together with a prudent estimate of the financial effect (i.e. refer to the directors' opinion and legal advice).

A prudent provision for the legal fees should be made in the accounts.

(7) The movement in foreign exchange rates is a non-adjusting event as it does not affect conditions existing at the balance sheet date. As the effect is material to the company, the effect of the change in exchange rates should be disclosed by way of memorandum note as it may be necessary to enable users to assess the financial position.

ANSWER 5.10 (INTERMEDIATE)

Stock Exchange

ANSWER GUIDE

(a) Additional disclosure requirements – continuing obligations:
  (1) annual accounts disclosures e.g.:
    (i) reasons for significant departures from SSAPs
    (ii) explanation of reasons for trading results differing from published forecasts
    (iii) statement of borrowings – analysed 0–1,1–2, 2–5, 5 years +
    (iv) statement of interest capitalised during year
    (v) whether company is a close company for tax purposes
    (vi) name of principal country in which each subsidiary operates
    (vii) geographical analysis of net turnover and contribution to trading results of trading operations carried on outside UK.

(b)(1) *Stock Exchange objectives in regulating*
    (i) create efficient market
    (ii) avoid placing persons (S) in privileged dealing positions
    (iii) ensure proper conduct and disclosure of information likely to have significant effect on share price.
  (2) *Means of pursuing objectives*
    (i) control over publication of half-yearly reports of profits
    (ii) control over publication of preliminary profit statement for full year
    (iii) control over public announcements
    (iv) security over price–sensitive information
    (v) City Code on Mergers and Takeovers
    (vi) Control over profit forecasts.

ANSWER 5.11 (INTERMEDIATE)

Segmental reporting

ANSWER GUIDE

(a)(1) *Terminology* – analysis of information between parts of a business which are individually significant from an economic viewpoint:
    e.g. analysis of (i) turnover (ii) trading profits (iii) assets employed between different geographical markets and between different business segments.
  (2) need for further disclosure:
    (i) trend for larger business units, diversification of activities, takeovers (hence large groups) with danger of less information about component parts

(ii) different business (industry) segments and geographical segments may experience different profitability rates, growth opportunities, future prospects and investment risk
(iii) segmental reporting is needed to counter-balance consolidation reporting for ever-increasing sizes of groups
(iv) responses of Companies Act 1985 and Stock Exchange (give outline of requirements)
(v) interpretation of accounts – ratio analysis
(vi) need for further disclosure should be related to needs of different user groups.

(b) *Objections and problems*
  (1) identification of segments:
    (i) product/service
    (ii) industrial classification
    (iii) customer type
    (iv) geographical market
    – basis should be disclosed
    – CA 85 gives discretion to directors
    – relate to information needs of user groups.
  (2) disclosure:
    (i) turnover
    (ii) operating profit
    (iii) value added
    (iv) operating assets (capital employed)
    (v) numbers of employees.
  (3) measurement problems:
    (i) shared assets
    (ii) shared overheads.

ANSWER 5.12 (ADVANCED)

Angie

SOLUTION

(a)(1) Private companies – maximum distribution is accumulated realised profits (not previously distributed or capitalised) less accumulated realised losses (so far as not written off by a reduction or reorganisation of capital). A profit is realised provided it is treated as such under generally accepted accounting principles. It makes no difference whether the profit is revenue or capital in nature.
  (2) Public companies – in addition to the above an additional restriction applies. Net unrealised losses (the excess of accumulated unrealised losses over accumulated unrealised profits) must be deducted from the amount otherwise available for distribution (per (1) above).
  (3) Investment companies:
    (i) for a company to qualify as an investment company, the company must be a public limited company and its Memorandum or Articles of Association must prohibit the distribution of capital profits;
    (ii) may choose between
      (a) the maximum distribution permitted by the usual PLC rules and
      (b) a distribution out of accumulated realised *revenue* profits less accumulated revenue losses (realised or unrealised). Such a distribution must not reduce assets below 1.5 times liabilities.

(b)(1) *Angie plc*

Maximum amount available for distribution:	£'000
Realised capital profit	800
Accumulated realised revenue profits b/f	400
Current year profit	200
	1,400
Depreciation relating to revaluation surplus (2,000 − 900 ÷ 50)	22
	1,422

(2) *Betty plc*

Maximum amount available for distribution:

		£
Revenue profits b/f		500
Current year loss		(200)
		300
Net unrealised losses (since plc)		(200)
		100

(3) *Cathy Ltd*

Maximum amount available for distribution:

Revenue losses b/f	(1,600)
Current year profit	200
	(1,400)

No distribution could be made

(c) *Betty plc – investment company*

May choose between:
(1) Plc rules i.e. — £100,000

and
(2) accumulated realised revenue profits
less accumulated revenue losses i.e. — £300,000

subject to ensuring assets 1.5 times liabilities
or liabilities ⅔ assets

Total assets 380 + 180 =	460,000
Liabilities ⅔ × 460,000 =	373,333
Existing liabilities	160,000
∴ Distribution restricted to	213,333

∴ Choice of £100,000 and £213,333
∴ maximum distributable profit is — £213,333

ANSWER 6.1 (INTERMEDIATE)

Assumptions

ANSWER GUIDE

(1) Explain clearly terminology of SSAP 2:
   (i) fundamental accounting concepts
   (ii) accounting bases
   (iii) accounting policies
(2) Accounting bases cover wide range of businesses and transactions.
(3) Judgment is crucial – need to consider future events of uncertain financial effect e.g. useful lines of fixed assets, expected profits on long-term contracts.
(4) Bases provide limits to the areas subject to the exercise of judgment but companies have considerable discretion in choice of policies.
(5) The standard-setting programme should in theory assist in application of suitable bases to a particular business but some recently issued SSAPs have come in for much criticism.
(6) SSAP 2 requires a company to give clear disclosures of its key accounting policies – but some companies provide far more useful information to users than others.
(7) Problems of interpretation/comparability – if two companies in same business sector adopt different policies, does mere disclosure of policies always enable valid comparisons to be made (information may be verbal description rather than numerical data).

ANSWER 6.2 (INTERMEDIATE)

Accounting policies

ANSWER GUIDE

Part (a) of the question deals specifically with SSAP 2.

Part (b) is particularly topical in view of the controversies surrounding certain recently-issued standards such as SSAP 22 (goodwill) and SSAP 23 (acqusitions and mergers). The following is a brief synopsis of the relevant points which should be included in an acceptable solution:

(a)(1) Accounting concepts – broad basic assumptions underlying periodic financial statements. SSAP 2 refers to going concern, accruals, consistency and prudence. (Definitions should be given for each).

(2) Accounting bases – methods developed for the purpose of applying fundamental accounting concepts to financial transactions and items such as fixed asset depreciation and stock valuation.

(3) Accounting policies – specific accounting bases selected by enterprises as appropriate to their business and circumstances.

(b)(1) Policies are critical in determination of profit e.g. choice between deferral and immediate write-off of development costs (SSAP 13).

(2) One company can legitimately select from a wide range of acceptable bases, provided the consistency concept is followed.

(3) Because of (2) clear disclosure of policies is crucial.

(4) For quoted companies a wider range of user groups are concerned with appraisal of financial information.

(5) Comparisons include:
(i) intra-company : this year with last year
(ii) inter-company : one company with another similar company. Profit determines earnings per share (EPS) EPS is used to calculate price earnings (P/E ratio) – a standard investment ratio.

(6) Effect of earnings on share prices.

(7) Recent controversies and effect on group earnings:
(i) choice between merger method and acquisition method of accounting for business combinations;
(ii) treatment of exceptional and extraordinary items – similar transactions may be accounted for differently by different companies.

(8) Not all companies disclose policies in a clear and comprehensible way.

ANSWER 6.3 (INTERMEDIATE)

Matching

ANSWER GUIDE

(1) Accruals or matching concept:
(i) revenues and costs are accrued (as earned or incurred rather than simply when payment takes place)
(ii) revenues dealt with in P/L account (on realised basis per prudence concept) are matched with associated costs and expenses.

(2) Matching of sales and cost of sales.

(3) Cost of sales – costs in bringing goods to present location and condition:
(i) cost flow assumptions required in order to apply matching concept e.g. unit cost, FIFO, AVCO
(ii) cost of production includes a proportion of fixed production overheads – establish procedure for overhead cost recovery rate.

(4) Relevance of lower of cost and net realisable value rule – some goods sold this year may have previously been held in B/S at net realisable value (being lower than cost).

(5) Problems of applying matching concept to situations where factory is operating at well below capacity – need to write off 'irrecoverable' overheads in current year.

Note: As this question carries only 12 marks it is assumed that no discussion of long-term contract work in progress is required.

ANSWER 6.4 (ADVANCED)

Marvin and Welsh

ANSWER GUIDE

(1) *Cost of goods sold*
  (i)   treatment of production overheads (SSAP 9 requires absorption costing)
  (ii) different cost flow assumptions e.g. FIFO, AVCO, LIFO (LIFO not usually acceptable)
  (iii) different estimates of NRV where NRV is below cost (where provisions required).

(2) *R & D*
  (i)   different classifications of expenses
  (ii) different treatments of development costs (immediate W/O or deferral per SSAP 13).

(3) *Depreciation of plant etc.*
  (i)   different depreciation methods (S/L, RB etc)
  (ii) different estimates of useful life
  (iii) different estimates of residual value.

(4) *Depreciation of buildings*
  (i)   refurbishment and maintenance argument/effect on residual value. SSAP 12 requires depreciation charge unless immaterial effect.

(5) *Warranty costs*
  (i)   different views about likely claims re sales for the year
  (ii) different policies – provision at year end or charge costs as incurred (provision preferred).

(6) *Redundancy costs*
  (i)   difference of classification – extraordinary or exceptional (? SSAP 6 – continuing business segment)
  (ii) possible decision after year-end: SSAP 17 – adjusting or non-adjusting event?

(7) *Goodwill*
  (i)   amortisation or immediate W/O (SSAP 22)
  (ii) indication of business purchase during year – ensure goodwill properly measured
  (iii) ensure goodwill not C/F indefinitely.

Note:
The above points are not intended to cover all possibilities but rather to give an indication of useful areas of discussion. What is crucial is to emphasise two key points:

(1) the importance of subjective decisions within the historical cost convention;
(2) how crucial choice of accounting policy can be in the determination of reported profit.

ANSWER 6.5 (INTERMEDIATE)

Corporate report

ANSWER GUIDE

(a) *Potential users*
  (1) equity investor group
  (2) loan creditor group
  (3) employee group
  (4) analyst – adviser group
  (5) business contact group
  (6) government
  (7) public.

(b) *Information needs*
  (1) *equity investor* – information for share trading decisions, voting decisions, comparisons with other entities
  (2) *loan creditor*
    (i) long-term loans – economic stability and vulnerability of borrower
    (ii) short-term creditors – liquidity of enterprise, priority of claims

(3) *employee group*
   – security and prospects of employment, collective bargaining
(4) *analyst – adviser*
   (i) similar to equity investor etc.
   (ii) possible need for more detailed information
(5) *business contact group*
   (i) suppliers – ability to pay, longer-term viability, prospects, market conditions
   (ii) trade creditors – ability to pay, consequences of default
   (iii) customers – current and future supply of goods and services, terms and conditions
   (iv) competitors – takeover, information for comparison purposes
(6) *government* – assessment of government policy, as customers etc. in their own right
(7) *public* – role of entities, impact on community.

(c) *Influence on financial reporting*
   (1) financial reports should provide information to assist decision-making by different users
   (2) different users have different needs – one set of information may not satisfy all requirements
   (3) some require more detailed information, some more simplified information
   (4) types of reports – statutory, employee statements, reports, corporate objectives etc.

ANSWER 6.6 (INTERMEDIATE)

True and fair

ANSWER GUIDE

(1) Important concept – under CA 85, T & F view is overriding.
(2) Fundamental to financial reporting by companies and auditors.
(3) No agreed definition despite attempts to define.
(4) Concept is dynamic – interpretation of T and F is likely to vary over time.
(5) Needs to recognise complexity of business transactions – there is no unique T and F view for a company (so talk about *a* T and F view).
(6) Only courts can say whether particular set of accounts give a T and F view.
(7) Role of SSAPs.
(8) Role of SORPs (statement of recommended practice).
(9) Practice of majority of companies at present time.
(10) Role of judgment and opinion.

ANSWER 7.1 (INTERMEDIATE)

Jupiter

SOLUTION

a Tangible fixed assets note

	Freehold land & buildings £'000	Plant & machinery £'000	Fixtures & equip. £'000	Motor vehicles £'000	Total £'000
Cost or valuation					
At 1.11.X5	390	475	395	50	1,310
Additions	—	100	8	28	136
Revaluation	400	—	—	—	400
Disposals				(6)	(6)
At 31.10.X6	790	575	403	72	1,840
Cost	—	575	403	72	1,050
Valuation 19X5	790	—	—	—	790
	790	575	403	72	1,840

	Freehold land & buildings £'000	Plant & machinery £'000	Fixtures & equip. £'000	Motor vehicles £'000	Total £'000
Depreciation					
At 1.11.X5	60	365	125	35	585
Provided during year	10	52.5	94.75	15.25	172.5
Eliminated on					
– revaluation	(60)				(60)
– disposal	—			(5.75)	(5.75)
At 31.10.X6	10	417.5	219.75	44.5	691.75
Net book value					
31.10.X6	780	157.5	183.25	27.5	1,148.25
31.10.X5	330	110.0	270.0	15.0	725.0

NOTES TO THE ACCOUNTS
(1) On 1 November 19X5 all freehold land and buildings were revalued on an open market value for existing use basis by C Star, Chartered Surveyor. The revaluation was incorporated into the accounts.
(2) The comparable historical cost figures for the property are as follows:

	£'000
Cost	390
Depreciation	67
	323

WORKINGS

(1) Depreciation charges:

Factory	240 ÷ 40	6
Salesroom	150 ÷ 37.5	4
		10

Plant	475 ÷ 10	47.5
	100 ÷ 10 × 6/12	5.0
		52.5

Fixtures		
Computer	295 ÷ 4	73.75
Furniture	100 ÷ 5	20.0
Computer	8 ÷ 4 × 6/12	1.0
		94.75

Motor vehicles		
(50 − 6) ÷ 4		11.0
6 ÷ 4 × 6/12		0.75
28 ÷ 4 × 6/12		3.5
		15.25

(2) Comparable HC depreciation provision:

	£'000
Balance b/f	60
Factory 150 ÷ 50	3
Salesroom 180 ÷ 45	4
	67

b(1) The practice of permitting companies to incorporate fixed asset revaluations into the balance sheet is often referred to as modified historical cost (MHC) and has been permitted practice in the UK for many years.

MHC is also permitted (but not required) by the Companies Act 1985 under the alternative accounting rules. MHC may be applied to all tangible fixed assets or just a particular category such as land and buildings. MHC was given approval by ASC in its review of SSAP 6.

The advantages of MHC include:

(i) as regards the balance sheet the inclusion of assets at valuation may help to mitigate some of the misleading effects of inflation on reported figures;

(ii) as regards profit and loss account it allows the depreciation charge to be based on a going rate (in today's prices) for services consumed i.e. approximating to a CCA depreciation charge.

The disadvantages of MHC include:

(a) its inconsistent application both within companies (where it may not be universally applied) and between companies. This will result in loss of comparability;

(b) companies which practise MHC will have a higher depreciation charge (in numerical terms) compared with a charge based on historical cost. This may put them at a competitive disadvantage with companies which adhere to pure historical cost;

(c) valuation is subjective and is not necessarily carried out by a professional valuer.

(2) Where asset valuations are incorporated into the balance sheet, the depreciation charge should be based on the revalued amount. There should be consistency between B/S and P/L treatment. To leave the P/L charge based on HC whilst including the asset at valuation would be inconsistent and unacceptable.

As regards determination of profit on sale, two approaches giving different figures are currently used:

(i) by comparing sales proceeds with net book value (based on revaluation figures) at the date of sale. This approach is consistent with the depreciation approach, namely MHC in the balance sheet does affect depreciation and profit on sale in P/L. Any amount previously held in revaluation reserve now becomes realised and should be transferred to P/L reserves (no entry to P/L);

(ii) by comparing sales proceeds with depreciated historical cost as though no valuation had ever taken place. An amount previously held in revaluation reserve now becomes part of the reported profit on sale figure in P/L account.

ASC are presently reviewing the above matter as part of their study of the effect of fixed asset revaluation on financial reporting.

In the meantime inconsistent application of MHC between companies can lead to anomalous profit comparisons between companies.

ANSWER 7.2 (INTERMEDIATE)

Morecombe Malt

SOLUTION

(1) *Freehold factory*

As the property is owned and occupied by the company for its own purposes, the property does not fall within the definition of investment property (SSAP 19). Accordingly the buildings element of the property should be depreciated over its economic useful life per SSAP 12. SSAP 12 requires the depreciation charge to be based on cost (or revaluation) less estimated residual value divided by useful life. The property should be included under tangible fixed assets – freehold property.

(2) *Village*

The village represents land and buildings held for investment potential. The village falls within the definition of investment property per SSAP 19.

All assets in the village should be included in successive balance sheets at open market value. No depreciation should be charged on freehold buildings. However, leases with less than 20 years to run at the balance sheet date should be amortised over the remaining term of the lease. Subject to the latter changes in market values of investment properties between one balance sheet and the next should be taken to investment revaluation reserve. If the change is a deficit it should be debited to Investment Revaluation Reserve unless the balance on the latter account is insufficient in which case profit and loss account should be debited.

(3) *Factory leased to subsidiary*

This is specifically excluded from the SSAP 19 definition of investment property. The buildings element should be depreciated over economic useful life.

ANSWER 7.3 (ADVANCED)

Metals
WORKINGS

(1) *Tin Ltd*	£'000
Freehold and plant	465
Stocks and work in progress	847
Knowhow	110
	1,422
Purchase consideration (1,422 + 188 − 110)	1,500
Purchased goodwill	78

(2) *Manganese Ltd*	
Fair value of net assets	2,460
Purchase consideration	2,312
Negative goodwill	(148)

(3) *Copper Ltd*	
Fair value of net assets (324 + 512 − 487)	349
Purchase consideration	647
Purchased goodwill	298

(4) *Zinc Ltd*	
Fair value of net assets other than goodwill (1,728 + 3,126 − 1,174 + 80)	3,760
Purchased consideration (3m × 126p)	3,780
Purchased goodwill	20

Summary	£'000
Tin	78
Manganese	(148)
Copper	298
Zinc	20
	248

SOLUTION

(a) *Accounting policy (extract)*

Positive goodwill – where the fair value of the purchase consideration exceeds the aggregate of the fair values of the separable net assets, goodwill is eliminated by immediate write-off against reserves.

Negative goodwill – where the aggregate of the fair values of the separable net assets acquired exceeds the fair value of the purchase consideration, the difference is credited to unrealised reserves.

(b) *Notes to the group financial statements at 30 June 19X5*

	Share premium £'000	Other reserves (unrealised) £'000	Profit & loss a/c £'000	Total £'000
At 1 July 19X4	1,126	175	478	1,779
Retained profit	—	—	368	368
Premium on issue of shares – merger reserve (CA85, S131) 3m × (126p − 25p)		3,030	—	3,030
Goodwill arising during the year		(248)	—	(248)
At 30 June 19X5	1,126	2,957	846	4,929

(1) The premium on the issue of shares to acquire Zinc Ltd has been credited to a merger reserve account in accordance with section 131, Companies Act 1985.
(2) Goodwill arising as a result of acquisitions during the year:

	£'000
Tin Ltd	78
Manganese Ltd	(148)
Copper Ltd	298
Zinc Ltd	20
	248

(c) Factors which should be considered in determining the useful economic life of purchased goodwill include:
(1) expected changes in products, markets of technology
(2) the expected period of future service of certain employees
(3) expected future demand, competition or other economic factors which may affect current advantages.

The above factors should be assessed at the date of acquisition.

ANSWER 7.4 (INTERMEDIATE)

New Products

SOLUTION

(a)(1) pure research expenditure – original investigation undertaken in order to gain new scientific or technical knowledge but not primarily directed towards any specific practical aim or application
(2) applied research expenditure – as above but directed towards a specific practical aim or objective
(3) development expenditure – use of scientific or technical knowledge in order to produce new or substantially improved materials, products or services etc. prior to the commencement of commercial production.

(b) Circumstances in which it may be appropriate to carry forward development costs to future periods:
(1) clearly defined project
(2) separately identifiable related expenditure
(3) outcome of project
    (i) technically feasible
    (ii) commercially viable
(4) future developments costs likely to be covered by related future revenues
(5) adequacy of resources to enable completion of the project.

(c)(1) *Project 3:* Expenditure should be written off as incurred (there is no justification for carry forward on the grounds that recovery of expenditure can reasonably be regarded as assured).
(2) *Project 4:* Expenditure has been carried forward – savings of £30,000 (50% – 20% × £100,000) more than cover costs of £22,000. Plant is depreciated over its useful life of 10 years
(3) *Project 5:* Work carried out on behalf of a client should be carried forward as work in progress.

Summary of effect on financial statements

(1) BALANCE SHEET
Tangible fixed assets

	£
Machinery at cost	35,000
less accumulated depreciation	3,500
	31,500

Intangible fixed assets

Deferred development expenditure (10,000 + 12,000)	22,000

	£
Current assets	
Work in progress (20,000 + 24,000 + 500)	44,500

(2) PROFIT AND LOSS ACCOUNT	£
Research and development expenditure (5,000 + 6,000)	11,000
Depreciation	3,500

Note: The development costs of £22,000 should be amortised over an appropriate period of time or other basis. No charge was made above in the absence of further information.

ANSWER 7.5 (INTERMEDIATE)

R & D

ANSWER GUIDE

(1) Accruals concept – accrual of revenues and costs, matching of revenues with associated costs.
(2) Prudence concept – profits not recognised until realised: provision made for all known expenses and losses.
(3) Problems with R & D:
    (i) determining whether expenditure incurred will provide higher profits in later years
    (ii) determining periods over which benefits expected to be received
    (iii) nature and categorisation of R and D expenditure
        (a) pure research
        (b) applied research
        (c) development expenditure.
(4) Conflict between accruals concept and prudence concept – in the case of expenditure on pure research and applied research difficult to relate benefits to particular periods, expenditure regarded as necessary to maintain 'status quo' of the company's business and hence written off to P/L as incurred.
(5) For development costs there are theoretical grounds for permitting costs to be deferred and matched against reserves of future periods subject to considerations of prudence. In practice a deferral policy may be difficult or costly to operate. SSAP 13 gives a choice between:
    (i) immediate charge to P/L (immediate write-off policy), and
    (ii) capitalisation with expenditure being amortised over several periods (deferral policy), can only be used if a company can satisfy several stringent criteria such as clearly defined project, separately identifiable expenditure, ultimate commercial viability etc.

ANSWER 7.6 (INTERMEDIATE)

Capsule

ANSWER GUIDE

(1) *Stocks of Banoline*
    (i) SSAP 9 principles:
        (a) lower of cost and NRV
        (b) cost includes expenditure required to bring product to present location and condition.
    (ii) Cost should not include proportion of selling expenses.
    (iii) Current asset stocks should include £382,000 (i.e. 200,000 + 144,000 + 38,000), assuming NRV > £382,000.
    (iv) Accounting policy should be disclosed.

(2) *Research costs re Calindown*
    (i) Development work carried out on behalf of third parties where related expenditure is to be fully reimbursed should be included in work in progress (SSAP 13).
    (ii) In accordance with SSAP 13 include £348,000 as WIP provided there is no evidence suggesting this expenditure will not be reimbursed.

(3) *Stocks of Apentone*
    (i) SSAP 9 – lower of cost and NRV.
   (ii) Cost £340,000 + £260,000 + £47,000 = £647,000 (selling office expenses do not relate to bringing goods to present location and condition so should not be included.
  (iii) NRV

Assume selling price of £35 per 100 gross (max)

– sales revenue (13 × £35 × 1,000) =		£455,000
less packing costs	20,000	
advertising costs	30,000	
		50,000
		405,000

It is assumed that selling office expenses are incurred whatever happens and thus charged to P/L in that year i.e. they do not fall within all costs to be incurred in marketing, selling and distributing as such selling costs have already been incurred.
  (iv) ∴ stocks should be stated at the lower of £647,000 and £405,000 i.e. £405,000.
   (v) Disclosure is required of accounting policy.

(4) *Research costs into chemical substitute*
    (i) Research costs should be charged to P/L as incurred (in accordance with SSAP 13 and CA 85) i.e. £265,000.
   (ii) Fixed assets used in research activities should be depreciated over their useful lives i.e. £100,000 should be depreciated over a reasonable period with unamortised cost included under tangible fixed assets.
  (iii) Accounting policies for R & D and depreciation should be disclosed.

ANSWER 8.1 (BASIC)

Pamina

ANSWER GUIDE

(a)(i) **Weighted average price**

	Quantity	Price per unit £	Total £
Balance at 1.4.X3	7,240	11.00	79,640
2/4 Transfer to work in progress (WIP)	4,170	11.00	45,870
Balance	3,070	11.00	33,770
3/4 Purchases	4,240	12.00	50,880
	7,310	11.58	84,650
12/4 Transfer to WIP	6,716	11.58	77,771
Balance	594	11.58	6,879
12/5 Transfer to WIP	494	11.58	5,721
Balance	100	11.58	1,158
15/5 Purchases	9,217	13.00	119,821
	9,317	12.985	120,979
1/6 Transfer to WIP	7,460	12.985	96,868
Balance	1,857	12.985	24,111
17/6 Purchases	2,490	10.00	24,900
Balance	4,347	11.275	49,011

(ii) **First in – first out (FIFO)**

	Quantity	Price per unit £	£	Total £
Balance at 1.4.X3	7,240	11		79,640
2/4 Transfer to WIP	(4,170)	11		(45,870)

	Quantity	Price per unit		Total
		£	£	£
Balance	3,070			33,770
3/4 Purchases	4,240	12		50,880
	7,310			84,650
12/4 Transfer to WIP (3,070)		11 (33,770)		
(3,646)	(6,716)	12 (43,752)		(77,522)
Balance	594			7,128
12/5 Transfer to WIP	(494)	12		5,928
	100			1,200
15/5 Purchases	9,217	13		119,821
	9,317			121,021
1/6 Transfer to WIP (100)		12 (1,200)		
7,360	(7,460)	13 (95,680)		(96,880)
Balance	1,857			24,141
17/6 Purchases	2,490	10		24,900
Balance	4,347			49,041

(b) Two other methods to record receipt and issue of raw materials:

   (i) last in – first out (LIFO)
   (ii) standard cost.

ANSWER 8.2 (INTERMEDIATE)

Thornfield

SOLUTION

	Contract 1	Contract 2	Contract 3
	£	£	£
Materials and subcontract work	41,000	38,000	13,500
Direct wages	80,000	74,500	12,000
General expenses	3,700	2,400	1,300
Depreciation of plant	4,000	2,000	500
Overheads	1,600	1,490	240
	130,300	118,390	27,540
Attributable profits	11,000	—	—
Foreseeable losses	—	(5,000)	—
	141,300	113,390	27,540

WORKINGS

(1) *Contract 1*

Estimated total costs to completion of contract: as no specific information is given, one possible approach is to assume that costs increase at the same rate throughout the contract (for alternative approaches, see notes below).

i.e. Costs of (130,300 − 4,000 = 126,300) are equivalent to value of work done of £150,000.

$\therefore$ Costs equivalent to £210,000 value of work done are $\frac{210}{150} \times £126,300 = £176,820$

$\therefore$ Attributable profits may be calculated as follows:

	£	£
Contract price		210,000
Costs incurred to date	130,300	
Rectification costs	10,000	
Further costs to complete		
(176,820 − 130,300)	46,520	186,820
Estimated total profit on contract		23,180

Per company's accounting policy, attributable profit

$$= \frac{150}{210} \times \frac{2}{3} \times £23,180 = £11,038, \text{ say } \underline{£11,000}$$

Notes

(a) If attributable profit of, say, £11,000 is to be taken up then it is important to ensure that the rectification provision is adequate.

(b) Other approaches for calculation of attributable profit could be acceptable, e.g.

(i) $\frac{130,300}{176,820} \times \frac{2}{3} \times £23,180 = £11,388$ (a similar result).

(ii) $\frac{2}{3}(150,000 - (130,300 - 4,000 + 10,000)) = £9,133.$

(2) *Contract 2*

Using a similar approach to above, estimated total cost to completion would be

$$\frac{215}{110} \times (118,390 - 6,000) = £219,671$$

Over the life of the contract the expected outcome is:

	£	£
Contract price		215,000
Costs incurred to date	118,390	
Further costs to complete (219,671 − 118,390)	101,281	219,671
Estimated loss		4,671

The full amount of the expected loss, say, £5,000, should now be provided for. Clearly it is important to ensure that all contingencies have been provided for.

(3) *Contract 3*

Estimated total costs to completion of contract:

$$\frac{190}{20} \times (27,540 - 9,000) = £176,130$$

Since the contract price is £190,000 the contract is likely to result in a profit. However, the contract is at an early stage of completion and so it is not prudent to take up any profit this year. Furthermore the company's policy is not to take any profit before the contract is one-third complete which this contract clearly is not. The contract should therefore be stated at cost.

Amounts to be included in work-in-progress:

	Contract 1 £	Contract 2 £	Contract 3 £
Work-in-progress valuation	141,300	113,390	27,540
Less: progress payments (80% × value to date)	120,000	88,000	16,000
Balance sheet totals	21,300	25,390	11.540
Overall total		£58,230	

ANSWER 8.3 (INTERMEDIATE)
Barlow
SOLUTION
Contract accounts in summarised form

		Sewerage works £		New school £
	$(\frac{12}{36})$		$(\frac{9}{24})$	
Depreciation of plant		91,067		9,000
Purchases		352,000		69,000
Wages and salaries		240,000		76,000
Sundry expenses		6,400		17,200
		689,467		171,200
Profit (loss)		100,500		(7,200)
Value of work in progress		789,967		164,000

WORKINGS

Calculation of profit or loss to date on contracts:

(1) *Sewerage works*

It could be argued that the contract is at a relatively early stage and so no profit should be taken up. This view could be further supported by the lack of information regarding estimated costs to complete. Where the outcome of a contract cannot be assessed with reasonable certainty no attributable profit should be taken up.

A contrary view is that the nature of the information regarding interim certificates etc. requires some attempt at calculating profit. This was probably the aim of the question.

A possible calculation would be as follows:

Value of contract work to date:	
Certified 100/80 × 620,000	775,000
Uncertified	15,000
	790,000
Cost to date	689,467
∴ Profit to date	100,533

(say £100,500)

(2) *New school*

Value of contract work to date:		
Certified	145,000	
Retentions	12,000	
Uncertified	7,000	
	164,000	
Cost to date	171,200	
∴ Loss to date	(7,200)	

Clearly the lack of information here is a major problem. SSAP 9 requires the estimated total loss over the contract life to be taken into account immediately. £7,200 may well be considerably below the eventual loss. In the absence of further information, the loss of £7,200 is taken to profit and loss account.

ANSWER 8.4 (ADVANCED)
Project X
SOLUTION

(a) **Extracts from balance sheet**

Current assets	£
Stock and work-in-progress (see note x)	146,500

Note to accounts – stock and work-in-progress	£
Work-in-progress	81,500
Finished goods	65,000
	146,500

Accounting policy note: Finished goods stocks are valued at the lower of cost and net realisable value. Cost includes direct costs and a proportion of production overheads. Work-in-progress is valued at cost plus any attributable profit less progress payments invoiced.

WORKINGS

(1) *Finished goods stocks*

Ratio of direct labour to overheads is 250,000:250,000. Assume that overheads are allocated on basis of direct labour costs (100%).

	Item 1 £	Item 2 £	Total £
Direct material	20,000	15,000	35,000
Direct labour	10,000	5,000	15,000
Overheads	10,000	5,000	15,000
Total	40,000	25,000	65,000

(2) *Work-in-progress (Project X)*

Costs to date
Direct material	25,000
Direct labour	35,000

Overheads
- manufacturing (based on direct labour of £20,000)   20,000
- assembly

$$\frac{\text{Overheads}}{\text{Direct labour}} = \frac{10,000}{100,000} = 10\%$$

10% × £15,000	1,500
	81,500

To ensure that contract is expected to be profitable:

	£	£
Contract price		190,000
Estimated total costs to completion		
Direct costs (50 + 50 + 30)	130,000	
Overheads – manufacturing	50,000	
– assembly 10% × 30,000	3,000	183,000
Estimated total profit		7,000

Two possible viewpoints:
(1) take up attributable profit of 50% × £7,000 = £3,500 as contract is half complete;
(2) take view that at this stage of contract it is not prudent to take up *any* attributable profits (too many uncertainties, contingencies not allowed for, etc.).
This solution prefers the second viewpoint – so contract work-in-progress is carried forward at £81,500.

(b) Reasons why SSAP 9 was required:

- prior to introduction of SSAP 9, wide differences between companies regarding basis of computation of stocks and work-in-progress (for example, treatment of overheads in stock valuation).

Objectives of SSAP 9:
- to define practices of stock computation
- to narrow the differences

- to ensure adequate disclosure in accounts
  - (1) breakdown of stock figure in balance sheet
  - (2) statement of accounting policies.

ANSWER 9.1 (BASIC)

Pasedena

SOLUTION

Profit and loss account extracts

	£	£
Income from fixed asset investments (16,700 × 10/7)		23,857
Tax on profit on ordinary activities		
Corporation tax at 35%		73,000
Tax overprovided in previous years (55,200 − 51,000)		(4,200)
Tax credit on UK dividends received (23,857 − 16,700)		7,157
		75,957

Balance sheet extracts

	£
Debtor − ACT recoverable (3/7 × (49,000 − 16,700))	13,843
Creditors − amounts falling due within one year	
Tax and social security	86,843
Proposed dividends	49,000

Workings – tax and social security	£
Mainstream corporation tax	73,000
ACT payable	13,843
	86,843

ANSWER 9.2 (BASIC)

Charleston

SOLUTION

Profit and loss account extracts

	£	£
Tax on profit on ordinary activities		
Corporation tax at 35%		85,072
Tax underprovided in previous years (63,050 − 58,240)		4,810
		89,882
Dividends on ordinary shares		
Paid	15,230	
Proposed	22,130	37,360

Balance sheet extracts

	£
Debtor − ACT recoverable (3/7 × 22,130)	9,484
Creditors − amounts falling due within one year	
Tax and social security	88,029
Proposed dividends	22,130

Workings – tax and social security	£
Mainstream corporation tax (85,072 − 3/7 × 15,230)	78,545
ACT payable	9,484
	88,029

ANSWER 9.3 (INTERMEDIATE)

Hardy

SOLUTION

Corporation tax account

	£		£
Cash (19X2)	81,400	MCT (19X2) b/d	81,400
ACT a/c	7,286	MCT (19X3) b/d	71,760
MCT (19X3) c/d	79,530	P/L (19X4)	92,000
MCT (19X4) (92,000 − 7,286)	84,714	P/L (unprovided in previous years) (79,530 − 71,760)	7,770
	252,930		252,930

Advance corporation tax account

	£		£
Cash (3/7 × 17,000)	7,286	Corporation tax account	7,286
ACT on prop. div. c/d	11,143	ACT on proposed div. c/d (3/7 × 26,000)	11,143
	18,429		18,429
Bal b/d	11,143	Bal b/d	11,143
	↑		↑
	Non-current (deferred asset)		Current

Deferred tax account

	£		£
Balance c/d	32,070	Bal b/d	21,600
		P/L a/c (32,070 − 21,600)	10,470
	32,070		32,070

Note: For presentation purposes, the asset of £11,143 is offset against the deferred tax provision of £32,070.

Profit and loss account extracts

	£
Tax on profit on ordinary activities	
Corporation tax at 35%	92,000
Corporation tax underprovided in previous years	7,770
Transfer to deferred tax	10,470
	110,240

Balance sheet extracts

Creditors due within one year	
Corporation tax	79,530
Advanced corporation tax (3/7 × 26,000)	11,143
Creditors due after more than one year	
Corporation tax payable 1.1.X6	84,714
Provisions for liabilities and charges	
Deferred taxation	20,927

	£
NOTE TO ACCOUNTS – DEFERRED TAXATION	
Deferred tax	32,070
ACT recoverable	11,143
	20,927

ANSWER 9.4 (INTERMEDIATE)

Corax

WORKINGS

Corporation tax account

	£		£
Cash (19X3)	16,300	MCT (19X3) b/d	16,300
P/L (over provided)	1,200	MCT (19X4) b/d	5,000
ACT a/c	5,940	P/L (19X5)	36,000
MCT (19X4) c/d	3,800		
MCT (19X5) (36,000 − 5,940)	30,060		
	57,300		57,300

Advance corporation tax account

	£		£
Cash 3/7 × 13,860	5,940	Corporation tax a/c	5,940
ACT on proposed div c/d	11,880	ACT on proposed div c/d	11,880
	17,820		17,820
Bal b/d	11,880	Bal b/d	11,880
	↑		↑
	Non-current		Current

Deferred tax account

	£		£
Balance c/d	36,400	Balance b/d	29,400
		P/L a/c	7,000
	36,400		36,400

SOLUTION

Extract from profit and loss account

	£	£
Profit on ordinary activities before tax		88,800
Taxation		
Corporation tax on profits for the year	36,000	
Corporation tax over-provided in previous year	(1,200)	
Transfer to deferred tax	7,000	41,800
Profit on ordinary activities after tax		47,000
Dividends		
Interim (paid)	13,860	
Final (proposed)	27,720	41,580
Retained profit		5,420
Profit and loss account balance at 1.1.X5		43,000
Profit and loss account balance at 31.12.X5		48,420

Extracts from balance sheet

Creditors: amounts falling due within one year

	£
Corporation tax	3,800
Advance corporation tax	11,880
Proposed dividends	27,720

Creditors: amounts falling due after more than one year

	£
Corporation tax	30,060

Provisions for liabilities and charges

Deferred taxation	24,520

Note to accounts – deferred taxation

Deferred tax	36,400
ACT recoverable	11,880
	24,520

ANSWER 9.5 (INTERMEDIATE)

Tax items

ANSWER GUIDE

(i) Disclose in P/L at gross amount (cash plus tax credit). Disclose tax credit as separate part of tax charge.

(ii) Proposed dividend – cash amount under creditors within one year.
ACT payable – creditors within one year.

(iii) If deferred tax account – deduct from deferred tax balance.
If no deferred tax account – show as deferred asset provided evidence of recoverability within foreseeable future.

(iv) Charge to P/L – separate part of tax charge.

(v) Disclose turnover – exclusive of VAT.
VAT credited to VAT (Customs and Excise) account.

(vi) Include as part of FA capital cost.

(vii) Through VAT (Customs and Excise) account.

ANSWER 9.6 (INTERMEDIATE)

Shannon

WORKINGS

(1) Total potential deferred tax at 31 December:

	19X5 £	19X6 £	19X7 £	19X8 £	19X9 £
(Acs NBV – tax WDV)	1,250	1,270	1,300	1,220	1,260 ✓
Tax at 35%	438	445	455	427	441

(2) Provisions required – calculation of cumulative originating or reversing timing differences:

	Net originating (reversing) £	CUMULATIVE AT THE FOLLOWING BALANCE SHEET DATES				
		19X5 £	19X6 £	19X7 £	19X8 £	19X9 £
19X6	20	20	—	—	—	—
19X7	30	50	30	—	—	—
19X8	(80)	(30)	(50)	(80)	—	—
19X9	40	10	(10)	(40)	40	—
19X10	35	45	25	(5)	75	35
Maximum cumulative net reversal foreseen		(30)	(50)	(80)	Nil	Nil
∴ Provision required (at 35%)		(11)	(18)	(28)	Nil	Nil

(3) Profit and loss debits (credits) – difference between provision at beginning of year and provision at end of year:

19X5	£11 – 0 = 11 (debit)
19X6	£18 – 11 = 7 (debit)
19X7	£28 – 18 = 10 (debit)
19X8	£0 – 28 = 28 (credit)
19X9	£0 – £0 = 0

(4) Deferred tax on timing differences arising during year (for purposes of calculating whether further memorandum disclosure is required):

	Timing differences £	At 35% £
19X5	50	18
19X6	20	7
19X7	30	10
19X8	(80)	(28)
19X9	40	14

SOLUTION

Summary

	19X5 £	19X6 £	19X7 £	19X8 £	19X9 £
B/S – provided	11	18	28	Nil	Nil
– unprovided*	427	427	427	427	441
P/L – charge (credit)	11	7	10	(28)	Nil
– unprovided**	7	—	—	—	14

Notes
*   This is the difference between total potential deferred tax and provided (see workings above) – it is provided for memorandum information only.
** Difference between working (4) and working (3) – memorandum disclosure only.

ANSWER 9.7 (ADVANCED)

Forsters ·

SOLUTION

(a) *Accounting policy note – deferred taxation*
Deferred tax is accounted for in respect of the tax effects arising from all material timing differences to the extent that it is probable that a liability or asset will crystallise. Deferred tax is not accounted for where it is considered probable that a liability or asset will not crystallise. Deferred tax is computed using the liability method.

(b) *Balance sheet note on deferred tax at 30.11.X12*

	Provided £	Unprovided £
Capital allowances	51,219	169,281
Short-term timing differences	—	15,859
Revaluation surplus	—	30,000
	51,219	215,140
Less advance corporation tax	(45,000)	—
	6,219	215,140

WORKINGS

(1) Calculation of total potential deferred tax at 30.6.19X12 (NB – it will then be necessary later in the workings to calculate how much of this should be provided in the balance sheet. The balance will be disclosed by way of memo note as unprovided.)

$10\% (600 + 100)$ deps for the yr

(i) Capital allowances

	£
Acs NBV (600,000 + 100,000 − 70,000)	630,000
Tax WDV	Nil
Difference	630,000

Tax at 35% = £220,500

(ii) Interest receivable

Debtor in B/S	50,000 ✓

Tax at 35% = £17,500

(iii) Interest payable

Creditor in B/S (15% × 3/12 × 125,000)	4,688

Tax at 35% = £1,641

(iv) Revaluation surplus   100,000

Tax at 30% = £30,000

(2) Calculation of required provision at 30.6.19X12 considering overall position on *all* timing differences other than revaluation surplus:

	Capital expenditure			Short-term			
	CAs	Dep	Net	Int.	Int.	Net for	
	£	£	£	pay	received	year	Cumulative
19X13	10,000	64,000	(54,000)	Nil	Nil	(54,000)	(54,000)
19X14	10,000	58,600	(48,600)	Nil	Nil	(48,600)	(102,600)
19X15	10,000	53,740	(43,740)	Nil	Nil	(43,740)	(146,340)
19X16	[No detailed figures but no reversals anticipated]						

Maximum cumulative reversal foreseen = £146,340

∴ Provision required = 35% × £146,340 = £51,219

∴ Unprovided = £220,500 (see (1) (i)) − £51,219 = £169,281

(i) Depreciation calcs.

19X13	10%	(630,000 + 10,000)	=	64,000
19X14	10%	(640,000 − 64,000 + 10,000)	=	58,600
19X15	10%	(586,000 − 58,600 + 10,000)	=	53,740

(ii) Interest paid and received: amounts in accounts and tax computations expected to be the same each year.

∴ Potential deferred tax of £17,500 − £1,641 = £15,859 (see (1)(ii) and (iii)) should be referred to by way of memorandum note as unprovided.

(iii) ACT = 3/7 × £105,000 = £45,000

ANSWER 9.8 (ADVANCED)

County Manufacturing

SOLUTION

(a) The additional amount of deferred tax referred to in the question results from a change in fiscal policy (e.g. a switch from accelerated capital allowances to a reduction in the rate of corporation tax). The additional amount involved should be charged to profit and loss account as an extraordinary item. It should not be dealt with as a movement on reserves.

(*Note:* This point in the question referred to the financial effects of the changes in the 1984 Budget.)

(b) *Tax on profit on ordinary activities*

	£
UK corporation tax based on profit for the year at 35% (19X3 : X%)	81,194
Transfer to deferred tax	25,953
Share of tax charge of associated company	9,270
Overseas taxation	26,400
	142,817

(1) The tax charge for the year has been reduced by £7,581 as a result of tax losses brought forward.

(2) The unrelieved tax losses available to the group to carry forward to future years amount to £23,940.

WORKINGS

(i) UK corporation tax

	£	£
County		25,140
Essex		286,360
Avon's losses – group relief thereon		(79,290)
Cumbria	21,660	
Less losses brought forward	21,660	—
(leaving 45,600 – 21,660 = 23,940 to c/f as memo note)		
		232,210
Corporation tax at 35%		81,274
Tax overprovided in previous year (3,680 + 40,600) – (3,700 + 40,500)		(80)
		81,194

(ii) Transfer to deferred tax

		£
Timing differences – Essex (70,160 – 36,340) =		33,820
– Avon (56,810 – 16,480) =		40,330
		74,150

Deferred tax at 35% = £25,953

(iii) Associated company 25% × £37,080 = 9,270

(iv) Reduction in tax charge 35% × £21,660 = 7,581

(c) *Taxation liabilities to be included in creditors*

	£
Holding company balance sheet	8,619
Group balance sheet	107,124

(v)

	County £	Essex £	Total £
Profits liable	25,140	207,070*	232,210
Corporation tax at 35%	8,799	72,475	81,274
ACT on divs paid	(4,650)		(4,650)
Tax on interest received	(180)	(370)	(550)
MCT liability	3,969		76,074
ACT on divs prop	4,650		4,650
Total	8,619	72,105	80,724

∴ Group total (including overseas) £80,724 + £26,400 = £107,124.

* Assume Avon group relief against Essex.

ANSWER 10.1 (BASIC)

Westbury

SOLUTION

(a) (i) **Actuarial method (14%)**

Year	B/F £	Rental £		Finance charge £	C/F £
19X2	25,000	(6,387)	18,613	2,606	21,219
19X3	21,219	(6,387)	14,832	2,076	16,908
19X4	16,908	(6,387)	10,521	1,473	11,994
19X5	11,994	(6,387)	5,607	780	6,387
19X6	6,387	(6,387)	—	—	
		31,935		6,935	

(ii) Sum of the digits methods

Year		£
19X2	$^4/_{10} \times £6,935$	2,774
19X3	$^3/_{10} \times £6,935$	2,080
19X4	$^2/_{10} \times £6,935$	1,387
19X5	$^1/_{10} \times £6,935$	694
		6,935

(b) Disclosures in financial statements:

Accounting policy note
Where assets are financed by leasing agreements that give rights approximating to ownership (finance leases), the assets are treated as if they had been purchased outright at their fair values. The corresponding leasing commitments are shown as obligations to the lessor.

Depreciation is provided on a straight-line basis at an annual rate of 10%. Finance charges are allocated using the actuarial method.

Profit and loss disclosures
Profit on ordinary activities before tax is arrived at after charging:

	£
depreciation of assets held under finance leases	2,500
finance charges payable – finance leases	2,606

Balance sheet disclosures
(1) The net book value of fixed assets includes an amount of £22,500 in respect of assets held under finance leases.
(2) Finance lease obligations (disclosed under separate creditor headings) are;

– falling due within one year	4,311
– falling due after more than one year	16,908
	21,219

ANSWER 10.2 (INTERMEDIATE)

Lessor and Lessee

SOLUTION

(a) *Definition of finance lease* – a lease that transfers substantially all the risks and rewards of ownership of an asset to the lessee (presumed if at start of lease the present value of the minimum lease payments amounts to 90% or more of the fair value of the asset).

Distinguishing features of a finance lease:
(1) lease may relate to the useful life of the asset.
(2) lessee is responsible for repairs, maintenance and insurance and may suffer disruptions as a result of breakdowns
(3) the substance of the transaction is the acquisition of an asset over its useful life by means of credit (i.e. a finance lease is an alternative to hire purchase etc.)

(b) *Financial statements of lessee*

WORKINGS
(1) finance charge $(20 \times 74) - 1,000$ = £480
(2) sum of digits $\dfrac{20(21)}{2}$ = 210
(3) finance charges

19X9	$\dfrac{(20 + 19 + 18 + 17)}{210} \times £480$	= £169
19X10	$\dfrac{(16 + 15 + 14 + 13)}{210} \times £480$	= £133

(4) obligations under finance leases	£
1/9/X8 BF	1,000
Finance charges 19X9	169
Cash (4 × 74)	(296)
31/8/X9 C/F	873
Finance charges 19X10	133
Cash	(296)
31/8/X10 C/F	710

(5) depreciation 20% × £1,000   200

Financial statements of lessee

Profit and loss account 31/8/X9   £
    Finance charges   169
    Depreciation   200

Balance sheet at 31/8/X9

	£
Fixed assets	
– cost	1,000
– depreciation	200
	800
Creditors within one year	
– obligations under finance leases (873 − 710)	163
Creditors due more than one year	
– obligations under finance leases	710

Financial statements of lessor

	£
Profit and loss account 31/8/X9	
Gross earnings from finance leases	169
Balance sheet at 31/8/X9	
Debtors – finance lease receivables	
Current	163
Non-current	710

(c) *Minimum legal disclosure requirements (Companies Act 1985)*
   – plant hire charges (£296)
   – financial commitments not provided for and which are relevant to assessing the company's state of affairs (remaining leasing payments)
   The Companies Act 1985 does not require capitalisation of finance leases although this practice is becoming increasingly common as a result of SSAP 21.

ANSWER 10.3 (INTERMEDIATE)

Mewslade

WORKINGS

Table of cash flows

	B/F	Cash	Sub-total (o/s for one year)	Interest at 10%	C/F
	£	£	£	£	£
19X2	200,150	(48,000)	152,150	15,215	167,365
19X3	167,365	(48,000)	119,365	11,936	131,301

	B/F	Cash	Sub-total (o/s for one year)	Interest at 10%	C/F
	£	£	£	£	£
19X4	131,301	(48,000)	83,301	8,330	91,631
19X5	91,631	(48,000)	43,631	4,369*	48,000
19X6	48,000	(48,000)	—	—	—
				39,850	

* Rounding difference.

SOLUTION

a Balance sheet extracts

	19X2	19X3
	£	£
Debtor – net investment in finance lease		
Non-current	131,301	91,631
Current	36,064**	39,670**
	167,365	131,301

** Calculated as balancing figures.

b Profit and loss account extracts

	19X2	19X3	19X4	19X5	19X6
	£	£	£	£	£
Finance charges	15,215	11,936	8,330	4,369	—
Interest	(x)	(x)	(x)	(x)	(x)
Overheads	(x)	(x)	(x)	(x)	(x)
Bad debts	(x)	(x)	(x)	(x)	(x)
Profits on ordinary activities before tax	x	x	x	x	x
Rentals receivable (memorandum note)	48,000	48,000	48,000	48,000	48,000

ANSWER 10.4 (ADVANCED)

Lessor

SOLUTION

a(1) *Finance leases*

SSAP 21 requires a lessor to allocate the total gross earnings of a finance lease over accounting periods so as to give a constant periodic rate of return on the lessor's net cash investment in the lease in each period.

Gross earnings means the lessor's gross finance income over the lease term. Gross earnings is determined by comparing:
(i) total minimum lease payments and any unguaranteed residual value accruing to the lessor, and
(ii) the cost of the leased asset less any grants receivable.
Net cash investment means at any time the amount of funds invested in a lease by the lessor and comprises the cost of the asset, plus or minus the following payments or receipts as applicable:
(i) grants receivable towards the purchase or use of the asset
(ii) rentals receivable
(iii) taxation payments and receipts including the effect of capital allowances
(iv) residual values, if any, at end of lease term
(v) interest payments, where applicable
(vi) interest received on cash surplus
(vii) profit taken out of the lease.
As rentals are received, the net cash investment (NCI) in the lease falls. Eventually, NCI becomes zero (or close to zero) although this takes some time because of the delayed effects of taxation. Gross earnings are allocated in such a way that profit taken out of the lease gives a constant periodic rate of return on NCI.

(2) *Hire purchase agreements*
The principles of allocation of gross earnings are similar to those for finance leases except that earnings may be allocated on the basis of net investment (NI) rather than NCI.

(3) *Operating leases*
Rental income should be recognised on a straight-hire basis over the lease period. The only exception to this is where another systematic and rational basis is more representative of the time pattern in which the benefit from the leased asset is receivable.

b(1) *Calculation or profit taken out of lease*

Period (6 months)	Net cash Investment (NCI) at start of period £	Cash flows in period Costs, rentals tax		Ave NCI in period	Profit taken out of lease (5.4%)	NCI at end of period
1/x4	—	(50,000)	8,000	(42,000)	(2,268)	(44,268)
2/x4	(44,268)	—	8,000	(36,268)	(1,958)	(38,226)
			16,000		(4,226)	
1/x5	(38,226)	—	8,000	(30,226)	(1,632)	(31,858)
2/x5	(31,858)	—	8,000	(23,858)	(1,288)	(25,146)
			16,000		(2,920)	
1/x6	(25,146)	(1,225)	8,000	(18,371)	(992)	(19,363)
2/x6	(19,363)	—	8,000	(11,363)	(614)	(11,977)
			16,000		(1,606)	

(Remaining parts of table completed purely for purposes of additional explanation – not required for question.)

1/x7	(11,977)	(2,319)	8,000	(6,296)	(340)	(6,636)
2/x7	(6,636)	—	8,000	1,364	74	1,438
			16,000		(266)	
1/x8	1,438	(3,139)	—	(1,701)	(92)	(1,793)
2/x8	(1,793)	—	—	(1,793)	(97)	(1,890)
			—		(189)	
1/x9	(1,890)	1,783		(107)	107	Nil
Totals					9,100	

WORKINGS – TAX

19 × 4	35%	(£16,000 − 25% × £50,000) = £1,225
19 × 5	35%	(£16,000 − 25% × £37,500) = £2,319
19 × 6	35%	(£16,000 − 25% × £28,125) = £3,139
19 × 7	35%	(£16,000 − tax wdv £21,094) = (£1,783)

(2) *Allocation of gross earnings between years*

	£
Gross earnings before tax	
Total rentals	64,000
Cost of asset	50,000
Therefore gross earnings	14,000

	19X4 £	19X5 £	19X6 £	19X7 £	19X8 £	(and beyond)	Total £
Profit taken out of lease (post tax) – per previous calculations	4,226	2,920	1,606	266	82		9,100
Notional tax (x 35/65)	2,276	1,572	865	143	44		4,900
Gross earnings (x 110/65)	6,502	4,492	2,471	409	126		14,000
Rentals received	16,000	16,000	16,000	16,000	—		64,000

(3) *Extracts from financial statements of lessor*

(A) PROFIT AND LOSS ACCOUNTS

	19X4	19X5	19X6	19X7	19X8	(and beyond)
	£	£	£	£	£	
Gross earnings	6,502	4,492	2,471	409	126	

(Items such as tax and overheads would be calculated on a global basis for the company as a whole. Gross earnings are determined on a lease-by-lease basis and the results aggregated to determine the figures for the company as a whole.)

Note para. 130, Guidance Notes SSAP 21:

'In the case of finance leases, a lessor should disclose gross earnings as turnover . . . However, as this provides an incomplete measure of a lessor's activity, disclosure should also be made in the notes of the aggregate rentals receivable under finance leases and of the cost of assets acquired for letting under finance leases.'

(B) BALANCE SHEETS
 — net investment in finance lease

19X4	19X5	19X6
£	£	£
40,502	28,994	15,465

Workings	£
B/F	50,000
P/L 19 × 4	6,502
cash	(16,000)
C/F	40,502
P/L 19 × 5	4,492
cash	(16,000)
C/F	28,994
P/L 19 × 6	2,471
cash	(16,000)
C/F	15,465

ANSWER 11.1 (INTERMEDIATE)

Pension costs

SOLUTION

(a) Several factors have contributed to the difficulties of producing an acceptable standard on pension cost accounting. These include:
  (1) the problems of getting actuaries to agree on the basis (bases) of actuarial valuations;
  (2) the problems of defined benefit schemes where pensions are often linked to salary at retirement. The cost to the employer of providing pension benefits can only be estimated on the basis of critical assumptions on matters such as future inflation, earnings on pension fund investments, pay increases and changes in the workforce;
  (3) the problems of accounting for special situations such as changes in benefits or conditions and increases to pensions in payment;
  (4) in recent years the problem of substantial surpluses in pension funds and how to deal with the related funding and accounting.
(b) Conventional methods of accounting for pension costs essentially involve charging pension contributions to the profit and loss account of the employer company as the payments are made. In some situations where a pension fund is in considerable surplus the company may take a 'contribution holiday' and make no further payments for a year or two. The present practice is for such companies to make no charge to profit and loss account.

(c) The accruals concept requires the cost of pensions to be charged against profits on a systematic basis over the service lives of employees in the scheme. The traditional approach referred to in (b) above fails to distinguish between funding (which is a matter of financial management) and accounting (which requires an appropriate annual charge against revenues). The traditional accounting treatment can distort income comparisons between one year and another.

(d) An appropriate approach is that outlined in ED39 (Accounting for pension costs). The charge for pension costs in the profit and loss account should consist of two elements:

(1) regular costs – the method chosen should provide a substantially level percentage of the current and expected future pensionable payroll;

(2) variations from regular cost (relating to experience deficiencies or surpluses, changes in assumptions, changes in benefits or conditions, increases to pensions in payment) – these should be allocated over the expected average remaining service lives of employees in the scheme. The justification for this treatment is that these past service costs relate to services to be provided in the future. The company should benefit in the future as a result of being able to attract and retain employees.

Differences between actual payments and cumulative charges to profit and loss account should be treated as net pension liabilities or prepayments as appropriate.

ANSWER 11.2 (INTERMEDIATE)

Southgate

SOLUTION

(a) Main assumptions include those relating to:
(1) future rates of inflation
(2) future rates of pay increases
(3) increases to pensions in payment
(4) earnings on investments
(5) number of employees joining scheme
(6) probability that employees will die or leave before reaching retiring age.

(b) The retractive change in benefits (i.e. backdating benefit entitlement according to previous years of service) were decided in the current year. A prior year adjustment is therefore not appropriate. ED39 takes the view that although past service costs are calculated by reference to past years of service, such costs relate to services to be provided in the future. In the case of Southgate plc, the company as a result of improving benefits would normally expect the business to benefit as a result of being able to attract and retain employees. The benefit will extend to future periods, not just the one in which the improvement is granted. ED39 considers that it would normally be excessively prudent to write off the costs wholly against the revenues of the year in which the improvement is granted. The recommendation therefore is that past service costs should normally be written off over the average remaining services lives of the employees.

The past service cost of £400,000 should be amortised over ten years (the expected average remaining service lives of employees) giving a charge for 19X10 and 19X11 of £40,000.

(c) Extracts from financial statements:

(1) *Profit and loss account*	19X11		19X10	
	£'000	£'000	£'000	£'000
Staff costs				
Wages and salaries		X		X
Social security costs		X		X
Other pension costs				
regular cost	205		175	
variation from regular costs	40		40	
		245		215

(2) *Balance sheet*	19X11	19X10
Prepayments (100,000 − 40,000)		60,000
(200,000 − 80,000)	120,000	

ANSWER 12.1 (INTERMEDIATE)

SORPs

SOLUTION

(a) The primary aims in issuing SORPs are:
   (1) to narrow the areas of difference and variety in the accounting treatment of the particular topic;
   (2) to enhance the usefulness of published accounting information.
(b) The main points of difference between SSAPs and SORPs are:
   (1) Scope – SORPs are issued on subjects which it is not considered appropriate to issue an accounting standard at that point in time. This could be for example because the topic is not regarded as fundamental to the concept of truth and fairness, or because the topic relates to a specific sector of industry (e.g. accounting for exploration and development expenditure in the oil industry).
   (2) Status – unlike SSAPs, SORPs are not mandatory on members of the individual CCAB bodies.
   (3) Authority – SSAPs can only be issued by the various councils of the constituent members of CCAB (e.g. ICAEW, ACCA etc). SORPs can be issued by ASC itself or, in the case of franked SORPs (see (d)) by the industry group.
(c) The explanatory foreword states that SORPs will always take account of the principles laid down in accounting standards. SORPs can never be taken as authority to depart from the requirements of standards or to extend to scope of particular standards. SORPs may give a useful indication of acceptable accounting treatments which might be appropriate in situations not covered by accounting standards.
(d) The two main types of SORPs are:
   (1) Ordinary SORPs – these are developed and issued by ASC.
   (2) Franked SORPs – these are developed by an industry group. After approval and 'franking' by ASC, the SORPs are issued by the industry group.

ANSWER 12.2 (INTERMEDIATE)

Support Association

SOLUTION

A. Smith Esq.,
Secretary,
The Support Association,
16 Longport Street,
London, SW12 2PY.   5 May 19X8

Dear Mr Smith,

Thank you for your letter dated 21 April 19X8 together with enclosures. I have pleasure in setting out below information relating to the various points which you have raised:

Restricted funds
These are funds which are subject to specific conditions imposed by the donor. These conditions are binding on the trustees. The funds represent unspent restricted income and the assets whose use is restricted.

Designated funds
These are unrestricted funds (or elements of unrestricted funds) which have been allocated or earmarked for specific purposes by the charity itself. The use to which these funds are put is at the discretion of the trustees.

Revenue account
The following groupings are suggested:

(a) Income:
   (1) Donations, identifying separately
      (i) covenants

   (ii) legacies
   (iii) life subscriptions
   (iv) other donations
(2) Investment income
(3) Surplus from the sale of books
(4) Income from property occupied by beneficiaries.

(b) Expenditure:
   (1) Charitable expenditure
      (i) grants to hospitals
      (ii) maintenance to families
      (iii) expenditure on schools
   (2) Administration expenses
      (i) salaries and wages
      (ii) sundry office expenses
   (3) Depreciation on properties.

Balance sheet
The following groupings are suggested:

(1) Fixed assets
   (i) properties held for the use of the Support Association
   (ii) assets deployed for charitable purposes
   (iii) office equipment
(2) Investments
   (i) special fund investments
   (ii) properties held for investment
(3) Net current assets
(4) General fund
(5) Special fund.

The net total of (1), (2) and (3) should equal the total of (4) and (5).

Application of accounting for commercial undertakings to charities
Reasons why accounting for commercial undertakings may be inappropriate for charities include:

(1) Difference in objectives:
   – commercial organisations set out to maximise profits. Charities usually aim to maximise expenditure on charitable purposes (for example, grants to hospitals and maintenance to families of handicapped children).

(2) Relationship between costs and revenue:
   – for many commercial organisations there is a fairly well-defined relationship between costs and revenues (for example cost of sales as a percentage of sales). For charities such relationships are usually tenuous.

(3) Users of financial statements:
   – the primary users of financial statements of commercial organisations are the shareholders, although other important users include lenders of funds and employees. The presentation of information is largely specified by the Companies Act 1985 and reflects the needs of the primary users. Users of charity accounts are far more diverse in nature and include donors and beneficiaries. Because the information needs of uses of charity accounts differ significantly from those of commercial organisations charity accounts need to be presented in a different way. Special features may include reference to restricted funds and designated funds as indicated above.

I hope that the above information is helpful for your purposes but I will be pleased to supply further information should you require it.
Yours sincerely,

David Hillwood

ANSWER 12.3 (ADVANCED)

Daffodil Bulb

SOLUTION

a The report of the actuary refers to two different actuarial approaches in assessing the amount required to provide pensions:
  (1) a discontinuance basis (or discontinuance actuarial valuation) – this is concerned with judging whether the existing assets are sufficient to secure the benefits of existing pensioners and members assuming the scheme is to be wound up on the valuation date (30.6.19X12). This basis is designed to test the solvency of the scheme. It does not imply that the scheme is to be wound up.
  (2) a going concern basis (or ongoing actuarial valuation) – this is concerned with the continuous funding of the scheme and whether the fund will be able to meet its future obligations. The basis assumes that contributions will continue to be paid by the employer and members.
  The actuaries consider that the scheme is solvent on a discontinuance basis but report a deficiency on a going concern basis. The company has accordingly decided to increase its funding rate to the level suggested by the actuaries. This new rate will continue until the next actuarial valuation in 19X15 when the position is reviewed.

b **Revenue account of the Daffodil Bulb Co plc pension fund for the year ended 30 June 19X13**

	£'000	£'000
Contributions receivable:		
from Daffodil Bulb Co	344	
from members	181	
transfers in from other schemes	8	
	533	
Investment income		
income from fixed interest securities and dividends from investments		
$(137 \times \frac{100}{70})$	196	
net rents from properties (50 – 10)	40	
interest on deposits	35	
		271
		804
Benefits payable		
pensions	21	
death benefits and commutation payments	167	
payments to and on account of leavers		
– refund of contributions	5	
transfers to other schemes	4	
		9
		197
Excess of income over expenditure for the year		607

NET ASSET STATEMENT AS AT 30 JUNE 19X13

	£'000
Investment assets	
Fixed interest government securities	710
Quoted securities	1,207
Freehold property (note 2)	1,050
Cash deposits – term	149
– ordinary	14
Loan to Daffodil Bulb Co plc (note 3)	150
	3,280
Current assets	
Tax recoverable	5

	£'000	£'000
Creditors – amounts falling due within one year		
Bank overdraft	1	
Accruals and deferred income	10	
Liabilities for commutations	100	
	111	(106)
		3,174

MOVEMENT IN NET ASSETS OF THE SCHEME FOR THE YEAR ENDED 30 JUNE 19X13

	£'000	£'000
Net assets of the scheme at 1 July 19X12		1,696
Net new money invested per revenue account		607
Change in market value of investments		
– unrealised	874	
– realised	(3)	871
Net assets of the scheme at 30 June 19X12		3,174

Workings

(1) Tax recoverable

	£'000
Tax credits (196 – 137)	59
Less tax recovered	54
	5

(2) Unrealised gains less losses

		£'000
Equity	1,207 – 861	346
Gov. stocks	710 – 732	(22)
Freehold	1,050 – 500	550
		874

Notes to the pension scheme accounts

(1) Accounting policies:
  (i) The accounts have been prepared in accordance with Statement of Recommended Practice No. 1 on the basis of the accruals concept.
  (ii) The accounts do not take account of liabilities to pay pensions and other benefits in the future.
  (iii) Investments are included at valuation.
  (iv) The scheme is an exempt approved fund and therefore tax deductions and credits are recoverable.
(2) The freehold property was valued on 30 June 19X13 by Hulls, Chartered Surveyors. The property is included in the net assets statement at the valuation of £1,050,000. The property is leased to Daffodil Bulb Co for a period of 50 years from 19X7 at a current annual rental of £40,000.
(3) The loan to the Daffodil Bulb Co plc is for a period of 5 years at a rate of 2% above interbank rate.

c The report of the trustees should refer to the following main matters:

(1) Membership statistics.
(2) Major changes in benefits, constitution or legal requirements.
(3) Financial development of the scheme as disclosed in the accounts.
(4) Actuarial position of the scheme as disclosed in the actuary's statement.
(5) Investment policy and performance of scheme. This should include details of any delegation by the trustees of investment management responsibilities.

ANSWER 13.1 (BASIC)

Hop and Skotch
WORKINGS

a Analysis of equity of Skotch

	Total £	Group share pre-acq. £	Group share post-acq. £
OSC	40,000	40,000	—
P/L at acq.	6,000	6,000	—
P/L since acq.	19,000	—	19,000
	65,000	46,000	
Cost of investment		48,000	
Goodwill w/o against reserves		2,000	(2,000)
Hop P/L			75,000
Consol. B/S			92,000

b Analysis of equity of Skotch

	Total £	Group share (60%) pre-acq. £	Group share post-acq. £	MI £
OSC	40,000	24,000		16,000
P/L at acq.	16,000	9,600		6,400
P/L since acq.	9,000		5,400	3,600
	65,000	33,600		
Cost of investment		48,000		
Goodwill w/o against reserves		14,400	(14,400)	
Hop P/L			75,000	
Consol. B/S			66,000	26,000

SOLUTION

Consolidated balance sheets (abridged) at 31.12.X8

	(a)	(b)
Tangible fixed assets	96,700	96,700
Current assets	181,900	181,900
Current liabilities	(86,600)	(86,600)
	192,000	192,000
Called up share capital	100,000	100,000
Profit and loss account	92,000	66,000
	192,000	166,000
Minority interest	—	26,000
	192,000	192,000

ANSWER 13.2 (BASIC)

Helston and Sands (Part 1)

WORKINGS

Analysis of equity of Sands

	Total £	Group share (90%) pre-acq. £	Group share post-acq. £	Minority interest (10%) £
OSC	200	180		20
P/L at acq.	400	360		40
P/L since acq. (700 − 400)	300		270	30
	900	540		
Cost of investment		630		
Goodwill w/o against reserves		90	(90)	
Helston P/L			2,250	
Consol B/S			2,430	90

SOLUTION

Consolidated balance sheet

	£
Fixed assets	2,700
Net current assets	820
	3,520
Called up share capital	1,000
profit and loss account	2,430
	3,430
minority interest	90
	3,520

ANSWER 13.3 (BASIC)

Helston and Sands (Part 2)

WORKINGS

The balance sheet of Sands would now show a proposed dividend of £50 and a profit and loss account balance of £650. Helston's balance sheet would remain unchanged. However Helston would eventually (before finalising its own accounts) have to accrue £45 (90% × £50) dividend receivable, by setting up a debtor of £45 and increasing its own P/L balance to £2,295 (i.e. 2,250 + 45).

Analysis of equity of Sands

	Total £	Group share (90%) pre acq. £	Group share post-acq. £	Minority interest (10%) £
OSC	200	180		20
P/L at acq.	400	360		40
P/L since acq. (650 − 400)	250		225	25
	850	540		
Cost of investment		630		
Goodwill w/o against reserves		90	(90)	
Helston P/L per draft acs		2,250		
add Share of Sands div. 90% × 50		45	2,295	
Consol B/S			2,430	85

SOLUTION

Consolidated balance sheet

	£	£
Fixed assets		2,700
Net current assets	820	
less dividend payable to minority (10% × 50)	5	815
		3,515
Called up share capital		1,000
profit and loss account		2,430
		3,430
Minority interest		85
		3,515

Note: MI is still £90 in total but B/S presentation includes £5 in current liabilities reflecting the cash that will leave the group within 12 months of B/S date.

ANSWER 13.4 (BASIC)

Ainsdale and Churchtown

SOLUTION

(a) **Consolidated profit and loss account**

	£
Turnover (6,000 + 3,000)	9,000
Operating expenses (900 + 400)	1,300
Operating profit	7,700
Taxation (2,000 + 1,000)	3,000
Profit after tax	4,700
Balance brought forward (working)	11,000
Balance carried forward	15,700

Workings		
Ainsdale b/f		8,000
Churchtown b/f	5,000	
less pre-acquisition element	2,000	
∴ post-acquisition element		3,000
		11,000

(b) If Churchtown had proposed a dividend of £400 its retained profit would have been £1,200 and its reserves c/f £6,200. Ainsdale would have shown dividend receivable of £400 immediately following operating profit and hence retained profit of £3,500 and carry forward of £11,500.

Note that although the profit and loss accounts of the two individual companies would be altered, the consolidated profit and loss account would be exactly the same.

ANSWER 13.5 (BASIC)

Thomas and Percy

SOLUTION

(a) **Consolidated profit and loss account**

	£
Turnover (96,000 + 25,000)	121,000
Operating expenses (18,000 + 8,000)	26,000

	£
Operating profit	95,000
Taxation	37,000
Profit after tax	58,000
Minority interest (20% × 10,000)	2,000
Profit attributable to members of holding company	56,000
Balance brought forward (working)	138,400
Balance carried forward	194,400

Working		
Thomas b/f		120,000
Percy b/f	35,000	
less pre-acquisition element	12,000	
∴ post-acquisition element	23,000	
Group share 80% × 23,000		18,400
		138,400

(b) Effect of proposed dividends:
   (i) by Thomas – the holding company's proposed dividend of £15,000 will be reflected in the consolidated accounts;
   (ii) by Percy – the subsidiaries' proposed dividend, although changing the reserves of the two individual companies, has no effect on aggregate group reserves. Nor will it affect the figure of minority interest.

The consolidated profit and loss account will therefore be the same as for part (i) except as follows:

	£
Profit attributable to members of holding company	56,000
Proposed dividends of holding company	15,000
Retained profit	41,000
Balance b/f	138,400
Balance c/f	179,400

ANSWER 13.6 (BASIC)

James and Gordon

WORKINGS

(1) Before attempting to complete the consolidated profit and loss account, check carefully the inter-company dividends. Clearly James's £4,500 and £9,000 are 90% of the respective dividends paid and proposed. These inter-company dividends should be eliminated on consolidation. This will leave £2,100 to be dealt with as investment income in the consolidated profit and loss account. However for presentation purposes it will be displayed as:

investment income $\left(2,100 \times \dfrac{100}{70}\right)$	3,000
tax credit on dividends	(900)
	2,100

(2) Minority interest is based on profit after tax but before deducting ordinary dividends i.e. 10% of £20,000 = £2,000.

SOLUTION

Consolidated profit and loss account for the year ended . . .

	£	£
Turnover		184,000
Operating expenses		43,000

	£	£
Operating profit		141,000
Investment income		3,000
		144,000
Profit before tax		
Corporation tax	59,000	
Tax credit on dividends received	900	
		59,900
Profit after tax		84,100
Minority interest		2,000
Profit attributable to members of holding company		82,100
Dividends – paid	20,000	
– proposed	30,000	
		50,000
Retained profit		32,100
Balance b/f (working)		127,800
Balance c/f		159,900
WORKINGS		
James		108,000
Gordon 90% (33,000 – 11,000)		19,800
		127,800

ANSWER 14.1 (BASIC)

Terence and Toby

WORKINGS

Points to note:

(1) The current accounts agree so they can simply be cancelled against each other for the purposes of the consolidated balance sheet.

(2) In calculating the goodwill on consolidation relating to the investment in ordinary shares it is necessary to analyse the revaluation reserve of Toby between pre-acquisition and post-acquisition.

(3) The premium on the purchase of the preference shares of £100 (£3,100 – £3,000) may be dealt with in the same way as consolidation goodwill on ordinary shares.

(4) *Analysis of equity of Toby*

(A) ORDINARY SHARES

	Total £	Group share (80%) pre-acq. £	Group share P/L post-acq. £	Group share revaluation post-acq. £	MI (20%) £
OSC	20,000	16,000			4,000
P/L at acq.	8,000	6,400			1,600
P/L since acq.	22,400		17,920		4,480
Reval. at acq.	1,200	960			240
Reval. since acq.	3,000			2,400	600
	54,600	23,360			
Cost of investment		25,000			
Goodwill w/o (see below)		1,640			
					MI (70%)
(B) PREF. SHARES	10,000	3,000			7,000
Cost of investment		3,100			
Premium w/o (see below)		100			
Goodwill w/o (1,640 + 100)			(1,740)		
Terence			48,000	15,000	
Consol. B/S			64,180	17,400	17,920

SOLUTION

Consolidated balance sheet at . . .

	£	£
Tangible fixed assets		180,100
Current assets		
Stock	49,000	
Debtors	32,700	
Cash	4,300	
	86,000	
less creditors due within one year	31,600	54,400
		234,500
less creditors due more than one year		55,000
		179,500
Called up share capital		
– ordinary share capital		50,000
– preference share capital		30,000
Revaluation reserve		17,400
Profit and loss account		64,180
		161,580
Minority interest		17,920
		179,500

ANSWER 14.2 (INTERMEDIATE)

Tom and Jerry

WORKINGS

Analysis of equity of Jerry

(1)   Ordinary shares

	Total £	Group share (75%) pre-acq. £	Group share post-acq. £	MI (25%) £
OSC	50,000	37,500		12,500
P/L at acq.	20,000	15,000		5,000
P/L since acq.	18,000		13,500	4,500
	88,000	52,500		
Cost of investment		58,000		
Goodwill on consolidation (w/o – see below)		5,500		

(2)   Preference shares

		Group share (40%)		MI (60%)
PSC	40,000	16,000		24,000
Cost of investment		15,000		
Discount (see below)		(1,000)		

(3)   Tom P/L

Per draft acs	120,000		
Ord. div receiv. 75% × 2,500	1,875		
Pref. div receiv. 40% × 1,400	560	122,435	

(4) Goodwill w/o (5,500 – 1,000)		(4,500)
(5) Unrealised profit $^{20}/_{120}$ × £42,000		(7,000)
Consol. B/S	124,435	46,000

Dividend payable to MI (current liability):

		£
Ords	25% × 2,500	625
Prefs	60% × 1,400	840
		1,465

SOLUTION
Consolidated balance sheet at 31.12.X9

	£	£	£
Tangible fixed assets			320,600
Current assets (113,100 + 43,400 − 7,000)		149,500	
less creditors amounts falling due within one year:			
Creditors	78,200		
Proposed dividends			
Holding company	20,000		
Minority	1,465	99,665	
Net current assets			49,835
Total assets less current liabilities			370,435
Called up share capital			200,000
Profit and loss account			124,435
			324,435
Minority interest			46,000
			370,435

ANSWER 14.3 (ADVANCED)

Black Root
WORKINGS

(1) Unrealised profit on transfer of fixed assets

	£
– profit on transfer $\frac{40}{140}$ × 126,000	36,000
– depreciation effect 20% × 36,000	(7,200)
	28,800

(2) Current account reconciliation

Books of:	Black Root	Confectioners
Per B/S	70 (Dr)	57 (Cr)
Goods in transit (485 − 475)		10
Cash in transit (418 − 415)	(3)	
	67	67

(3) Unrealised profit in stock at year-end

Stock per count	50
In transit	10
	60

$$URP = \frac{25}{125} \times 60 = 12$$

(4) Consolidated stock

Black root	1,397
Confectioners	640
In transit	10
Unrealised profit adjustment	(12)
	2,035

Analysis of equity

(1) Ordinary shares – Confectioners:

	Total £	Group Share (60%) pre-acq.	Group share post-acq. P/L	(60%) share premium	MI (40%)
OSC	2,352	1,411.2		—	940.8
Share premium	504			302.4	201.6
P/L – at acq.	300	180.0			120.0
– since acq.	99		59.4		39.6
	3,255	1,591.2			
Cost of investment		3,709.0			
Goodwill on consolidation W/O		2,117.8			

(2) Preference shares:

– Confectioners	320				320.0

(3) Black Root: | | | 5,468 | 2,110.0 | |

(4) Goodwill W/O: | | | (2,117.8) | | |

(5) Unrealised profit adjustments:

– fixed assets			(28.8)		
– stock			(12.0)		
Consol. B/S			3,368.8	2,412.4	1,622.0
MI – current 40% × 235					94.0

SOLUTION

Summarised consolidated balance sheet as at 31 December 19X3 for Black Root Ltd and its subsidiary Confectioners Ltd

	£'000	£'000
Tangible fixed assets (22,080 + 2,176 − 28.8)		24,227.2
Investment in Health Sales Ltd		1,190.0
		25,417.2
Current assets		
Stock	2,035.0	
Debtors (5,060 + 1,600 − 60% × 235)	6,519.0	
ACT recoverable (446 + 101)	547.0	
Current account with Health Sales Ltd	140.0	
Cash (2,297 + 1,052 + 3)	3,352.0	
	12,593.0	
Creditors – amounts due within one year		
Trade creditors (1,044 + 384)	1,428.0	
Taxation (2,070 + 257 + 446 + 101)	2,874.0	
Proposed dividend of Black Root	1,041.0	
Dividend payable to minority shareholders	94.0	
	5,437.0	
Net current assets		7,156.0
Total assets less current liabilities		32,573.2
Creditors – amounts due after more than one year		
Debenture stock (9,200 + 960)		(10,160.0)
		22,413.2
Capital and reserves		
Share capital – ordinary shares		10,410.0
– preference shares		4,600.0
Share premium account		2,412.4
Profit and loss account		3,368.8

	£'000	£'000
		20,791.2
		1,622.0
Minority interest		
		22,413.2

ANSWER 14.4 (BASIC)

Nicklaus and Palmer

WORKINGS

(1) Ensure inter-company dividends agree – they do!
   None of these dividends appear in the consolidated P/L – they are eliminated on consolidation.

(2) Calculate MI carefully! Recommended approach:

	£	MI	£
Profit after tax	34,000		
less preference div.	6,000	(80%)	4,800
available for ords.	28,000	(40%)	11,200
Total MI			16,000

(3) Balance b/f

	£
Nicklaus	102,000
Palmer 60% (62,000 – 30,000)	19,200
	121,200

SOLUTION

Consolidated profit and loss account (abbreviated)

	£	£
Operating profit		179,000
Tax		70,000
Profit after tax		109,000
Minority interest		16,000
		93,000
Dividends – paid	20,000	
– proposed	30,000	50,000
Retained profit		43,000
Balance b/f		121,200
Balance c/f		164,200

ANSWER 14.5 (INTERMEDIATE)

Hydrogen

WORKINGS

(1) Only 3 months of Chlorine's turnover, cost of sales etc. should be included in the consolidated P/L.

(2) MI is calculated as follows:

	£
Bromine 10% × 370	37
Chlorine 20% × $^3/_{12}$ × 120	6
	43

(3) Group reserves B/F are as follows: £

Hydrogen	2,000
Bromine 90% (800 − 200)	540
Chlorine (acquired during year)	—
	2,540

(4) Dividends from subsidiaries

Bromine – all post-acq. 90% × 140   = 126
Chlorine – total 80% × 60   = 48
(of which post-acquisition part is
restricted to 80% × $^{3}/_{12}$ × 70   = 14)
– i.e. pre-acq. element wrongly credited to P/L = 48 − 14 = 34

(5) Retained profit allocation:

retained by holding company
– per draft acs (274) less pre-acq. div (34) i.e. 240

retained by subsidiaries
Bromine 90% × 230   = 207
Chlorine 80% × $^{3}/_{12}$ × 50   = 10
      217

SOLUTION

Consolidated profit and loss for the year ended 31 March 19X4

	£	£
Turnover (2,000 + 1,750 + $^{3}/_{12}$ × 600)		3,900
Cost of sales (700 + 950 + 75)		1,725
Gross profit		2,175
Distribution costs (50 + 60 + 5)	115	
Administration expenses (350 + 170 + 15)	535	
		650
Profit on ordinary activities before tax		1,525
Taxation (400 + 200 + 25)		625
Profit on ordinary activities after tax		900
Minority interest		43
Profit attributable to holding company shareholders		857
Dividends on ordinary shares – paid	100	
– proposed	300	
		400
Retained profit		457
Holding company	240	
Subsidiaries	217	
	457	
Balance at 1.4.X3		2,540
Balance at 31.3.X3		2,997

ANSWER 14.6 (INTERMEDIATE)

Holds

WORKINGS

(1) Inter-company dividends received by Holds are replaced on consolidation by attributable profits of subsidiaries:

Ord. divs – Alton   90% × 7,000 = 6,300
Pref. divs – Alton   20% × 1,000 =   200
Ord. divs – Brown 70% × 5,000 = 3,500

(2) Divs from trade investments (1,200 + 300 = 1,500) should be included in consol. P/L. These should be grossed up at 30% per SSAP 8 i.e.

£1,500 × $\frac{100}{70}$ = 2,143 and the tax credit of £643 (2,143 – 1,500) included as part of the tax charge.

(3) Minority interest working:

Alton			MI
Profit after tax	11,000		
less pref. divs	1,000	(80%)	800
available for ords	10,000	(10%)	1,000
Brown			
Profit after tax	7,300	(30%)	2,190
Total MI			3,990

(4) Unrealised profit adjustment (assuming 100% elimination):

$^{20}/_{120}$ × ⅙ × £36,000 = £1,000 (note the effect on cost of sales).

Inter-company turnover is £36,000
(reduce both turnover and cost of sales)

(5) Retained profit allocation:

	£	£
Holds – per acs		9,200
Alton 90% × 3,000	2,700	
Brown 70% × 2,300	1,610	
Unrealised profit	(1,000)	3,310

(6) Balance b/f:

Holds	40,000
Alton 90% (20,600 – 4,600)	14,400
Brown 70% (10,500 – 1,500)	6,300
	60,700

SOLUTION

Consolidated profit and loss account for the year ended 31 December 19X9

	£	£
Turnover (500 + 200 + 100 – 36)		764,000
Cost of sales (410 + 170 + 84 – 36 + 1)		629,000
Gross profit		135,000
Distribution costs	15,000	
Administrative expenses	30,000	45,000
Operating profit		90,000
Income from fixed asset investments		2,143
Profit on ordinary activities before tax		92,143
Tax		
Corporation tax	43,000	
Tax credit on dividends received	643	43,643
Profit on ordinary activities after tax		48,500
Minority interest		3,990
Profit attributable to holding company shareholders		44,510

	£	£
Dividends on ordinary shares – paid	12,000	
– proposed	20,00	
		32,000
Retained profit		12,510
Holding company	9,200	
Subsidiaries	3,310	
	12,510	
Balance at 1.1.X9		60,700
Balance at 31.12.X9		73,210

ANSWER 14.7 (ADVANCED)

Redland and Kingsdown

WORKINGS

Analysis of equity schedule

	Total	At acquisition	P/L since acq.	Reval. reserve since acq.	MI
Kingsdown					
OSC	300,000	240,000	—	—	60,000
P/L*					
– at acq.	75,000	60,000	—	—	15,000
– since	126,000	—	100,800	—	25,200
Share premium	80,000	64,000			16,000
Revaluation					
– at acq.	95,000	76,000			19,000
– since	92,350			73,880	18,470
	768,350	440,000	100,800	73,880	153,670
PSC	100,000	20,000			
					80,000
		460,000			
Cost of investment		256,840			
Capital reserve on consolidation		203,160			
Redland					
– per draft acs	561,230			396,450	
div receivable	72,000				
management charge receiv.	84,000				
		717,230			
Unrealised profit in stock		(13,800)			
Consol B/S		804,230	470,330	233,670	

* After adjusting for management charges payable (285,000 − 84,000 = 201,000).

SOLUTION

Redland plc

Consolidated balance sheet at 31.12.X9

	£	£
Tangible fixed assets		
Freehold land and buildings		2,161,539
Plant and machinery		
Cost	1,585,626	
Depreciation	961,276	624,350
		2,785,889

	£	£
Current assets		
Stocks	805,956	
Debtors	563,960	
Prepayments	46,473	
Cash	19,582	
	1,435,971	
Creditors – amounts falling due within 1 year		
Creditors	176,930	
Accruals	19,680	
Taxation	494,110	
Bank overdraft	86,750	
Dividends – Holding company	240,000	
– minority	18,000	
	1,035,470	
Net current assets		400,501
		3,186,390
Creditors amounts falling due after more than one year		
– loan stock		(500,000)
		£2,686,390

	£
Capital and reserves	
Ordinary share capital	800,000
Share premium account	175,000
Revaluation reserve	470,330
Capital reserve on consolidation	203,160
Profit and loss account	804,230
	2,452,720
Minority interest	233,670
	2,686,390

ANSWER 15.1 (INTERMEDIATE)

Greendale

WORKINGS
(using indirect consolidation method)

Stage 1 – Consolidation of Langdale group

Analysis of equity of Treeside (Langdale 90%, minority 10%)

	Total	Group share pre-acq.	Group share post-acq.	Minority interest
	£	£	£	£
Ordinary share capital	150	135	—	15
Reserves at acquisition by Langdale	80	72		8
Reserves since acquisition	340	—	306	34
Total	570	207	306	57
Cost of investment by Langdale		242		
Goodwill on consolidation written off against reserves		35	(35)	
Reserves of Langdale			732	
Totals for Langdale group			1,003	57

Stage 2 – Consolidation of Greendale and Langdale group

Analysis of equity of Langdale (Greendale share 60%, minority 40%)

	Total	Group share pre-acq.	Group share post-acq.	Minority interest
	£	£	£	£
Ordinary share capital	500	300	—	200
Reserves at acquisition by Greendale (see below)	640	384		256
Reserves since acquisition (1,003 − 640)	363		218	145
	1,503	684		
Cost of investment by Greendale		820		
Goodwill on consolidation written off against reserves		136	(136)	
Reserves of Greendale			960	
Minority interest – Langdale Group				57
Consolidated balance sheet totals			1,042	658

Note: The consolidated P/L reserves of Langdale group at date of acquisition by Greendale is calculated as follows:

	£
P/L reserves of Langdale	550
Langdale's share of post-acquisition reserves of Treeside 90% (180 − 80)	90
	640

SOLUTION

Consolidated balance sheet of Greendale group

	£
Tangible fixed assets (800 + 700 + 400)	1,900
Net current assets (340 + 290 + 170)	800
	2,700
Ordinary share capital	1,000
Profit and loss account	1,042
	2,042
Minority interest	658
	2,700

ANSWER 15.2 (ADVANCED)

Machinery

WORKINGS

(1) Unrealised profit in stock 20% × £25,000 — 5,000

(2) Unrealised profit in machinery transfer
Cost adjustment	2,000
Depreciation adjustment 2 years × 10% × 2,000	(400)
Net adjustment	1,600

(3) Inter-company balances

	Dr	Cr
Sales		45.6
		28.9
Machinery	56.9	
Components	28.9	
	85.8	74.5
Cash in transit		11.3
	85.8	85.8

(4) MI in dividends
      Components
         Ord 20% × 10,000   2,000
         Pref   2,000
      Machinery
         Ord 25% × 48,000   12,000
                                  _____
                                  16,000
                                  _____

(5) Debtors

	Debtors £'000	Creditors £'000
S	196.7	160.0
M	124.8	152.7
C	83.5	59.2
Divs. 80% × 10	(8.0)	—
75% × 48	(36.0)	—
I/C balances	(85.8)	(74.5)
	275.2	297.4

(6) **Analysis of equity of Components Ltd** (Group holding 80%, minority 20%)

	Total £	Group share pre-acq. £	Group share post-acq. £	Minority interest £
Ordinary share capital	100,000	80,000		20,000
Reserves at acquisition by Machinery	20,000	16,000		4,000
Reserves since acquisition	54,000		43,200	10,800
	174,000	96,000		
Cost of investment by Machinery		96,000		
Goodwill on consolidation		—		
Preference share capital				40,000
Reserves of Machinery			85,000	
Totals for Machinery Group			128,200	74,800

(7) **Analysis of equity of Machinery Ltd** (Group holding 75%, minority 25%)

	Total £	Group share pre-acq. £	Group share post-acq. £	Minority interest £
Ordinary share capital	120,000	90,000		30,000
Reserves at acquisition by Sales (see (8) below)	72,000	54,000		18,000
Reserves since acquisition (128,200 − 72,000)	56,200		42,150	14,050
	248,200	144,000		
Cost of investment by Sales		135,000		
Capital reserve on consolidation		9,000		
Reserves of Sales			154,000	
Minority interest – Machinery Group				74,800
Unrealised profits:				
Stock			(5,000)	
Fixed assets			(1,600)	
Consolidated B/S totals			189,550	136,850

(Assumption: no adjustment to MI in respect of unrealised profits.)

(8) The consolidated P/L reserves of Machinery Group at date of acquisition by Sales is calculated as follows:

	£
P/L reserves of machinery	40,000
Machinery's share of post-acquisition reserves of Components 80% (60,000 − 20,000)	32,000
	72,000

SOLUTION

SALES LTD AND ITS SUBSIDIARIES

Consolidated balance sheet as at 31 October 19X5

	Cost £	Depreciation £	Net £
Tangible fixed assets			
Land	184,000	—	184,000
Buildings	260,000	92,400	167,600
(102.9 + 170 + 92 − 2)	362,900		
(69.9 + 86 + 48.2 − 0.4)		203,700	159,200
	806,900	296,100	510,800

	£
Current assets	
Stock (108,5 + 75.5 + 68.4 − 5)	247,400
Debtor (see above)	275,200
Cash (25.2 + 25.4)	50,600
	573,200

	£
Creditors – amounts due within one year	
Creditors (see above)	297,400
Overdraft (37.4 − 11.3)	26,100
Corporation tax (57.4 + 47.2 + 24.5)	129,100
Dividends payable to shareholders of Sales	80,000
Dividends payable to minority shareholders	16,000
	548,600

	£
Net current assets	24,600
	535,400

	£
Capital and reserves	
Ordinary shares of £1	200,000
Profit and loss account	189,550
Capital reserve on consolidation	9,000
	398,550
Minority interest	136,850
	535,400

ANSWER 16.1 (INTERMEDIATE)

Merger Corporation

ANSWER GUIDE

	£
(1) *Company A*	
Cash consideration	80
Share consideration	800
	880

Since cash is below 10% of total and other conditions are satisfied, combination may be accounted for on a merger accounting basis.

(2) *Company B*   £
   Cash consideration   320
   Share consideration   2,000
                                 ―――――
                                 2,320
                                 ―――――

Cash exceeds 10% of total, merger conditions cannot be satisfied.

(3) *Company C*   £
   Cash consideration   100 × 175p   175
   Share consideration   450 × £4   1,800
                                      ―――――
                                      1,975
                                      ―――――

Merger conditions are satisfied.

(4) *Company D*
   (i) Immediately prior to offer – holding 160 shares (below 20%).
   (ii) Merger conditions satisfied.

(5) *Company E*
   Merger conditions satisfied.

ANSWER 16.2 (INTERMEDIATE)

Holdings

ANSWER GUIDE

Note marks for style/layout.

(a) Conditions for merger accounting:
   (1) other to holders of all shares
   (2) ... secured 90% of equity shares ...
   (3) holding prior to offer below 20%
   (4) not less than 90% of fair value in the form of equity.

(b) Differences between acquisition accounting and merger accounting:
   (1) merger: – share for share exchange
                – current year profits all post-acq.
                – comparatives restated
      (treated as joined since formation of the respective companies).
   (2) acquisition: – only post-acquisition profits included in consolidated P/L
                – consolidation goodwill is recognised.

(c)(1) calculation – difference between carrying value of investment (= nominal value of shares
                issued plus fair value of non-equity consideration) and nominal value received.
   (2) Accounting treatment:
      (i) CV greater than NV: treat as reduction of reserves
      (ii) CV less than NV: treat as reserve on consolidation.

(d)(1) Acquisition accounting:
   (i) advantages:
      – composition of consideration not restricted
      – reflects fair value of consideration
      – computes goodwill figure.
   (ii) disadvantages:
      – only includes profits from date of acquisition
      – gives lower figure for group P/L reserves (although this does not affect individual
        companies).
      – higher depreciation charge in consolidated P/L.

(2) Merger accounting:
  (i) advantages:
    – larger figure in consolidated B/S for P/L reserves
    – full year profits included in year of acquisition
    – depreciation charge unaffected
    – no goodwill to be accounted for.
  (ii) disadvantages:
    – consolidation difference is not meaningful.

ANSWER 16.3 (ADVANCED)

Hillside

WORKINGS

(a) *Books of holding company*
  (1) If acquisition accounting is to be used for consolidation purposes, the *usual* entry will be:

Dr Cost of investment		Cr OSC	£150,000
	£450,000	Merger reserve	£300,000

  (2) If merger accounting is to be used for consolidation purposes, the *usual* entry will be:

Dr Cost of investment		Cr OSC	£150,000
	£150,000		

(b) *Consolidated accounts – acquisition accounting*
  (1) Profit and loss – include 3 months figures for Birkdale, e.g. turnover $165 + \frac{3}{12} \times 88 = 187$.
  (2) Tangible fixed assets $423 + 310 = 733$.
  (3) Goodwill calculation:

		£
Cost of investment		450,000
Share capital and reserves at acquisition		
SC	100,000	
SP	20,000	
Revaluation	65,000	
Revaluation adjustment (310 − 174)	136,000	
P/L	80,000	401,000
		49,000

(c) *Consolidated accounts – merger accounting*

	£
'Cost' of investment	150,000
Shares received	100,000
Difference adjusted against reserves	50,000

SOLUTION

Comparison of consolidated profit and loss accounts

	Acquisition accounting £'000	Merger accounting £'000
Turnover	187	253
Operating expenses	79	121
Operating profit	108	132
Tax	33	42
Profit after tax	75	90
Balance b/f	158	223
Balance c/f	233	313

Comparison of consolidated balance sheets

	Acquisition accounting £'000	Merger accounting £'000
Tangible fixed assets	733	597
Net current assets	368	368
	1,101	965
Ordinary share capital	450	450
Share premium account	72	92
Merger reserve 300 − 49 goodwill w/o)	251	—
Revaluation reserve	95	160
Profit and loss account	233 (313 − 50)	263
	1,101	965

ANSWER 16.4 (ADVANCED)

Consolidated Furniture Group

SOLUTION

a(1)

	Acquired	Consideration	£
1.8.19X3	5%	80,000 × 125p	100,000
30.9.19X3	95%	190,000 × 20 × 135p	5,130,000
		190,000 × £3	570,000
			5,700,000

(i) Initial holding is below 20%.
(ii) Total value of consideration £5,800,000
   Equity part of £5,230 is greater than 90% of £5,800,000.
   ∴ merger accounting may be used in accordance with SSAP 23.

(2) Carrying value of investment	80,000 × 125p	100,000
	190,000 × 20 × 25p	950,000
	190,000 × £3	570,000
		1,620,000
Nominal value received		1,600,000
Difference adjusted against reserves (1,620 − 1,600)		20,000

(3) **Consolidated balance sheet at 30 November 19X3**

	£'000
Fixed assets (4,563 + 3,092)	7,655
Goodwill (800 − 20% × 800)	640
Investments (175 − 100 re Table and Chairs)	75
Current assets (2,369 + 3,626)	5,995
Current liabilities (2,286 + 4,207)	(6,493)
Proposed dividend (12,000 × 1p)	(120)
Loan stock	(570)
	7,182
Share capital (3,000 + 950)	3,950
Share premium account	140
Revenue reserves	3,092
	7,182

Working − revenue reserves	
CFG	1,681
T & C	1,711
Div	(120)
Merger difference	(20)
Goodwill amortisation	(160)
	3,092

Consolidated profit and loss account		£'000
Turnover (36,873 + 25,003)		61,876
Profit before tax (1,151 + 127 − 160)		1,118
Taxation		260
Profit after tax		858
Dividends – paid	288	
– proposed	120	408
Retained profit		450

b Statement of reserves

	Profit and loss £'000	Share premium £'000	Total £'000
At 1.12.X2 (as restated for effects of merger)	2,642	140	2,782
Retained profit	450	—	450
At 30.11.X3	3,092	140	3,232

WORKING	£'000
CFG 1,681 − 603	1,078
T & C 1,711 − 127	1,584
Merger difference	(20)
Restated opening P/L reserves	2,642

ASSUMPTION
Purchased goodwill in the balance sheet of Table and Chairs arose during YE 30.11.X3 so only one year's amortisation is required.

c In essence the above business combination reflects a pooling or uniting of interests. Although there is a pre-merger holding this is only 5%. Also the non-equity part of the consideration (£570,000) is less than 10% of the total value of the consideration. Essentially no resources leave the group and there is continuity of ownership between the two groups of shareholders. Overall therefore merger accounting is appropriate for the combination.

The advantages which may arise from the use of merger accounting include:

(1) It presents the situation as though the two companies have been merged since their respective incorporations. Comparative figures are restated to reflect this.
(2) It usually gives a larger group profit and loss reserves in the consolidated balance sheet compared with merger accounting. However, this has no direct effect on the distributable reserves of the individual companies.
(3) Goodwill does not arise and thus the problem of how to write off goodwill is avoided.
(4) Merger accounting does not require the fixed assets of the 'acquired' company to be revalued. Thus the depreciation charge is based on existing figures.

ANSWER 16.5 (ADVANCED)

Willow

WORKINGS

Merger of Willow and Pourwell – merger terms

	£
Pourwell is valued at 200,000 × 50p	100,000

Willow issues £1 shares at value £2.50
∴ number of shares issued is 40,000

(1) merger method (part (a))	£
Nominal value of shares issued by Willow	40,000
Nominal value of shares in Pourwell	(200,000)
capital reserve on merger	(160,000)

(2) acquisition method

(i) accounts of Willow

			£
cost of investment in Pourwell	– dr		100,000
ordinary share capital	– cr		40,000
Merger reserve	– cr		60,000
(CA 85, S 131)			

(ii) consolidated accounts

	£	£
cost of investment		100,000
share capital and reserves		
at acquisition		
OSC	200,000	
P/L	(124,502)	75,498
Goodwill on consolidation		24,502

SOLUTION

Solution to part (a)

Consolidated balance sheet of Willow Ltd and its subsidiary Pourwell Ltd as at 31 December 19X5

Fixed assets

		£
Intangible assets		
Goodwill		135,000
Development expenditure		87,500
		222,500
Tangible assets		
Land and buildings	320,800	
Plant and machinery	150,920	
Fixtures	5,280	477,000
Investments		42,500
		742,000

Current assets

Stocks – raw materials	76,410	
– work in progress	73,103	
– finished goods	267,462	
	416,975	
Debtors	263,765	
Cash	45,636	
	726,376	

Creditors: amounts due in less than one year		
Creditors (137,148 + 208,550 + 17,350)	363,048	
Corporation tax	97,600	
Bank overdraft	38,022	
Proposed dividends	40,000	
	538,670	

Net current assets	187,706
Total assets less current liabilities	929,706
Creditors: amounts falling due after more than one year	(250,000)
	679,706

Capital and reserves	
Share capital – ordinary shares (250 + 40)	290,000
Capital reserve arising on merger	160,000
Profit and loss account (254,208 – 124,502)	129,706
Minority interest in preference shares	100,000
	679,706

Solution to part (b)

Capital and reserves section	£
Ordinary shares	290,000
Merger reserve	60,000
Profit and loss account	254,208
	604,208
Minority interest in preference shares	100,000
	704,208

Goodwill on consolidation of £24,502 may be treated in the following ways:
(1) carried forward in the consolidated balance sheet amortised over a number of years, or
(2) written off against reserves – for example £24,502 could be written off against either £60,000 (merger reserve) or £254,208 (profit and loss).

Solution to part (c)

(1) *Net asset comparison*
   (i) *Present position:* Net assets of Pourwell at 31.12.19X5 attributable to the ordinary shareholders

   = 175,498 – 100,000 prefs. i.e. £75,498

   Net assets per share

   $= \dfrac{75,498}{200,000} = 38p$

   Net assets per 100 shares = £38

   (ii) *Taking account of merger:* Net assets of group at 31.12.19X5 attributable to the ordinary shareholders

   = (679,706 – 100,000) i.e. £579,706

   Holder of 100 shares in Pourwell receives 20 shares in Willow.

   Net assets attributable to 20 shares is

   $\dfrac{20}{290,000} \times £579,706 = £40$

(2) *Conclusions*
   (i) *Dividends*
      – at present no dividends and little prospect of payment in the future
      – under merger terms, good chance of reasonable level of dividends.

   (ii) *Asset backing*
      – modest improvement if comparison made at 31.12.X5 (note that Pourwell's net assets are declining rapidly).

ANSWER 17.1 (BASIC)

H, S, A

SOLUTION

Summarised consolidated balance sheet at 31 December 19X4

	£	£
Tangible fixed assets (6,000 + 12,100)		18,100
Investment in associated company (25% × 8,000)		2,000
Current assets (8,500 + 7,500)		16,000

	£	£
Debtor – associated company:		
dividend 25% × 600	150	
current accounts	1,000	1,150
Current liabilities (5,000 + 4,000)		(9,000)
Proposed dividends – H		(2,000)
– minority (20% × 1,000)		(200)
		26,050
Called up share capital		10,000
Profit and loss account (working)		9,150
Revaluation reserve (working)		4,380
		23,530
Minority interest (20% × 12,600)		2,520
		26,050

WORKINGS

(1) P/L

	£
H	8,550
S 80% (3,600 – 1,200)	1,920
A 25% (3,400 – 700)	675
Goodwill re S (8,000 – 80% (7,000 + 1,200 + 400))	(1,120)
Premium re A (2,100 – 25% (3,000 + 700 + 1,200))	(875)
	9,150

(2) Revaluation

	£
H	3,000
S 80% (2,000 – 400)	1,280
A 25% (1,600 – 1,200)	100
	4,380

ANSWER 17.2 (INTERMEDIATE)

Kettlewell

SOLUTION

	(a) All companies consolidated £	(b) Dale excluded from consolidation £
Consolidated balance sheets		
Tangible fixed assets	629	399
Goodwill*	52	25
Non-consolidated subsidiary	—	291
Net current assets	246	146
	927	861
Called up share capital	200	200
Profit and loss	625	625
Minority interest	102	36
	927	861
Note re non-consolidated subsidiary		
Net assets		264
Premium		27
		291

* Left in balance sheet for purposes of comparison. Goodwill should be dealt with per SSAP 22.

WORKINGS

(1) Goodwill

D	235 − 80% (100 + 160) =	27
F	88 − 70% (50 + 40) =	25
		52

(2) Non-consolidated subsidiary

Net assets 80% × 330	264
Premium (as per (1))	27
	291

(3) P/L

K		548
D	80% (230 − 160)	56
F	70% (70 − 40)	21
		625

(4) MI

D	20% × 330	66
F	30% × 120	36
		102

ANSWER 17.3 (ADVANCED)

Falcondale

WORKINGS

(1) *Investment in Henleaze – equity method*

	£
Cost of investment	6,500
Post-acquisition reserves 90% (3,900 − 950)	2,655
	9,155

		£
Alternatively:		
Proportion of net assets 90% × £8,900		8,010
Premium		
Cost	6,500	
SC & res (5,000 + 950) × 90%	5,355	1,145
		9,155

(2) *Reserves*

Falcondale	11,240
Henleaze	2,655
	13,895

(3) *Equity method*

Share of profits 90% × 4,800	=	4,320
Tax 7,200 + 90% × 2,400	=	9,360
P/L B/F 6,500 + 90% (2,100 − 950)	=	7,535

(4) *Normal consolidation*

MI – current (600 − 540)	=	60
– non-current 10% × 8,900	=	890
– P/L 10% × 2,400	=	240

(5) *Pro-rata consolidation*

FA	25,180 + 90% × 7,260	=	31,714
Stock	3,100 + 90% × 1,900	=	4,810
Debtors	2,950 + 90% × 1,350	=	4,165
Cash	870 + 90% × 690	=	1,491
Creditors	4,900 + 90% × 1,700	=	6,430
Turnover	30,000 + 90% × 8,000	=	37,200
Expenses	15,600 + 90% × 3,200	=	18,480
Tax	7,200 + 90% × 2,400	=	9,360

SOLUTION

Consolidated balance sheets

	Cost method £	Equity method £	Normal consolidation £	Pro-rata (proportional equity consolidation) £
Fixed assets				
Intangible goodwill	—	—	1,145	1,145
Tangible	25,180	25,180	32,440	31,714
Investments	6,500	9,155	—	—
Stock	3,100	3,100	5,000	4,810
Debtors	2,950	2,950	4,300	4,165
Dividends receivable	540	540	—	—
Cash	870	870	1,560	1,491
Creditors	(4,900)	(4,900)	(6,600)	(6,430)
Proposed dividends	(3,000)	(3,000)	(3,000)	(3,000)
	31,240	33,895	34,845	33,895
Ordinary share capital	20,000	20,000	20,000	20,000
Profit and loss account	11,240	13,895	13,895	13,895
Minority interest				
– non current	—	—	890	—
– current	—	—	60	—
	31,240	33,895	34,845	33,895

Consolidated profit and loss accounts

	Cost method £	Equity method £	Normal consolidation £	Pro-rata (proportional equity consolidation) £
Turnover	30,000	30,000	38,000	37,200
Operating expenses	15,600	15,600	18,800	18,480
	14,400	14,400	19,200	18,720
Share of profits of Henleaze	—	4,320	—	—
Dividends received	540	—	—	—
Profit on ordinary activities before tax	14,940	18,720	19,200	18,720
Tax	7,200	9,360	9,600	9,360
Profit on ordinary activities after tax	7,740	9,360	9,600	9,360
Minority interest	—	—	240	—
	7,740	9,360	9,360	9,360
Dividends proposed	3,000	3,000	3,000	3,000
Retained profit	4,740	6,360	6,360	6,360
Balance B/F	6,500	7,535	7,535	7,535
Balance C/F	11,240	13,895	13,895	13,895

ANSWER 17.4 (ADVANCED)

Plural Publishers
WORKINGS

	PP £'000	VH (80%) £'000	Sub total £'000	CST (40%) £'000
Turnover	17,280	7,560	24,840	3,825
Materials	(10,368)	(4,158)	(14,526)	(2,056)
Services	(3,430)	(936)	(4,366)	(431)
Salaries and wages	(1,322)	(1,386)	(2,708)	(573)
Directors emoluments	(225)	(78)	(303)	(68)
Audit fees	(58)	(7)	(65)	(4)
Depreciation	(360)	(180)	(540)	(93)
Operating profit	1,517	815	2,332	600
Assoc. Co. Share (40%)				240
Debenture interest	(60)	(5)	(65)	
Tax – group	(630)	(360)	(990)	
– assoc. 40% × 315				(126)
Profit after tax	827	450	1,277	114
MI (20%)		(90)	(90)	
Divs. – VH (80%)	240	(240)		
– CST (40%)	60		60	(60)
Proposed divs. – PP	(900)		(900)	
Retained profits	227	120	347	54
Balance b/f	8,080	(120)	7,960	140
Balance c/f	8,307	—	8,307	194

8,501

Notes
(1) The majority holding in VH was acquired during the previous year. The post-acquisition balance b/f is taken from the information in Appendix 2.

(2) No information is given regarding the reserves of CST at the date of purchase of the shares. The whole of the 350 balance b/f (Appendix 4) is therefore taken as post-acquisition, giving 40% × 350 = 140 for the group.

The balances b/f (8,080 − 120 + 140 = 8,100) reconciles with the reserves figure in Appendix 3.

SOLUTION

Consolidated profit and loss account for the year ended 30 September 19X14

	£'000	£'000
Turnover		24,840
Operating expenses (14,526 + 4,366 + 2,708 + 303 + 65 + 540)		22,508
Operating profit		2,332
Share of profit of associated company		240
Interest payable		(65)
Profit on ordinary activities before tax		2,507
Taxation		
Plural Publishers and subsidiary	990	
Associated company	126	1,116
Profit on ordinary activities after tax		1,391
Minority interest		90
Profit attributable to holding company shareholders		1,301
Dividends on ordinary shares – proposed		900
Retained profit		401

	£'000	£'000
Holding company	227	
Subsidiary	120	
Associated company	54	
	401	
Balance brought forward		8,100
Balance carried forward		8,501
By holding company	8,307	
Subsidiary	—	
Associated company	194	
	8,501	

ANSWER 18.1 (INTERMEDIATE)

Methods

SOLUTION

(a) *Methods of foreign currency translation*
  (1) closing rate/net investment method:
    - assets and liabilities are translated into sterling at closing rate of exchange
    - profit and loss items may be translated at either average or closing rate (provided a company is consistent from year to year)
    - exchange gains and losses arising as a result of translation of financial statements should be taken direct to reserves.
  (2) temporal method:
    - the financial statements of the foreign enterprise are included in the consolidated accounts as though the transactions had been entered into by the investing company itself. Fixed assets and stocks are translated at historical rates, monetary items are translated at closing rates. Most profit and loss items, with the notable exception of depreciation, are translated at average rate. Exchange differences are taken to profit and loss account.

(b) *Circumstances in which each method is mandatory*
  (1) Closing rate/net investment method:
    - mandatory where entity operates as a separate or quasi-independent entity. This may be indicated by the following factors:
      (i) investment in net worth rather than individual assets and liabilities
      (ii) net current assets and fixed assets financed partly by local currency borrowings
      (iii) foreign enterprise not normally dependent in its day to day operations on the reporting currency of the investing company
      (iv) investing company expects stream of dividends but expects investment to remain until business is liquidated or disposed of.
  (2) Temporal method:
    - mandatory where foreign entity's trade is effectively extension of trade of investing company. An important factor is to determine which currency is the dominant currency as regards the environment in which the foreign enterprise operates. The following should be taken into account in determining dominant currency:
      (i) extent to which enterprise's cash flows have direct impact on cash flows of investing company
      (ii) extent to which functioning of enterprise depends directly on the investing company
      (iii) currency in which majority of trading transactions are denominated
      (iv) major currency to which operation is exposed in its financing structure.

(c) *Justification of treatment of overseas investment financed by overseas borrowing*
  Overseas investment financed by overseas borrowing may be considered at two different levels – individual company accounts and consolidated accounts. For the purpose of this solution consolidated accounts only are considered.
    SSAP 20 refers to the situation within a group of companies where foreign borrowings may

have been used either (1) to finance group investments in foreign enterprises or (2) to provide a hedge against the exchange risk associated with similar existing investments. The currencies of the loan(s) and investment(s) need not be the same.

Any exchange rate movements will affect both the carrying amount of the assets underlying the investments as well as the borrowings, one being covered by the other. The group would apparently be covered in economic terms against any movement in exchange rates. It appears logical therefore to allow exchange differences on borrowings and investments to be offset and taken to reserves with no effect on consolidated profit and loss account. The 'cover' method can only be used if certain stringent conditions are satisfied.

ANSWER 18.2 (INTERMEDIATE)

Factors

SOLUTION

(a) The closing rate/net investment methods recognises that the company's investment is in the net worth of a foreign enterprise (for example, foreign subsidiary) rather than a direct investment in individual assets and liabilities. Three other features typify this method:
   (1) the foreign enterprise will normally have working capital and fixed assets possibly part-financed by local borrowings;
   (2) the foreign enterprise is not normally dependent in its day-to-day operations on the investing company's reporting currency;
   (3) the investing company looks for a stream of dividends but intends to leave the investment intact until sale of business or liquidation.
   The label 'closing rate' effectively specifies that the asset and liabilities of the foreign enterprise are translated at the closing rate of exchange. However, under the version of the method specified in SSAP 20, profit and loss items may be translated at either average or closing rate. The 'net investment' label refers to the concept of investment in net worth referred to above. The retranslation of net investment at each balance sheet date is effectively a revaluation and so logically the financial effects of the retranslation should be taken direct to reserve without being passed through profit and loss account.

(b) The temporal method recognises the operations of the foreign entity as direct extensions of the trade of the investment company, i.e. effectively a direct investment in individual assets and liabilities. The translation 'rules' are consequently similar to those for translation of foreign currency transactions entered into by individual companies.
   Accordingly:
   (1) non-monetary assets (stock and fixed assets) are translated at historical rates;
   (2) monetary assets and liabilities are translated at closing rates;
   (3) profit and loss transactions (except depreciation) are translated at average rate. Depreciation charge is translated at the same rate as for fixed assets;
   (4) exchange differences are passed through profit and loss account.

(c) The temporal method should normally be used for translation of foreign currency transactions in the accounts of individual companies.

As regards group situations, in order to decide whether the temporal method should be used it is useful to consider which currency is the dominant currency. If the investing company's currency (£ sterling) is the dominant currency in the economic environment in which the foreign enterprise operates, the temporal method should be used.

Relevant factors in determining dominant currency include:

(1) the extent to which the cash flows of the enterprise have a direct impact upon those of the investing company;
(2) the extent to which the functioning of the enterprise is dependent directly upon the investing company;
(3) the currency in which the majority of the trading transactions are denominated;
(4) the major currency to which the operation is exposed in its financing structure.

Two examples of situations where temporal method may be the most appropriate include:

(i) where the foreign enterprise acts as a selling agency receiving stocks of goods from the investing company and remitting the proceeds back to the company;

(ii) where the foreign enterprise is located overseas for tax, exchange controls or similar reasons and is essentially a means of raising finance for other companies in the group.

SSAP 20 envisages that the temporal method will only be appropriate for consolidation purposes in a limited number of situations.

ANSWER 18.3 (INTERMEDIATE)

Terrier and Spaniel
ANSWER GUIDE
(a) Refer to solution to question R1.
(b) (1) *Terrier Ltd*
    (i) South American branch
       – operates as direct extension of trade of Terrier
       – similar to SSAP 20 example
       – dominant currency £ sterling
       – temporal method
       – translation gains/losses through P/L.
    (ii) West German branch
       – similar considerations to (i)
       – translation gains/losses through P/L
         (1) part re trading transactions under other operating income/expenses
         (2) part re loan under interest receivable and other similar income or interest payable and other similar charges.

   (2) *Spaniel plc*
    (i) Alsatian
       – operates as separate or quasi-independent entity
       – closing rate/net investment method
       – exchange gains/losses direct to reserves
    (ii) Boxer
       – operates as direct extension of trade of Spaniel
       – similar to example given in SSAP 20
       – temporal method appropriate
       – translation gains/losses through P/L (other operating income/expenses).

ANSWER 18.4 (INTERMEDIATE)

Overseas
WORKINGS

(1) *Translation of balance sheet of subsidiary*

	$	Rate	£
Fixed assets	2,400	2	1,200
Net current assets	1,200	2	600
	3,600		1,800
Loans	(600)	2	(300)
	3,000		1,500
Ordinary share capital	1,300	3	433
Pre-acquisition reserves	200	3	67
Post-acquisition reserves	1,500	Balance	1,000
	3,000		1,500

	$	Rate	£
(2) Translation of profit and loss account of subsidiary			
Sales	800	2.3	348
Operating expenses	500	2.3	217
Operating profit	300	2.3	131
Balance b/f	1,400	} See below	
Balance c/f	1,700		
(3) Calculation of exchange differences			
Equity interest at 1.1.X4	2,700	2.6	1,038
Gain on restatement (balance)	—	—	312*
Equity interest restated at closing rate	2,700	2	1,350
Profit and loss	300	2.3	131
Exchange difference on P/L $\frac{300}{2} - \frac{300}{2.3}$	—	—	19*
Equity interest at 31.12.X4	3,000	2	1,500

* Group share of exchange gain = 80% (312 + 19) = 265.

(4) Analysis of equity of overseas

	Total £	Group share (80%) pre-acq. £	Group share post-acq. £	MI (20%) £
OSC	433	346	—	87
P/L at acq.	67	54	—	13
P/L since acq.	1,000	—	800	200
	1,500	400		
Cost of investment		650		
Goodwill W/O against reserves		250	(250)	
Howe P/L			6,500	
Consol. B/S			7,050	300

(5) Group reserves b/f

	£	£
Howe		5,000
Overseas		
Equity at 1.1.X4 (working 3)	1,038	
Equity at acquisition (working 4)	500	
	538	
80% × 538		430
Goodwill w/o		(250)
		5,180

SOLUTION

Summarised consolidated balance sheet at 31.12.X4

	£
Tangible fixed assets (7,350 + 1,200)	8,550
Net current assets 1,500 + 600)	2,100
Loans (1,000 + 300)	(1,300)
	9,350
Ordinary share capital	2,000
Profit and loss account	7,050
Minority interest	300
	9,350

Summarised consolidated profit and loss account for the year ended 31 December 19X4

	£
Sales (2,000 + 348)	2,348
Operating expenses (500 + 217)	717
Operating profit (1,500 + 131)	1,631
Minority interest (20% × 131)	26
Retained profit	1,605

	£
STATEMENT OF RESERVES	
Balance at 1.1.X4	5,180
Retained profit	1,605
Exchange difference (80% (312 + 19))	265
Balance at 31.12.X4	7,050

ANSWER 18.5 (ADVANCED)

Basil's Hotels – closing rate

WORKINGS

(1) *Translation of balance sheet of subsidiary*

	P	Rate	£
Fixed assets			
– cost	2,650		780
– depreciation	1,447		426
	1,203		354
Stock	309		91
Debtors	234	3.4	69
Cash at bank	96		28
Loans	(200)		(59)
Creditors	(172)		(51)
Taxation	(300)		(88)
Proposed dividends	(120)		(35)
	1,050		309
Share capital	300	7.1	42
Pre-acq. reserves	225	7.1	32
Post-acq. reserves	525	Balance	235
	1,050		309

(2) *Translation of profit and loss account of subsidiary (at average rate)*

	P	Rate	£
Turnover	900		243
Operating expenses	(240)		(65)
Operating profit	660		178
Interest paid	(20)	3.7	(5)
Profit before tax	640		173
Tax	300		81
Profit after tax	340		92
Dividends – paid	(80)	3.5	(23)
– proposed	(120)	3.4	(35)
Retained profit	140		34

(3) *Calculation of exchange differences*

	P	Rate	£
Equity interest at 1.1.X9	910	4	227
Gain on restatement			41*

	P	Rate	£
Equity interest at 31.12.X9	910	3.4	268
Retained profit	140		34
Exchange difference − P/L			
$\frac{140}{3.4} - 34$	—	—	7*
Equity interest at 21.12.X9	1,050	3.4	309

* Group share of exchange difference 90% (41 + 7) = 43.

(4) *Analysis of equity of Manuel*

	Total £	Group share (90%) pre-acq. £	Group share post-acq. £	MI (10%) £
OSC	42	38		4
P/L at acq.	32	29		3
P/L since acq.	235		211	24
	309	67		
Cost of investment		84		
Goodwill w/o against reserves		17	(17)	
Basil's Hotels P/L			1,092	
Consol B/S			1,286	31

(5) *Group reserves b/f*

	£	£
Basil's Hotels		725
Manuel		
Equity at 1.1.X9 (working 3)	227	
Equity at acquisition (working 4)	74	
	153	
90% × 153		137
Goodwill w/o		(17)
		845

SOLUTION

Summarised consolidated balance sheet at 31.12.X9

	£	£	£
Tangible fixed assets			
Cost (3,076 + 780)			3,856
Depreciation (1,322 + 426)			1,748
			2,108
Current assets			
Stock (737 + 91)		828	
Debtors (698 + 69)		767	
Cash (211 + 28)		239	
		1,834	
Creditors due within one year			
Creditors (229 + 51)	280		
Taxation (405 + 88)	493		
Dividends			
− holding company	90		
− minority	3	866	968
			3,076

	£	£	£
Long term loans (900 + 59)			(959)
			2,117
Ordinary share capital			800
Profit and loss account			1,286
			2,086
Minority interest			31
			2,117

Summarised consolidated profit and loss account for the year ended 31 December 19X9

	£	£
Turnover (1,500 + 243)		1,743
Operating expenses (630 + 65)		(695)
Operating profit (870 + 178)		1,048
Interest paid (10 + 5)		(15)
Profit on ordinary activities before tax		1,033
Taxation (405 + 81)		(486)
Profit on ordinary activities after tax		547
Minority interest (10% × 92)		(9)
Profit attributable to holding company shareholders		538
Dividends – paid	50	
– proposed	90	(140)
Retained profit		398

STATEMENT OF RESERVES	£
Balance at 1.1.X9	845
Retained profit	398
Exchange difference (90% × (41 + 7))	43
Balance at 31.12.X9	1,286

ANSWER 18.6 (ADVANCED)

Basil's Hotels – temporal

WORKINGS

(1) *Translation of balance sheet of subsidiary*

	P	Rate	£
Fixed assets – cost	2,650 }	5.9	449
– depreciation	1,447 }		245
	1,203 }		204
Stock	309 }		91
Debtors	234 }		69
Cash	96 }		28
Loans	(200) }	3.4	(59)
Creditors	(172) }		(51)
Tax	(300) }		(88)
Divs.	(120) }		(35)
	1,050		159
Share capital	300	7.1	42
Pre-acq. reserves	225	7.1	32
Post-acq. reserves	525	Balance	85
	1,050		159

(2) *Translation of profit and loss account of subsidiary*

	P	Rate	£
Turnover	900	3.7	243
Operating expenses (excl. depreciation)	(88)	3.7	(24)
Depreciation	(152)	5.9	(26)
Operating profit	660		193
Interest paid	(20)	3.4	(6)
Profit before tax	640		187
Tax	(300)	3.7	(81)
Profit after tax	340		106
Dividends – paid	(80)	3.5	(23)
– proposed	(120)	3.4	(35)
Retained profit	140		48

(3) *Calculation of exchange difference*

(a) Reconstruction of balance sheet at 1.1.X9:

	P	Rate	£
TFA (1,203 + 152)	1,355	5.9	230
NCA (bal. fig.)	(445)	4	(111)
	910		119
OSC	300	7.1	42
Pre-acq. reserves	225	7.1	32
Post-acq. reserves	385	Balance	45
	910		119

(b)

	£
Equity interest at 1.1.X9	119
Equity interest at 31.12.X9	159
	40
Retained profit	48
∴ Exchange loss	(8)

(4) *Analysis of equity of Manuel*

	Total £	Group share (90%) pre-acq. £	Group share post-acq. £	MI (10%) £
OSC	42	38		4
P/L at acq.	32	29		3
P/L since acq.	85		76	9
	159	67		
Cost of investment		84		
Goodwill w/o against reserves		17	(17)	
Basil's Hotels plc			1,092	
Consol B/S			1,151	16

(5) *Group reserves b/f*

	£	£
Basil's Hotels		725
Manuel		
Equity at 1.1.X9 (working 3)	119	
Equity at acquisition (working 4)	74	
	45	
90% × 45		40
Goodwill w/o		(17)
		748

SOLUTION

Summarised consolidated balance sheet at 31.12.X9

	£	£	£
Tangible fixed assets			
Cost (3,076 + 449)			3,525
Depreciation (1,322 + 245)			1,567
			1,958
Current assets			
Stock (737 + 91)		828	
Debtors (698 + 69)		767	
Cash (211 + 28)		239	
		1,834	
Creditors due within one year			
Creditors (229 + 51)	280		
Taxation (405 + 88)	493		
Dividends			
holding company	90		
minority	3	866	968
			2,926
Long term loans (900 + 59)			(959)
			1,967
Ordinary share capital			800
Profit and loss account			1,151
			1,951
Minority interest			16
			1,967

Summarised consolidated profit and loss account for the year ended 31 December 19X9

	£	£
Turnover (1,500 + 243)		1,743
Operating expenses (630 + 24 + 26 + 8)*		(688)
Operating profit		1,055
Interest paid (10 + 6)		(16)
Profit on ordinary activities before tax		1,039
Taxation (405 + 81)		(486)
Profit on ordinary activities after tax		553
Minority interest (working)		10
Profit attributable to holding company shareholders		543
Dividends – paid	50	
– proposed	90	140
Retained profit		403
Balance b/f		748
Balance c/f		1,151

WORKING – MINORITY INTEREST		£
Profit after tax	10% × 106	11
Exchange losses	10% × (8)	(1)
		10

* Operating expenses include exchange loss of £8.

ANSWER 18.7 (ADVANCED)

Basil's cover

SOLUTION

(a) *Loan of 320 pesetas*
   (1) Individual accounts of Basil's Hotels:

    (i) without relief

– cost of investment	£84
– loan 31.12.X8 $\dfrac{P\ 320}{4}$	£80
31.12.X9 $\dfrac{P\ 320}{3.4}$	£94

       (translation loss of £14 charged to P/L)

    (ii) with relief
        – shares are denominated in foreign currency, i.e.

£84 × 7.1 =	P 596.4
31.12.X8 B/S $\dfrac{P\ 596.4}{4}$ =	£149.1
31.12.X9 B/S $\dfrac{P\ 596.4}{3.4}$ =	£175.4

        (translation gain = £26.3)
        – loan

31.12.X8 B/S (as above)	£80
31.12.X9 B/S (as above)	£94

        (translation loss = £14)
        – no effect on P/L account. Reserves credited with net gain of £12.3 (26.3 − 14.0).

  (2) Consolidated accounts:

    (i) without relief
        – 90% × exchange difference of £48 (see solution to closing rate question = £41 credit direct to consolidated reserves
        – loss on loan of £14 (charged to consolidated P/L).

    (ii) with relief

– exchange gain on retranslation of opening net investment 90% × £41	37
less: loss on loan	14
	23
– exchange gain on P/L translation 90% × £7	6
Credited direct to consolidated reserves	29

(b) *Loan of 2,060 pesetas*
   (1) Individual accounts of Basil's Hotels:

    (i)   without relief

	£
– cost of investment	84
– loan 31.12.X8 $\dfrac{P\ 1,060}{4}$	265
31.12.X9 $\dfrac{P\ 1,060}{3.4}$	312

       (translation loss of £47 charged to P/L).

    (ii) with relief
        – shares (as part (a))

31.12.X8 B/S	£149.1
31.12.X9 B/S	£175.4
(translation gain	£26.3)

        – loan

31.12.X8 B/S (as above)	265
31.12.X9 B/S (as above)	312

        (translation loss £47)

Per SSAP 20, gains/losses on borrowings may be offset only to extent of exchange differences on equity investments).

∴ Net loss of £20.7 (47.0 − 26.3) must be charged to P/L.

(2) Consolidated accounts:

   (i) without relief
- £41 exchange gain direct to reserves
- £47 loss on loan direct to consolidated P/L

   (ii) with relief

− exchange gain on retranslation of opening net investment 90% × £41	37
loss on loan	47
− net loss to be charged to consolidated P/L	10
− exchange gain on P/L translation (90% × 7) to be credited direct to consolidated reserves	6

ANSWER 19.1 (INTERMEDIATE)

Sandilands

WORKINGS

CPP		£
(i) Sales	1,200 × 116/108	1,289
	1,320 × 116/116	1,320
		2,609
(ii) Cost of sales	1,000 × 116/100	1,160
	1,100 × 116/108	1,181
		2,341

(iii) Fixed assets

Cost	1,000 × 116/100	1,160
Depreciation	10% × 1,160	116
		1,044

(iv) Monetary gains and losses

Gain on loan 500 × 116/100 − 500	80
Loss on monetary assets per summarised cash account	(8)
	72

(v) Total CPP profit (check)

Shareholders' funds at 1/1 restated for changes in purchasing power £1,500 × 116/100	1,740
Less shareholders funds at 31/12	1,914
∴ Total CPP profit	174

RC	£
(i) Cost of sales − replacement cost at date of sale	
30/6	1,100
31/12	1,200
	2,300
(ii) depreciation charge (year end RC) 10% × 1,300	130
(iii) fixed assets 1,300 − 10% × 1,300	1,170

(iv) replacement reserve
- realised holding gains (RC − HC) stock (cost of sales) 2,300 − 2,100   200

	£
Fixed assets (depreciation) 130 – 100	30
	230
– unrealised holding gains (RC NBV – HC NBV) (i.e. 1,170 – 900)	270
	500

SOLUTION

(a)1 Profit and loss accounts for year ended 31 December

	Historical cost (HC) £	Historical cost (HC) £	Current purchasing power (CPP) £	Current purchasing power (CPP) £	Replacement cost (RC) £	Replacement cost (RC) £
Sales		2,520		2,609		2,520
Purchases	3,300		3,541			
Less closing stock	1,200		1,200			
Cost of sales		2,100		2,341		2,300
Gross profit		420		268		220
Loan interest	50		50		50	
Depreciation	100	150	116	166	130	180
Net profit		270		102		40
Gain on long-term liability		—		80		—
Loss on short-term net monetary assets		—		(8)		—
		270		174		40

SOLUTION

2 Balance sheets at 31 December

	Historical cost (HC) £	Historical cost (HC) £	Current purchasing power (CPP) £	Current purchasing power (CPP) £	Replacement cost (RC) £	Replacement cost (RC) £
Tangible fixed assets						
Cost		1,000		1,160		1,300
Depreciation		100		116		130
		900		1,044		1,170
Current assets						
Stock	1,200		1,200		1,200	
Cash	170	1,370	170	1,370	170	1,370
		2,270		2,414		2,540
Loan		(500)		(500)		(500)
		1,770		1,914		2,040
Share capital		1,500		} 1,914		1,500
Profit and loss		270				40
Replacement reserve		—		—		500
		1,770		1,914		2,040

(b) Differences revealed by the three techniques

(1) HC reveals a profit of £270. This fails to take account of the increase in replacement costs of both stocks and fixed assets. HC also ignores the effect of inflation on monetary assets and liabilities. HC (unless modified by the incorporation of fixed asset values into the accounts) attempts only to protect the money amount of shareholders' equity. If the company were to distribute the whole of its HC profit (as it would be permitted to do by Companies Act 1985), capital would not be maintained intact in real terms.

(2) CPP reveals a profit of £174. The CPP model allows for general price increases (as reflected by

changes in the Retail Price Index) and requires shareholders capital to be maintained in purchasing power terms.
Total CPP profit is measured as follows:

Shareholders' funds (= net assets) at the end of the year stated in CPP terms
less
Shareholders' funds (= net assets) at the beginning of the year restated in terms of current purchasing power at the end of the year.
(allowance should be made for capital introduced during the year and dividend payments).

Total CPP profit has two elements:
(i) operating profit
(ii) monetary gains less losses.
During a period of inflation, the purchasing power of monetary assets such as cash is eroded. Conversely, the real burden of loan liabilities declines. While HC and RC ignore these, CPP takes them into account.
(3) RC (which exists in many different forms) attempts to maintain the operating capability of the business (the ability of the business to continue providing goods and services in the future). RC takes account of specific price changes of assets such as fixed assets and stock. RC is thus concerned with maintaining productive capacity as opposed to purchasing power of shareholders' funds.

ANSWER 19.2 (ADVANCED)

Martin (CPP)

WORKINGS

1 Translation and updating of balance sheet at 31.12.X4

	£ H	Factor	£ 31.12.X4	Factor	£ 31.12.X5
Fixed assets – cost	400	1.150	460		489
– depreciation	(120)	1.150	138		147
	280	1.150	322		342
Stocks	100	1.005	101		108
Debtors	140		140	1.064	149
Cash	191		191		203
Creditors	(70)	1.000	(70)		(75)
Dividends	(20)		(20)		(21)
Taxation	(17)		(17)		(18)
Debentures	(300)		(300)		(319)
	304		347		369
Shareholders' equity	304		347		369
	304		347		369

FACTORS
(a) *Translation*

Fixed assets $\dfrac{122.5}{106.5} = 1.150$

Stocks $\dfrac{122.5}{121.9} = 1.005$

(b) *Updating*

$\dfrac{130.4}{122.5} = 1.064$

2 Translation of balance sheet at 31.12.X5

	£ H	Factor	£ 31.12.X5
Fixed asset			
cost (19X2)	400	1.224	490
(19X5)	80	1.015	81
depn. (19X2)	(160)	1.224	(196)
(19X5)	(2)	1.015	(2)
Stocks	150	1.006	151
Debtors	160		160
Cash	124		124
Creditors	(80)		(80)
Dividends	(25)	1.000	(25)
Taxation	(20)		(20)
Debentures	(300)		(300)
	327		383
Shareholders' equity	327		383

TRANSLATION FACTORS

Fixed assets (19X2) $\dfrac{130.4}{106.5} = 1.224$

(19X5) $\dfrac{130.4}{128.5} = 1.015$

Stocks $\dfrac{130.4}{129.6} = 1.006$

3 Translation of detailed profit and loss account

	£ H	Factor	£ 31.12.X5
Sales	900	1.029	926
Opening stock	100	1.070	107
Purchases	690	1.029	710
	790		817
Closing stock	150	1.006	151
Cost of sales	640		666
Gross profit	260		260
Expenses	(126)	1.029	(130)
Depreciation (19X2)	(40)	1.224	(49)
Depreciation (19X4)	(2)	1.015	(2)
Interest payable	(24)	1.000	(24)
Tax	(20)	1.000	(20)
Dividends proposed	(25)	1.000	(25)
Retained profit for the year	23		10

TRANSLATION FACTORS

Sales etc. $\dfrac{130.4}{126.7} = 1.029$

Opening stock $\dfrac{130.4}{121.9} = 1.070$

Closing stock $\dfrac{130.4}{129.6} = 1.006$

Depreciation (19X2) $\dfrac{130.4}{106.5} = 1.224$

Depreciation (19X5) $\dfrac{130.4}{128.5} = 1.015$

4 Analysis of CPP profit

	£ *31.12.X5*
Total CPP profit	
Shareholders equity 31.12.X5	383
31.12.X4	369
	14
CPP retained profit per working (3)	10
Gain on net monetary items*	4
	14

* Calculated as a balancing figure, but reconciled below in working (5).

5 Reconciliation of gain in purchasing power

(a) *Long-term items – debentures*

	£ *31.12.X5*
Gain = 319 – 300	19

(b) *Short-term items*

	31.12.X5 £ H	*31.12.X4* £ H
Debtors	160	140
Cash	124	191
Current liabs.	(125)	(107)
	159	224

(c) *Reconciliation of movements on short-term items*

	£ H	Factor	£ *31.12.X9*
Short-term net monetary assets at 1.1.X5	224	1.064*	238
Sales	900	1.029	926
Purchases of goods	(690)	1.029	(710)
Expenses	(126)	1.029	(130)
Interest	(24)	1.000	(24)
Purchases of fixed assets	(80)	1.015	(81)
Dividends	(25)	1.000	(25)
Taxation	(20)	1.000	(20)
Short-term net monetary assets at 31.12.X5	159		174
Loss on short term net monetary assets (174 – 159)			15
Overall gain			4

* $\frac{130.4}{122.5}$

Summary of CPP profit

	£ *31.12.X9*
Profit after tax	35
Monetary gains – long term liabilities	19
Monetary losses – short-term net monetary assets	(15)
Dividends proposed	(25)
Total CPP profit	14

SOLUTION

Summary of results and financial position drawn up on a constant purchasing power basis

(a) *Results for the year*

	£ 19X5	£ 19X4
Sales	926	X
Profit before tax	59	X
Taxation	20	X
Profit after tax	39	X
Dividends	25	X
Retained profit for the year	14	X

Note: Profit before tax is after taking account of monetary gains on long-term liabilities of £19 less monetary loss on short-term net monetary assets of £15.

(b) *Financial position at end of year*

	£ 19X5	£ 19X4
Net current assets	310	342
Fixed assets less depreciation	373	346
	683	688
Less: debentures	300	319
Total equity interest	383	369

ANSWER 20.1 (INTERMEDIATE)

Golding

SOLUTION

(a) *Replacement cost balance sheet and profit and loss account*

1 Balance sheet at 31 December 19X3

	£	£
Fixed assets (7,000 − 700)		6,300
Stock (300 × £11)		3,300
Cash		12,600
		22,200
Creditors		(1,000)
		21,200
Shareholders' equity		
At 31.12.X2		8,000
Income for the year		
Operating income	9,400	
Holding gains	3,800	13,200
		21,200

2 Profit and loss account for the year ended 31 December 1983

	£
Sales	30,000
Replacement cost of sales	17,500
	12,500
Depreciation (10% × 7,000) – based on year-end costs	(700)
Other expenses	(2,400)
Operating income	9,400

Holding gains	£	£
(i) Realised		
– Stock (17,500 – 15,000)		2,500
– Fixed assets (700 – 600)		100
		2,600
(ii) Unrealised		
– Stock (3,300 – 3,000)	300	
– Fixed assets (6,300 – 5,400)	900	1,200
		3,800

(b) *Arguments for current entry value accounting*

The more usual term for current entry value accounting is replacement cost accounting. In the balance sheet, non-monetary assets are stated at replacement cost adjusted for, where appropriate, depreciation. The profit and loss or statement of total gains distinguishes between operating income (or gains) and holding gains.

The advantages of current entry value accounting include:

(1) the analysis of gains between operating income and holding gains provides useful information to those who wish to appraise a company's performance;
(2) operating income provides a far better guide than historical cost profit of the amount a business can distribute to shareholders without impairing its productive capacity;
(3) the replacement cost balance sheet offers an up-to-date measure of resources employed in the business;
(4) the profit and loss account indicates to what extent the business has maintained its operating capability.

ANSWER 20.2 (ADVANCED)

Martin (CCA)

WORKINGS

(1) *Fixed assets*

(a) B/S

	31.12.X4			31.12.X5		
	HC £		CC £	HC £		CC £
Cost (X2)	400	$\times \dfrac{236}{170}$	555	400	$\times \dfrac{266}{170}$	626
Cost (X5)	—		—	80	$\times \dfrac{266}{258}$	82
Dep (X2)	(120)	$\times \dfrac{236}{170}$	(166)	(160)	$\times \dfrac{266}{170}$	(250)
Dep (X5)	—		—	(2)	$\times \dfrac{266}{258}$	(2)
CC B/S			389			456
HC B/S			280			318
Gain on restatement			109			138

(b) P/L

Depreciation charge (year-end basis):

	HC £		CC £
X2 asset	40	$\times \dfrac{266}{170}$	63
X5 asset	2	$\times \dfrac{266}{258}$	2
	42		65

$\therefore$ Depreciation adjustment = 65 − 42 = <u>23</u>

(2) *Stocks*

(a) B/S

		31.12.X4		31.12.X5
CC B/S $100 \times \dfrac{129}{127}$	$=$	101	$150 \times \dfrac{142}{140}$	152
HC B/S		100		150
Gain on restatement		1		2

(b) P/L

Calculation of cost of sales adjustment (COSA) using averaging method:

	HC			Adjusted for cc
Opening stock	100	$\times$	$\dfrac{135}{127}$	106
Closing stock	150	$\times$	$\dfrac{135}{140}$	145
Increase (decrease)	50			39

COSA $=$ 50 (total change) $-$ 39 (volume change) $=$ 11

(3) *Monetary working capital*

Monetary working capital adjustment for P/L (MWCA) using averaging method and same indices as for stock:

	HC			Adjusted for cc
Opening MWC (140 − 70)	70	$\times$	$\dfrac{135}{127}$	74
Closing MWC (160 − 80)	80	$\times$	$\dfrac{135}{140}$	77
Increase (decrease)	10			3

MWCA $=$ 10 (total change) $-$ 3 (volume change) $=$ 7

(4) *Gearing adjustment (type 1)*

(a) Average net borrowing:

	19X4	19X5
Debentures	300	300
Tax	17	20
Cash	(191)	(124)
	126	196

AVERAGE 161

(b) Average shareholders' funds:

	19X4	19X5
Per HC acs.	304	327
Proposed divs.	20	25
Restatement from HC to CC		
− fixed assets	109	138
− stocks	1	2
Total	434	492

AVERAGE 463

(c) Gearing ratio $= \dfrac{\text{net borrowings}}{\text{net borrowings} + \text{S/hers' funds}} \times 100$

$= \dfrac{161}{161 + 463} \times 100 = 25.8\%$

(d) Current cost operating adjustments:

Dep. adjustment	23
COSA	11
MWCA	7
	41

∴ Gearing adjustment $= 25.8\% \times 41 = \underline{11}$

(5) *Gearing adjustment (type 2)*
  (a) Gearing ratio (as above) 25.8%
  (b) Adjustments (as above)   41
  Surpluses arising on restatement
  of assets to current costs
  – fixed assets (138 – 109)   29
  – stocks (2 – 1)   1
      71

∴ Gearing adjustment $= 25.8\% \times 71 = \underline{18}$

SOLUTION

Profit and loss account incorporating operating capital maintenance concept adjustments (including type 1 gearing adjustment)

	£	£
Turnover		900
Cost of sales		640
Gross profit		260
Expenses and depreciation		168
Profit before interest and tax on the historical cost basis		92
Less: current cost operating adjustments		
Cost of sales	11	
Monetary working capital	7	
Working capital	18	
Depreciation	23	41
Current cost operating profit		51
Gearing adjustment	(11)	
Interest payable	24	13
Current cost profit on ordinary activities before tax		38
Tax on profit on ordinary activities		20
Current cost profit for the financial year		18
Dividends proposed		25
Excess of dividends over retained profit		(7)

ANSWER 21.1 (BASIC)

Fozzie

SOLUTION

Source and application of funds statement for the year ended 31.12.X2

Source of funds	£	£
Profit before tax		231,000
Adjustment for items not involving movement of funds		
Depreciation		46,000
Total generated from operations		277,000
Funds from other sources		
Issue of shares		100,000
		377,000
Application of funds		
Dividends paid	83,000	
Tax paid	96,200	
Purchase of plant and machinery	60,000	
Repayment of loans	109,500	348,700
		28,300
Increase (decrease) in working capital)		
Increase in stocks	47,000	
Increase in debtors	3,100	
(Decrease) in creditors	1,500	
	51,600	
Movement in net liquid funds		
(Decrease) in bank balance	(23,300)	28,300

WORKINGS

(1)

Taxation ac			
Cash paid (bal. fig)	96,200	Bal. b/d	96,200
Bal. c/d	110,500	P/L ac.	110,500
	206,700		206,700

(2)

Dividends ac			
Cash paid (bal. fig.)	83,000	Bal. b/d	48,000
Bal. c/d	55,000	P/L	90,000
	138,000		138,000

ANSWER 21.2 (INTERMEDIATE)

Bamford

SOLUTION

Source and application of funds statement for the year ended 31 December 19X3

Sources of funds	£	£
Profit on ordinary activities before tax		760,000
Adjustment for items not involving the movement of funds		
depreciation	16,400	
profit on sale of fixed assets	(35,000)	(18,600)

	£	£
Total generated from operations		741,400
other sources		
disposal of property	125,000	
issue of shares	150,000	
		275,000
		1,016,400
Application of funds		
purchase of plant and machinery	81,800	
purchase of investments	200,000	
repayment of loans	170,000	
tax paid	230,000	
dividends paid	170,000	
		851,800
increase in working capital		164,600
increase in stocks	80,000	
increase in debtors	30,000	
increase in creditors	(14,000)	
		96,000
Increase in net liquid funds		
– cash at bank		68,600

WORKINGS

(1) freehold account

B/D	391	disposals	90
additions	0	C/D	301
	391		391

(2) plant & machinery

B/D	160.2	depreciation	16.4
additions		c/d	225.6
(bal. fig.)	81.8		
	242.0		242.0

(3) dividends

cash	170	b/d	90
(bal. fig.)			
C/D	120	P/L	200
	290		290

ANSWER 21.3 (ADVANCED)

Oxenholme

WORKINGS

(1) *Taxation account*

	£		£
P/I (extraord.)	23,400	Bal. B/d	98,250
cash (bal. fig.)	97,465	P/I (excl.	
Bal. c/d	146,300	assoc. co.)	168,915
	267,165		267,165

(2) *Investment grant suspense account*

	£		£
P/I	596	Bal. B/d	4,065
Bal. c/d	5,489	Cash (bal. fig.)	2,020
	6,085		6,085

(3) *Associated companies*

	£
Profit before tax (share)	11,075
Tax	4,225
	6,850
Retained profit (29,200 − 23,850)	5,350
∴ Dividends received	1,500

∴ Share of profits less dividends
  received = (11,075 − 1,500) = £9,575

(4) *Disposal of fixed assets*

	£
NBV of freehold (120,000 − 2,020)	117,980
NBV plant (67,200 − 25,080)	42,120
	160,100
Profit on sale (17,880 + 4,020)	21,900
Proceeds of sale	182,000

(5) *Minority interest at acquisition*
  10% × £70,250   7,025

(6) *Minority interest reconciliation*

	£		£
Cash paid	25,620	Bal. b/d OSC + res.	192,730
(bal. fig.)		divs.	12,120
Bal. c/d		P/L	49,760
OSC + res.	231,475	MI at acq.	7,025
divs.	18,940	Revaln.	
		20% × 72,000	14,400
	276,035		276,035

SOLUTION

(a) *Group source and application of funds statement for the year ended 31 December 19X2 – detailed breakdown method*

SOURCES OF FUNDS

Profit on ordinary activities before tax		386,420
Extraordinary loss before tax		(45,000)
		341,420
Adjustment for items not involving the movement of funds:		
Depreciation	19,270	
Amortisation of goodwill	7,500	
Amortisation of development costs	14,000	
Profit on disposal of fixed assets	(21,900)	
Release from deferred government grants	(596)	
Share of profits less dividends of assoc.	(9,575)	8,699
Total generated from operations		350,119
Funds from other sources:		
Proceeds of share issue	60,000	
Proceeds of disposal of tangible fixed assets	182,000	
Investment grant received	2,020	
Minority interest in new subsidiary	7,025	251,045
		601,164

Application of funds
  Dividends paid
    − minority shareholders   25,620
    − holding company shareholders   35,000
                                                                    60,620
  Tax paid   97,465
  Purchase of tangible fixed assets   196,020
  Purchase of goodwill on acquisition of a subsidiary   20,000
  Development costs incurred   30,000
  Loans to associated companies   15,000
                                                                                419,105
                                                                                182,059

Increase (decrease) in working capital
  Stocks   174,625
  Debtors and prepayments   55,687
  Creditors   (70,040)
                                                                                160,272
                                                                                 21,787

Movement in net liquid funds
  Cash balances   8,627
  Short-term investments   13,160
                                                                                 21,787

SUMMARY OF THE EFFECTS OF THE ACQUISITION OF SUBSIDIARY

Net assets acquired	£	*Discharged by*	£
Fixed assets	50,000	Shares issued	60,000
Goodwill	20,000	Cash paid	23,225
Stocks	22,100	Minority interest	7,025
Debtors	13,600		
Creditors	(15,450)		
	90,250		90,250

(b) *Group source and application of funds statement for the year ended 31 December 19X2 using the net outlay method*

Note: the key point is to feature the purchase of subsidiary (£83,225) as a one-line item. The first part of the statement is similar to (a) above and is this not reproduced below. All the items from fixed assets to creditors and MI need to be changed compared with the detailed breakdown method. Thus total sources are £594,139 (i.e. £601,164 − £7,025).

                                                                      £
Total sources   594,139

Application of funds
Dividends paid
  − MI   25,620
  − HC   35,000
                                                                    60,620
  Tax paid   97,465
  Purchase of tangible FA (196,020 − 50,000)   146,020
  Purchase of subsidiary   83,225
  Development costs   30,000
  Loans to assoc. cos.   15,000
                                                                                432,330
                                                                                161,809

In (dec.) in working capital
  Stocks (174,625 − 22,100)   152,525
  Debtors (55,687 − 13,600)   42,087
  Creditors (70,040 − 15,450)   (54,590)
                                                                                140,022
                                                                                 21,787

		£
Movement in net liquid funds		
Cash balances	8,627	
S/T inv.	13,160	21,787

Summary of effects . . . . (i.e. as for (a))

ANSWER 21.4 (ADVANCED)

Plural Publishers – funds flow

WORKINGS

(1) Establish group structure and changes during the year:
  (i) associated company (CST) from previous year
  (ii) partly-owned subsidiary (VH) acquired during year.
(2) Set out a pro-forma group funds flow statement (use detailed breakdown approach as no information about individual assets of VH acquired).
(3) Key workings:

	£
(i) *Acquisition of subsidiary*	
Shares 250,000 at £1.50	375,000
Cash	250,000
Total consideration	625,000
Net assets acquired	
80% × 575	460,000
∴ Goodwill (in B/S)	165,000

OSC increases by 250, SP by 125.

(ii) *Associated company*	
Share of profits	400
Share of tax	(150)
	250
Retained profit (per P/L and B/S comparison of investments 540 − 490)	50
∴ Divs. received	200

∴ Funds flow item 'share of profits less dividends received' is (400 − 200) i.e. 200

(iii) *Minority interest*	
At acquisition of new sub. 20% × 575	115
Share of loss (P/L) – note carefully!	(30)
Per closing B/S	85

(iv) *Divs*	
Balances B/D	745
P/L (450 + 800)	1,250
Cash (balancing figure)	(1,195)
Balances C/D	800

(v) *Tax*	
Balances B/D (1700 + 810 − 390)	2,120
P/L charge (excl. assoc. co.)	1,800
Cash (balancing figure)	(1,900)
Balances C/D (850 + 1640 − 470)	2,020

(vi) *Fixed assets*	
Balances B/D	5,685
Additions (balancing figure)	1,490
Disposals (NBV)	(75)
Depreciation charge	(700)
Balances C/D	6,400

Assumptions
(1) Tax on extraordinary items is not to be adjusted (no information regarding tax on this item).
(2) Goodwill is carried forward in B/S.
(3) Profit of 3,300 (per question) is after charging depreciation of 700 *and* crediting profit on sale of 25).

SOLUTION

Plural Publishers Group: statement of source and application of funds for the year ended 30 September 19X13
(based on the accounts of the group and showing the effects of acquiring Video Hire on the separate assets and liabilities of the group)

		£'000
Source of funds		
Profit before tax and extraordinary items		3,700
Extraordinary loss		(45)
		3,655
Adjustment of items not involving the movement of funds		
Depreciation	700	
Profit on sale of fixed assets	(25)	
Share of profits less dividends of associated company	(200)	475
Total generated from operations		4,130
Funds from other sources		
Shares issued in part consideration of the acquisition of Video Hire*	375	
Disposal of fixed assets	100	
Minority interest in Video Hire at date of acquisition	115	590
		4,720
Application of funds		
Dividends paid		
– holding company	1,195	
Tax paid	1,900	
Purchase of tangible fixed assets	1,490	
Purchase of goodwill on acquisition of Video Hire*	165	
Debentures redeemed	15	4,765
		(45)
Increase/decrease in working capital		
Increase in stocks	830	
Decrease in debtors	(550)	
Increase in creditors (excluding tax and dividends)	(140)	
	140	
Movement in net liquid funds		
Decrease in cash balance	(185)	(45)

* SUMMARY OF THE EFFECTS OF THE ACQUISITION OF VIDEO HIRE LTD

Net assets acquired	£,000	*Discharged by*	£'000
Fixed assets	X	Shares issued	375
Goodwill	165	Cash paid	250
Stocks	X		625
Debtors	X		
Creditors	(X)	Minority interest	115
(Check: 575 + 165)	740		740

ANSWER 21.5 (ADVANCED)

Plural Publishers – value added

WORKINGS PART (A)

	P	VH (80%)	CST (40%)
	£'000	£'000	£'000
TP	2,160	1,080	765
Dirs. emo.	(225)	(78)	(68)
Auditors	(58)	(7)	(4)
Depn.	(360)	(180)	(93)
Deb. int.	(60)	(5)	—
Operating profit	1,457	810	600
Assoc. co. share (40%)			240
Tax	(630)	(360) (40%)	(126)
Profit after tax	827	450	114
MI (20%)		(90)	
Divs. – VH (80%)	240	(240)	
– CST (40%)	60		(60)
Proposed dividends (P)	(900)		
Retained profits	227	120	54

∴ Total retained profits = 401

SOLUTION

(a) **Plural Publishers Group: statement of value added for the year ended 30 September 19X14**

	£'000	£'000	£'000
Turnover (17,280 + 7,560)			24,840
Bought-in materials, services and depreciation			
(10,368 + 4,158 + 3,430 + 936 + 58 + 7 + 360 + 180)			19,497
Net value added			5,343
Share of profits of associated company			
40% × (765 − 68 − 4 − 93)			240
Value added available for sharing			5,583

Applied as follows:

	£'000	£'000	£'000
To pay employees (1,322 + 1,386 + 225 + 78)		3,011	
To pay government (630 + 360 + 40% × 315)		1,116	
To pay providers of capital			
Interest on loans (60 + 5)	65		
Dividends to shareholders	900		
Minority interest	90	1,055	
To provide for expansion			
Retained profits		401	
			5,583

(b) Uses of a value-added statement to an existing shareholder:
  (1) The profit and loss account is a shareholder-orientated statement – it emphasises profits available for appropriation, earnings per share etc. Value added statements regard shareholders as members of a team comprising also employees, management and other providers of capital and thus gives less emphasis to the shareholders' position.
  (2) The value added statement is sometimes criticised as simply being a re-arrangement of the profit and loss account and one which may conceal certain key factors regarding the profitability of a business. For example, the statement does not reveal earnings per share.
  (3) Shareholders may regard the value added as a cake. The value added statement shows the

proportion of the cake taken by the various groups. For example, in the case above expressing each component as a percentage of value added available for sharing:

	%
Employees	53.9
Government	20.0
Providers of capital	18.9
Expansion	7.2
	100.0

Comparisons can be made with previous years in order to establish significant trends.
(4) Although value added statements are presented by a small minority of companies, some progressive companies such as Marks and Spencer (who present a statement of application of group sales revenue which although different in format is similar in principle to a value added statement) do feel that such statements are a useful supplement to 'traditional' statements.
(5) Statistics based on value added (for example, value added per employee) may be useful to shareholders, particularly if segmental information is available (for example, VA per employee by geographical areas).

(c) Alternative treatments:
   (i) *Minority interest.* The statement in (a) shows profits attributable to minority of 90 under providers of capital. Alternatively dividends of 60 (20% × 300) could be shown under this heading with the balance of 30 under providing for expansion.
   (ii) *Depreciation.* Depreciation could be included with retained profits under the overall caption 'providing for maintenance and expansion of assets'. This is less useful than the treatment suggested in (a) as fixed asset usage is just as much a charge in arriving at value added as is plant hire.

ANSWER 21.6 (ADVANCED)

Confectioners – value added

SOLUTION

a **Confectioners Ltd: value added statement for the year ended 31 December 19X3**

		£'000		£'000
		19X3		*19X2*
Turnover		3,536		2,492
Bought-in materials, services and depreciation		1,969		1,384
Net value added		1,567		1,108
Applied as follows:				
To pay employees		891		628
To pay government		224		240
To pay providers of capital				
Interest on loans	96		64	
Dividends	257	353	122	186
To provide for expansion				
(356 − 257)		99		
(176 − 122)				54
		1,567		1,108

WORKINGS

(1) Bought-in materials, services and depreciation (£'000):

	19X3	*19X2*
Turnover	3,536	2,492
Trading profit	868	608

	19X3	19X2
Operating expenses	2,668	1,884
Less wages and salaries	891	628
	1,777	1,256
Add depreciation	192	128
	1,969	1,384

b Five ratios derived from value added statement

	19X3	19X2	% change
(1) Sales per employee	$\dfrac{£3,536,000}{197}$ = £17,949	$\dfrac{£2,492,000}{143}$ = £17,426	+ 3.0%
(2) Value added per employee	$\dfrac{£1,567,000}{197}$ = £7,954	$\dfrac{£1,108,000}{143}$ = £7,748	+ 2.7%
(3) Value added as percentage of sales	$\dfrac{£1,567,000}{£3,536,000} \times 100$ = 44.3%	$\dfrac{£1,108,000}{£2,492,000} \times 100$ = 44.5%	Insignificant change
(4) Wages as percentage of value added	$\dfrac{£891,000}{£1,567,000} \times 100$ = 56.9%	$\dfrac{£628,000}{£1,108,000} \times 100$ = 56.7%	Insignificant change
(5) Value added as percentage of capital employed (shareholders' funds plus debentures)	$\dfrac{£1,567,000}{£4,535,000} \times 100$ = 34.5%	$\dfrac{£1,108,000}{£3,276,000} \times 100$ = 33.8%	+ 2.1%

Comments
(1) Sales per employee show an increase in money terms but a reduction in real terms (the RPI increased during the year by 10%).
(2) Value added per employee – similar comments to (1).
(3) Value added as percentage of sales – no significant change. Comparisons could be made with similar businesses.
(4) Wages as percentage of value added – no signs that employees are obtaining a larger slice of the cake. Employees would be particularly interested in this ratio. Some users regard this ratio as an indicator of labour productivity.
(5) Value added as percentage of capital employed – an improvement in what some regard as a measure of capital productivity.

ANSWER 21.7 (INTERMEDIATE)

Additional statements

ANSWER GUIDE

(a) Possible additional statements of assistance to employees are:

(1) value added statement
(2) employment report

(other possibilities which might be relevant: simplified financial statements, segmental information over and above statutory requirements).

(1) *Value added statement*
Shows wealth created by entity and application of wealth among its contributors (employees, providers of capital etc).
(i) turnover

(ii) bought-in materials, services and depreciation
(iii) value added
(iv) employees' (including directors') wages and salaries
(v) interest on loans
(vi) dividends
(vii) taxation
(viii) amount reinvested.
Usual to show comparatives and possible applications as percentage of value added.

(2) *Employment report*
(i) numbers of persons employed, changes during year, analysis male/female, full-time/part-time, location, function
(ii) location of centres of work
(iii) unions recognised
(iv) hours lost through illness, dispute
(v) training details
(vi) employee pension information

(b) Usefulness of statements:

(1) *Value added statement*
(i) puts profits into perspective i.e. shows contributions of those groups that help to create value added. Percentage changes (applications as percentage of value added) may highlight areas for investigation;
(ii) drawback – lack of standardisation of format and measurement of items; only presented by small minority of companies;
(iii) criticism of diverting away from 'true' profitability which is essential for long-term survival of a business.

(2) *Employment report*
(i) gives employees additional useful, non-statutory information;
(ii) recognises the key role that employees play in an organisation;
(iii) drawbacks are lack of standardisation, possibility employers may omit details not considered in a company's interest.

ANSWER 22.1 (BASIC)

Portishead

SOLUTION

Earnings = £895,000 − 30,000 = 865,000

Number of shares = 4 million

$\therefore$ EPS = $\dfrac{£865,000}{4 \text{ million}}$ = 21.6 pence per share

ANSWER 22.2 (INTERMEDIATE)

Orbison

SOLUTION

(1) Basic *EPS*

EPS = $\dfrac{£107,000}{400,000}$ = 26.7 pence per share

(2) *Fully diluted EPS* (FDEPS)

Earnings	£
– per basic calculation	107,000
– notional interest saving	
(net of corporation tax)	8,000
	115,000

Shares	
– per basic	400,000
– maximum number issuable in future	100,000
	500,000

So FDEPS $= \dfrac{£115,000}{500,000} = 23$ pence per share

Note: FDEPS would be disclosed as the effect of the dilution is material (a dilution of greater than 5% of basic EPS).

ANSWER 22.3 (INTERMEDIATE)

Earnings per share

SOLUTION

(a) The earnings per share statistic represents a measure of profits attributable to each share. The statistics can be used directly and indirectly. Shareholders can make a direct comparison of EPS this year with the previous year figure for the same company and thus evaluate the performance of their shares.

In addition, EPS can be used to calculate the price earnings ratio (P/E) thus enabling investors to make comparisons between different companies in the same industrial/commercial sectors. In theory this should indicate a particular company's standing in relation to the sector as a whole.

Earnings should be based on profit after tax, minority interest and preference dividends but before extraordinary items. Where a company has cumulative preference shares, the dividend for the period should be taken into account, whether or not it has been earned or declared. Preference dividend arrears paid during the year should be ignored.

(b) For some companies the size of the dividend payments may affect the total corporation tax paid. The net basis takes earnings after deducting the actual tax charge which may include irrecoverable advance corporation tax.

The nil basis uses a hypothetical tax charge calculated on the assumption that no dividends are paid during the year.

The advantage of the nil basis is that it produces an earnings figure which is not dependent on the level of a company's dividends. Proponents of this method argue that it provides a more useful indicator of a company's actual performance.

As against this, the advantage of the net method is that it takes all relevant facts into account including the tax consequences of a company's dividend policy. For this reason the net basis is the basis used and preferred by SSAP 3.

(c) (i) Equity shares not ranking for dividend in the period under review but ranking in the future – the company should calculate and publish the fully diluted EPS in addition to publishing the basic EPS. This calculation is based on the assumption that the new shares ranked for dividend from the beginning of the period.

(ii) A scrip (or bonus) issue of shares during the year – current year EPS is based on the new share capital. Comparative EPS should be restated as though the previous year calculation had been based on the new share capital.

(iii) Shares issued during the period as consideration for shares in a new subsidiary – EPS for current year should be calculated on the basis that the new securities were issued on the first day of the accounting period in which the new subsidiary's profits were included for the first time.

(d) Rights issue calculation for 19X3:

  (i) calculate theoretical ex rights price (TERPs) consider holder of 100 shares

					£
before	100	shares	× £2		200
rights	50	"	× £1.50		75
	150				275

$$\text{TERPs} = \frac{£275}{150} = 183.3 \text{ pence}$$

  (ii) earnings for 19X3 £750,000

  (iii) number of shares for EPS calculation

$$1.1. \times 3 - 30.6.X3 \quad 3 \text{ million} \times \frac{200p}{183.3p} = 3.27 \text{ million}$$

$$1.7. \times 3 - 31.12.X3 \qquad\qquad\qquad 4.5 \text{ million}$$

$$\text{Average for year} = (^6\!/_{12} \times 3.27) + (^6\!/_{12} \times 4.5)$$
$$= 3,885$$

$$\therefore \text{EPS} = \frac{£750,000}{3.885m} = 19.3 \text{ pence per share}$$

ANSWER 22.4 (ADVANCED)

Sandgrit

SOLUTION

(a) *EPS for 19X1 on net basis*

Earnings per share for year ended 31 December 19X2 disclosed on face of profit and loss account:

40 pence per share

Note to accounts: the calculation of earnings per share is based on earnings of £597,320 and a weighted average number of shares in issue of 14,804,344. Comparative figures for 19X1 have been adjusted to reflect the effect of the rights issue.

WORKINGS

(1) Earnings	£
Profit after tax	716,320
Less preference dividends 7% × 1,700,000	119,000
	597,320

(2) Number of ordinary shares

  (i) Effect of rights issue: Assume that the ex rights price of 30.6p is a suitable approximation for the theoretical ex rights price.

  (ii) Calculating a weighted average of the number of shares in issue throughout the year:

	Number
1 Jan – 31 May $^5\!/_{12} \times \dfrac{33.0p}{30.6p} \times 11,534$	5,182,761
1 June – 30 June $^1\!/_{12} \times (11,534 + 4,943)$	1,373,083
1 July – 31 Dec $^6\!/_{12} \times 16,497$	8,248,500
	14,804,344

$$. \ . \ \text{EPS} = \frac{£597,320}{14,804,344} = 4.0 \text{ pence per share}$$

(b) *Nil basis*

The 'nil distribution' basis of calculating earnings per share is based on a tax charge assuming hypothetically a nil dividend. The net basis takes account of all elements of the tax charge (those which are constant as well as those variable elements which vary with dividend payments) whereas the nil basis takes account of constant elements only. The nil basis thus excludes any irrecoverable ACT. The nil distribution permits an EPS comparison between different companies which is not distorted as a result of differing dividend policies.

(c) *EPS and smaller quoted companies*

Earnings per share is useful as a statistic in its own right, permitting a comparison within a company between this year and last year. More importantly, for quoted companies, it leads to a wider-used statistic, the price earnings ratio which expresses quoted price per share as a multiple of EPS. P/E ratios provide a useful yardstick of comparison between different companies in the same industrial or commercial sector. EPS is thus less relevant for small unquoted companies since a meaningful share price is rarely available.

In addition, family companies may pursue different directors remuneration/dividend policies purely for tax reasons. For some companies, therefore, earnings (being based on profit after tax) may not be a meaningful figure.

ANSWER 22.5 (ADVANCED)

Toff

SOLUTION

As the question requires only the amounts to be disclosed (i.e. on the face of the P/L ac), the descriptive note of the basis of calculation of EPS is not required:

Earnings per share:
- basic   80.9 pence per share
- fully diluted   56.3 pence per share

WORKINGS

a BASIC EPS

(1) *Earnings*	£'000
PAT before extraords	2,809
Less preference dividends	(100)
	2,709

(2) *Number of shares*

    (i) Effect of rights issue – bonus element:

        Theoretical ex rights price

$$\frac{(100 \times 50p) + (25 \times 40p)}{125} = 48p$$

        (Assumption: the Appendix to SSAP 3 refers to the theoretical ex rights price. The actual ex rights price has therefore been ignored.)

    (ii) Weighted average number of shares (allowing for 1:2 scrip):

1 July to 31 March	*Number*
Before adjusting for rights issue	
$^{9}/_{12} \times (2,000 \times ^{3}/_{2}) = 2,250$	
Allowing for bonus element	
$2,250 \times {}^{50}/_{48}$	2,343.75
1 April to 30 April	
$^{1}/_{12} \times (3,000 \times ^{5}/_{4})$	312.50
1 May to 30 June	
$^{2}/_{12} \times (3,750 + 400)$	691.67
Weighted average number of shares	3,347.92

(3) .. basic EPS $= \dfrac{£2,709,000}{3,347,920} = 80.9$ pence

b Fully diluted EPS

(1) *Adjusted to terms of option as a result of subsequent scrip or rights issues*

   (i) option price must be adjusted:
   40p $\times \frac{2}{3}$ (bonus) $\times \frac{48}{50}$ (scrip) $= 25.6$p

   (ii) number of option shares must be adjusted:
   $1,000 \times \frac{3}{2} \times \frac{50}{48} = 1,562,000$

(2) *Earnings*

Per basic calculation		2,709,000
Options actually exercised		
$10.6\% \times \frac{10}{12} \times 400,000 \times 25.6$p	9,045	
Options unexercised		
$10.6\% \times (1,562,500 - 400,000) \times 25.6$p	31,546	
	40,591	
Less: corporation tax at 50%	20,296	20,296
Fully diluted earnings		2,729,296

(3) *Number of shares*

Per basic calculations	3,347,920
Add option rights (as though exercised at beginning of period)	
Exercised $\frac{10}{12} \times 400,000$	333,333
Unexercised $(1,562,500 - 400,000)$	1,162,500
	4,843,753

(4) *Fully diluted EPS*
$= \dfrac{£2,729,296}{4,843,753} = 56.3$ pence

ANSWER 23.1 (INTERMEDIATE)

Hendale Contractors

ANSWER GUIDE

Key ratios	*19X6*	*19X5*
Return on capital employed	$\dfrac{221,000}{833,000} \times 100$	$\dfrac{361,000}{787,000} \times 100$
	= 26.5%	= 45.9%
$\dfrac{\text{Gross profit}}{\text{sales}}$	$\dfrac{364}{1,800} \times 100$	$\dfrac{501}{1,670} \times 100$
	= 20.2%	= 30.0%
$\dfrac{\text{Operating profit}}{\text{sales}}$	$\dfrac{221,000}{1,800,000} \times 100$	$\dfrac{361,000}{1,670,000} \times 100$
	= 12.3%	= 21.6%
$\dfrac{\text{Sales}}{\text{Capital employed}}$	$\dfrac{1,800,000}{833,000}$	$\dfrac{1,670,000}{787,000}$
	= 2.2 times	= 2.1 times
$\dfrac{\text{Sales}}{\text{Fixed assets}}$	$\dfrac{1,800}{526}$	$\dfrac{1,670}{395}$
	= 3.4 times	= 4.3 times
$\dfrac{\text{Sales}}{\text{Net current assets}}$	$\dfrac{1,800}{307}$	$\dfrac{1,670}{392}$
	= 5.9 times	= 4.3 times

	19X6	19X5
$\dfrac{\text{Overhead expenses}}{\text{Sales}}$	$\dfrac{143,000}{1,800,000} \times 100$	$\dfrac{140,000}{1,670,000} \times 100$
	= 7.9%	= 8.4%
Cost of sales per day	£3,934	£3,203
Stocks (days sales)	$\dfrac{407,000}{3,934}$	$\dfrac{221,000}{3,203}$
	= 103 days	= 69.0 days
Debtors (days sales)	$\dfrac{283,000}{4,931}$	$\dfrac{267,000}{4,575}$
	= 57.4 days	= 58.4 days
$\dfrac{\text{Current assets}}{\text{Current liabilities}}$	$\dfrac{698,000}{391,000}$	$\dfrac{798,000}{406,000}$
	= 1.8	= 1.9
$\dfrac{\text{Liquid assets}}{\text{Current liabilities}}$	$\dfrac{291,000}{391,000}$	$\dfrac{577,000}{406,000}$
	$= \dfrac{0.74}{1}$	$= \dfrac{1.42}{1}$
Gearing (debt/ debt + equity)	$\dfrac{150}{833} \times 100$	$\dfrac{150}{787} \times 100$
	= 18.0%	= 19.1%

Factors causing concern:
(1) drastic reduction in return on capital employed
(2) reduction in profitability of each items sold and reasons for this reduction (sales mix change, reduced selling prices etc.)
(3) rapid increase in stocks and possible need to realise at a low price
(4) extremely poor liquidity situation.

Information needed:
(1) nature of extraordinary item – is it a one-off?
(2) profit and cash forecasts for next twelve months
    – establish whether deterioration in profitability and liquidity is temporary or continuing
(3) reasonableness of property valuation
(4) other factors:
    (a) market prospects for sales of product, changes in competition from rivals
    (b) reasons why directors wish to sell their shares
    (c) other prospective purchasers of shares.

ANSWER 23.2 (INTERMEDIATE)
Financial terms

SOLUTION

A. D Viser & Co
15 Grand Street
Medport
Lowshire

5 March 19X8

D. R. Wilson, Esq.
Managing Director
Fig plc
Unit 6
High Trading Estate
Goswell
Lowshire

Dear Mr Wilson

Thank you for your recent letter referring to certain extracts from the *Financial Times*. I set out my explanations below:

(1) *Ordinary shares quoted in the Financial Times*
   (i) Price – the price is usually quoted in pence per share and represents the mid-market price quoted by buyers and sellers at the close of business.
   (ii) + or – shows the change in closing price compared with the closing price at the end of the previous day's trading.
   (iii) Dividend net – this represents the rate of dividend and is usually expressed as pence per share, representing the cash which will actually be received by the shareholder.
      For example, if a shareholder receives a dividend of £73 this is regarded for tax purposes as £100 gross (assuming income tax at 27%) with a tax credit of £27 attaching.
   (iv) Cover – this expresses profit after tax as a multiple of the dividend payment.
   (v) Yield gross – this expresses dividend per share, based on latest set of accounts and grossed up at the rate of income tax, as a percentage of the quoted share price.
   (vi) P/E – this refers to price/earnings ratio and expresses quoted price per share as a multiple of earnings per share based on the company's most recently published earnings.

(2) *Extracts from quotations page*
   (i) Net distribution basis and nil distribution basis: – in some circumstances the total tax liability of a company may vary according to the level of its dividend payments. Earnings on a 'net' basis reflect the company's actual tax charge. Earnings on a 'nil' basis are based on a hypothetical tax charge assuming a nil level of dividends.
      Statement of Standard Accounting Practice 3 (SSAP 3) on earnings per share requires listed companies to publish earnings per share on a 'net' basis. In addition, earnings per share on a 'nil' basis should also be published in the annual accounts if materially different from earnings per share calculated on the net basis. Thus bracketed figures referred to in the extract relate to companies whose tax charge is significantly affected by the level of dividend payments.
   (ii) Dividend cover – this indicates the number of times a dividend is covered by earnings available to pay dividends. Dividend cover reflects a margin of safety, for example a company whose dividend is covered 3 times may subsequently experience a fall in earnings to half the level of the current year. Cover would still be 1.5 times (assuming the same level of dividend) and the dividend could be paid out of current year profits without resorting to profits of previous years.
      As indicated above, a company's dividend level may on occasions significantly affect the company's tax charge. Maximum distribution cover is based on earnings which reflect the tax charge assuming the company pays the maximum distribution out of current year profits. Cover is then calculated by expressing the earnings per share measured on this maximum distribution basis as a multiple of dividend per share.

(3) *Sources of information*
   (a) daily share price of London quoted companies – this is given in the Stock Exchange Official List. Share price information is also available from several commercial data sources;
   (b) recent dividends and rights issues of UK listed companies – this is available from the Stock Exchange as well as commercial sources such as Extel;
   (c) copies of financial statements – for public companies. This information can be obtained direct from the companies themselves. For all companies, Companies House keep records of filed financial statements.

I hope the above provides the information which you require, but do please contact me if you require further information.

Yours sincerely,

R. A. Jones

ANSWER 23.3 (ADVANCED)

Hopeful Booksellers Ltd

ANSWER GUIDE

(a) *Points to be referred to in report interpreting inter-firm comparison*
   (1) Return on capital (net profit/operating assets) is very low compared with group average. Possible causes:
      (i) low profit percentage
      (ii) low asset utilisation.
   (2) Profit percentage: GP/sales and NP/sales are 50% above industry average
   (3) Assets utilisation – very low sales/operating assets compared with industry average
      (i) sales/fixed assets – low
      (ii) sales/current assets – low.
   (4) Sales per unit of area – good compared with average.
   (5) Fixed assets per unit of area – high.
   (6) Stock turnover – low.
   (7) High overheads in relation to sales.
   (8) High rent and rates in relation to sales (possibly expensive sites).
   (9) Product mix – concentration on retail sales (with high GP%) as against library sales. Result – good gross profit margins.

(b) *Questions to be put to directors*
   (1) Stocks – reasons for low stock turnover compared with industry average
      (i) 5 year trend
      (ii) control over budgets and purchasing
      (iii) stock control
      (iv) analysis of stock turnover by different products.
   (2) Rents – scope for less expensive premises? When does lease end?
   (3) Premises – is space properly utilised?
   (4) Fixed assets – effectively utilised?
   (5) Overheads – scope for economies?

ANSWER 23.4 (ADVANCED)

Olympic Group

ANSWER GUIDE

(a) *Opening*
   (1) Addressee
   (2) Recipient
   (3) Date
   (4) Title of report
   (5) Nature of businesses not directly comparable
      (i) Walkers – manufacture and sale of sports equipment
      (ii) Runners – manufacture and sale of sports clothing

(b) *Ratios*

	Walkers Ltd		Runners Ltd	
	19X6	*19X5*	*19X6*	*19X5*
(1) Return on capital employed	16.7%	12.0%	24.7%	33.8%
(2) Gross profit margin	15.0%	19.9%	34.1%	32.9%
(3) Asset ratios				
(i) stock turnover (days)	88.6	121.4	58.1	88.5
(ii) debt collection (days)	55.6	69.2	217.0	165.8
(4) Liquidity ratio	0.6	0.5	1.3	1.5

(c) *Walkers Ltd*
  (1) Return on capital:
      (i) significant improvement compared with last year in spite of worsening in gross profit percentage
      (ii) likely increase in efficiency with which assets generate sales (note improvement in stock turnover and debt collection)
      (iii) is return of 16.7% too low for this type of business?
  (2) Profitability:
      (i) reduction in gross profit percentage. Possibilities:
          – less cost-effective production methods
          – sales prices increase less than costs increase (market forces?)
          – change in sales mix
      (ii) is margin too low for this type of business?
      (iii) note also reduction in other costs
          – reasons?
          – effect of reduced loan/overdraft interest?
  (3) Asset management:
      (i) dramatic improvement in stock turnover
      (ii) modest improvement in debt collection
      (iii) increased sales despite reduction in fixed assets.
  (4) Liquidity:
      (i) ratio very low compared with 'rule of thumb' 1:1
      (ii) slight improvement – reduction in O/D
      (iii) classification of whole overdraft as 'current'.

(d) *Runners Ltd*
  (1) Return on capital:
      (i) percentage is fairly high but significant worsening compared with previous year, in spite of improvement in GP percentage
      (ii) area to investigate – asset utilisation (particularly debtors).
  (2) Profitability:
      (i) gross profit seems reasonable and shows improvement compared with last year
      (ii) significant increase in other costs, affecting net profit (? possible reasons – bad debts, higher interest charges).
  (3) Asset management:
      (i) significant improvement in stock turnover
      (ii) considerable deterioration in debt collection (possible danger of bad debts?)
  (4) Liquidity:
      (i) overall ratio seems reasonable
      (ii) slight deterioration compared with last year
      (iii) debtors' position should be investigated (62% increase in money terms).

(e) *General comments*
  Information is not available regarding profitability and performance of comparable businesses, nor of the degree of competition (and thus scope for sales price increases) in the respective trades. Inter-firm comparison information would provide critical yardsticks with which to appraise the two companies.

Tutorial note
A problem with this type of open-ended question is how to restrict the time to answer the question to approximately 30 minutes. The choice of *four* particular ratios is not an easy one (the answer gives *five* in order to give a broader picture. Another possibility would be net profit/sales).

WORKINGS

	Walkers Ltd		Runners Ltd	
	19X6	19X5	19X6	19X5
(1) Return on capital employed (PBT/cap + res + L/T)	$\dfrac{2.1}{12.6}$	$\dfrac{1.4}{11.7}$	$\dfrac{1.9}{7.7}$	$\dfrac{2.3}{6.8}$
	= 16.7%	= 12.0%	= 24.7%	= 33.8%

	Walkers Ltd		Runners Ltd	
	19X6	*19X5*	*19X6*	*19X5*
(2) Gross profit margin	6.8	7.6	5.8	4.6
(turnover – cos/turnover)	45.2	38.1	17.0	14.0
	= 15.0%	= 19.9%	= 34.1%	= 32.9%
(3) (i) Stock turnover	9.3	10.2	1.8	2.3
(stock/cos per day)	0.105	0.084	0.031	0.026
	= 88.6	= 121.4	= 58.1	= 88.5
(ii) Debt collection period	6.9	7.2	10.2	6.3
(debtors/sales per day)	0.124	0.104	0.047	0.038
	= 55.6	= 69.2	= 217	= 165.8
(4) Liquidity ratio	6.9	7.2	10.2	6.3
(Debtors + cash/creditors + O/D)	11.9	14.9	7.8	4.3
	= 0.6	= 0.5	= 1.3	= 1.5

ANSWER 24.1 (INTERMEDIATE)

International Standards

SOLUTION

(a) The objectives of the International Accounting Standards Committee include:

(1) formulating and publishing accounting standards and promoting their world-wide acceptance and observance;
(2) working for the improvement and harmonisation of regulations, accounting standards and procedures relating to the presentation of financial statements.

The obligations of the members in support of these objectives include:

(1) publishing international standards in members' own countries;
(2) ensuring that published financial standards comply with international standards;
(3) persuading governments, standard setting bodies and Stock Exchanges to give backing to compliance with international standards;
(4) ensuring that auditors satisfy themselves that published financial statements comply with international standards.

(b) Difficulties that arise from the existence of two sets of standards include:

(1) in drafting SSAPs, the Accounting Standards Committee takes account of UK law and practice. IASC have to take account of laws and practices of all member countries;
(2) the possibility that an international standard may conflict with a UK standard. In 1987 IASC announced that a new steering committee had been set up to consider whether alternative accounting treatments allowed by international standards could be eliminated or some preferences indicated. This may have implications at some future date.

(c) Steps taken to reconcile the demands of the two sets of Standards include:

(1) an objective of IASC is to harmonise as far as possible the diverse accounting standards and accounting policies of different countries;
(2) IASC will concentrate on essentials and not make International Standards so complex that they cannot be effectively applied on a worldwide basis;
(3) International Standards do not override local regulations. Where there is apparent conflict local members of IASC will try to persuade the relevant authorities of the benefits of harmonisation.

ANSWER 25.1 (INTERMEDIATE)

Ender

SOLUTION

a Journal entries

		Dr £	Cr £
(1)	Unsecured loan stock	60,000	
	Ordinary share capital		45,000
	Share premium		15,000

Issue of 90,000 ordinary shares as a result of conversion of £60,000 unsecured loan stock

		Dr £	Cr £
(2)	Bank	51,000	
	Investments		47,000
	Profit and loss account		4,000

Sales of investments to help finance redemptions of preference shares

		Dr £	Cr £
(3)	Bank	103,350	
	Ordinary share capital		
	(1,590,000 × 1/10 × 50p)		79,500
	Share premium		23,850

One for ten rights issue at 65p per share

		Dr £	Cr £
(4)	Preference shares	200,000	
	Profit and loss account	30,000	
	Bank		230,000

Redemption of preference shares at premium of 15p per share

		Dr £	Cr £
(5)	Share premium account	8,000	
	Bank account		8,000

Expenses of rights issue

		Dr £	Cr £
(6)	Profit and loss account	88,075	
	Capital redemption reserve		88,075

Transfer to capital redemption reserve

WORKING

	£
Nominal value redeemed	200,000
Proceeds of new issue (103,350 − 8,000)	95,350
∴ Transfer to CRR	104,650

(Assumption – proceeds of new issue is net of issue expenses).

b Summarised balance sheet after completion of the above matters

	£
Other assets, less liabilities	1,193,200
Less bank overdraft	(8,850)
	1,184,350
Less convertible loan stock	(170,000)
	1,014,350
Called up share capital – 50p ordinary shares	874,500
Share premium account	30,850
Profit and loss account	20,925
Capital redemption reserve	88,075
	1,014,350

WORKINGS

(1) *Cash at bank*

	£
Balance B/F	74,800
Proceeds of sale of investments	51,000
Rights issue	103,350
Expenses of issue	(8,000)
Redemption of shares	(230,000)
Bank overdraft	(8,850)

(2) *Ordinary share capital*

Balance B/F	750,000
Rights issue	79,500
Conversion of loan stock	45,000
	874,500

(3) *Share premium account*

Rights issue	23,850
Expenses of issue	(8,000)
Conversion of loan stock	15,000
	30,850

(4) *Profit and loss reserves*

Per summarised B/S	135,000
Profit on sale of investments	4,000
Premium on redemption of shares	(30,000)
Transfer CRR	(88,075)
	20,925

ANSWER 25.2 (ADVANCED)

Strawberry

WORKINGS AND SOLUTION

(1) *Strawberry plc*

Under the Companies Act 1985, shares may be purchased out of distributable reserves, the proceeds of a fresh issue or a combination of the two. Assuming that the purpose of the new share issue is to help finance the purchase:

	£
Nominal value purchased	20,000
Proceeds of new issue	13,000
∴ Transfer to capital redemption reserve (out of distributable reserves)	7,000

As this transfer is covered comfortably by distributable profits, the transaction is permitted.

Journal entries

	Dr £	Cr £
Cash	13,000	
Called up capital		13,000
Called up capital	20,000	
Cash		18,000
Profit and loss account		2,000
Profit and loss account	7,000	
Capital redemption reserve		7,000

Shareholders' funds after completing the above transactions

	£'000
Called up share capital (500 + 13 − 20)	493
Reserves – revaluation	100
– profit and loss account (300 + 2 − 7)	295
– capital redemption	7
	895

(2) *Greengage plc*

	£'000
Nominal value purchased	100,000
Proceeds of new issue	130,000

∴ No transfer to capital redemption reserve is required. Clearly the transaction is permitted.

The shares are being purchased at a premium. Share premium account may be utilised provided that the shares to be purchased were originally issued at a premium and provided there is a fresh issue of shares. Both these conditions are satisfied. The amount of share premium account which may be used is restricted to the lower of:

(i) Aggregate of premiums originally received on the issue of shares which are now being purchased, and   £10,000

(ii) present balance on share premium account including premium on fresh issue (20 + 30)   £50,000

i.e. *£10,000*. The balance of the premium on purchase (50 − 10 = 40) must come out of P/L.

Journal entries

Cash	130,000	
Called up share capital		100,000
Share premium account		30,000
Called up share capital	100,000	
Share premium	10,000	
Profit and loss account (50 − 10)	40,000	
Cash		150,000

Shareholders' fund

	£'000
Called up share capital (200 + 100 − 100)	200
Share premium account (20 + 30 − 10)	40
Profit and loss account (50 − 40)	10
	250

(3) *Peach Ltd*

The nominal value redeemed (£1,000) is not covered by the total of proceeds of fresh issue (£850) and profit and loss account (£50). However Peach Ltd is a private company. Subject to certain stringent conditions, a private company may make a purchase of shares out of capital. The transaction therefore may be permitted. The permissible capital payment (PCP) is determined as follows:

	£	£
Purchase cost		1,100
Proceeds of fresh issue	850	
Profit and loss account	50	900
∴ PCP		200

Comparing nominal value purchased (1,000) with total of proceeds of fresh issue and PCP (850 +

200 = 1,050): no transfer to capital redemption reserve is required. The excess of 50 may be used to reduce share premium account (which then becomes (500 − 50 = 450)).

Journal entries

Cash	850	
Called up share capital		850
Called up share capital	1,000	
Share premium account (see above)	50	
Profit and loss account	50	
Cash		1,100

Shareholders' funds

	£
Called up share capital (5,000 + 850 − 1,000)	4,850
Share premium account	450
Profit and loss account	—
	5,300

(4) *Plum Ltd*

Clearly there is no problem with this transaction in view of the size of Plum Ltd's distributable reserves.

Nominal value purchased	1,000
Proceeds of fresh issue	850
∴ Transfer to capital redemption reserve	150

The premium on purchase may come out of share premium account subject to the following limit:

Lower of:
(i) aggregate of premiums originally received
    on shares to be purchased, *and*   500

(ii) balance on share premium account including
    premium on fresh issue   850

i.e. 500

∴ Balance on SP becomes (500 + 350 − 500) i.e. 350

Journal entries

Cash	850	
Called up share capital		500
Share premium account		350
Called up share capital	1,000	
Share premium account	500	
Profit and loss account (600 − 500)	100	
Cash		1,600
Profit and loss account	150	
Capital redemption reserve		150

Shareholders' funds

Called up share capital (2,000 + 500 − 1,000)	1,500
Share premium account	350
Profit and loss account (5,000 − 100 − 150)	4,750
Capital redemption reserve	150
	6,750

(5) *Raspberry plc*

The distributable profits of £40,000 are insufficient to cover the purchase cost. The subsequent issue of shares purchased must be ignored as it occurs at a later date. The transaction is therefore not permitted.

ANSWER 25.3 (INTERMEDIATE)

Popular Furnishings
ANSWER GUIDE
a Considerations to be taken into account by loan stock holders

(1) If co. liquidates	£'000	£'000
Offices and showrooms		350
Factory and warehouse		230
Plant and machinery		125
Motor vehicles		120
Stock		150
Debtors		128
		1,103
Floating charge	520	
Liquidation costs	90	610
Available for unsecured creditors		493

Settlement:	Liabilities	(66p in £)
Loan stock		
Principal	400	
Interest	40	
	440	289
Creditors	310	204
	750	493

(Settlement = 493/750 = 66p in £)

(2) If scheme accepted:
(i) floating charge
(ii) interest £56,000 compared with £40,000
(iii) equity stake with votes/share of future prosperity
(iv) cash required to subscribe for rights issue.

Key point: how do loan stock holders assess future prospects of company?

b Journal entries

	Dr £'000	Cr £'000
(1) OSC (£1 shares)	300	
OSC (10p shares)		30
Capital reduction account		270
(2) PSC (£1 shares)	100	
OSC (10p shares)		20
Capital reduction account		80
(3) Offices and showrooms	100	
Factory and warehouse	38	
Plant and machinery		83
Motor vehicles		10
Stock		25
Debtors		15
Profit and loss account		293
Capital reduction account	288	
	426	426
(4) Bank overdraft	520	
Bank loan		520

		Dr £'000	Cr £'000
(5)	10% unsecured loan stock 19X16	400	
	14% secured loan stock 19X16		400
(6)	Arrears of interest	40	
	Cash		30
	OSC (10p shares)		10
(7)	Cash (10 × 30 + 20 + 10)	600	
	OSC (10p shares)		600
(8)	Capital reduction account (costs)	50	
	Cash		50
(9)	Creditors	310	
	Cash		310

WORKINGS

(i) Capital reduction account

OSC	270
PSC	80
Various Acs	(288)
Costs	(50)
Bal c/d	12

(ii) Cash

Rights issue	600
Interest	(30)
Costs	(50)
Creditors	(310)
Bal c/d	210

Summarised B/S after scheme	£'000	£'000
Offices		380
Factory		260
Plant		207
Vehicles		145
		992
Stock	225	
Debtors	165	
Cash	210	600
		1,592
Loans – bank		520
– unsecured		400
		920
Share capital	660	
Capital reserve	12	672
		1,592

c Comments

(1) General
- (i) development of new products
- (ii) marketing
- (iii) managerial quality
- (iv) future prospects – on realistic basis
- (v) opportunities for diversification
- (vi) financial backing from outside (confidence)
- (vii) takeover alternative to rights issue
- (viii) support of employees.

(2) Size of rights issue – too large?
    (i) working capital needs
    (ii) capital expenditure needs.
(3) Voting structure/board representation.
(4) Fairness of scheme (creditors paid in full)?
(5) Willingness of loan stock holders to put more cash in to company?

ANSWER 25.4 (ADVANCED)

Pourwell (reconstruction)

WORKINGS PART (A)

		£'000
(1)	L + B (120 − 100 + 19.2)	39.2
(2)	Goodwill w/o (150 − 10% × 150)	135.0
(3)	Development expenditure	
	Per B/S	87.5
	Contribution	
	15% (75 + 125 + 150 + 150)	75.0
	∴ w/o	12.5
(4)	Stocks $\frac{696}{6}$	116.0
(5)	Plant (58,824 − 90,800 + 47,880)	15.904
(6)	Pref. shares	
	50% × 100	50
	less ords 300,000 × 10p	30 20.0
(7)	Unpaid div 2 × 7,000	14.0
(8)	Ord. shares 200,000 × 90p	180.0

(9) P/L

B/F		(97,160)
Loss for year		
Gross profit		
(696,000 − 410,778)	285,222	
Distribution costs	(200,101)	
Admin. expenses	(105,113)	
Goodwill w/o	(15,000)	
Profit on sale of land	15,000	
Interest (7,100 + 5,250)	(12,350)	
Dividends received	5,000	(27,342)
C/F		(124,502)

SOLUTION PART (A)

Reduction and reconstruction account

	£		£
Goodwill	135,000	Land	39,200
Development expre	12,500	Plant	15,904
Stocks (170.102 − 116)	54,102	Directors loans waived	100,000
Debtors	19,200	Pref. shares	20,000
Pref. div.	14,000	Ord. shares	180,000
Profit and loss	124,502	Bal C/D	4,200*
	359,304		359,304

* Strictly speaking, the terms of the reconstruction should be arranged such that the final balance on this account is either nil or a credit balance.

WORKINGS PART (B)

(10) Stock

Raw material	20,210
WIP	10,103
Finished goods (W4)	116,000
	146,313

(11) Debtors

Control	89,505
Tax credit	1,500
Ins. prep.	4,000
W/O	(19,200)
	75,805

(12) Creditors

	less than one year	*more than one year*
App. (iii)	93,490	
	50,060	
	30,000	} 258,550
	35,000	50,000
Exp. Acc.	1,900	
Wages acc.	2,100	
Audit acc.	2,850	
Debentures		75,000
Less requiring		
immediate payment	(93,490)	
Per B/S	121,910	125,000

(13) Cash

note: rights issue to be made to raise sufficient cash to give
company a current ratio of 2:1

Current liabilities		121,910
∴ required current assets (X2)		243,820
Less stock	146,313	
debtors	75,805	
		222,118
∴ cash		21,702

Amount required from rights issue to
provide this closing balance:

	£
Present overdraft	38,022
Payment of creditors	93,490
Debenture interest	10,500
Preference dividends	14,000
	156,012
Required closing balance	21,702
∴ rights issue	177,714

(14) Share capital

		£
Ordinary shares less amounts w/o (200,000 − 180,000)		20,000
Issued to directors 250,000 10p shares		25,000
Issued to preference shareholders (6 × 50,000) 10p shares		30,000
Issued for cash at 18p		

$$\frac{177,714}{18p} = 987,300 \text{ shares}$$

i.e. nominal	98,730	98,730
premium	78,984	
	177,714	
Total		173,730

SOLUTION (PART B)

Balance sheet as at 31 December 19X5 (after reorganisation)

	£	£
Fixed assets		
Intangibles – development expenditure		75,000
Tangibles – land and buildings	120,000	
– plant and machinery	58,824	
– fixtures and fittings		
(9,900 − 4,620)	5,280	184,104
Investments		42,500
		301,604
Current assets		
Stock	146,313	
Debtors	75,805	
Cash	21,702	
	243,820	
Creditors due in less than one year	121,910	
Net current assets		121,910
Creditors due after more than one year		(125,000)
		298,514
Capital and reserves		
Ordinary share capital		173,730
Preference share capital		50,000
Share premium account		78,984
Reconstruction account		(4,200)
		298,514

ANSWER 25.5 (ADVANCED)

Combined Engineering

WORKINGS AND SOLUTION

		£'000
(1) *Properties – Rex*		
Per B/S		1,352
NBV of properties sold (1)		(950)
W/D on remaining property (4)		(100)
Adjusted figure		302
(2) *Stocks – Rex*		
Per B/S		3,368
Cost of stocks sold		
Loan to be repaid (1,000 + 150)	1,150	
Available from sales of properties		
(1,200 − 750)	450	
	700	
Cost of stocks sold $\frac{100}{70} \times 700$		1,000
Adjusted figure		2,368
(3) *Overdraft – Rex*		
Per B/S		1,817
Management Venture Capital		(600)
		1,217

(4) *External loans – Rex*

Per B/S	2,000
Repaid (1)	(750)
Repaid (4)	(150)
Venture Capital (7)	600
	1,700

(5) *Inter-co loans – Rex*

Per B/S	1,000
Temporary	150
Repaid (1,200 – 750)	(450)
Repaid – car stocks	(700)
	—

(6) *P/L reserves – Rex*

Per B/S	499
Profit on sale of property (1,200 – 950)	250
Write down on property	(100)
Loss on stocks (1,000 – 700)	(300)
	349

Pro-forma Balance Sheet of Rex Garages as at 31 July 19X2

	£'000	£'000
Tangible fixed assets		
Property		302
Plant and machinery		462
Vehicles		437
		1,201
Current assets		
Stock	2,368	
Debtors and prepayments	1,675	
Cash	8	
	4,051	
Creditors due within one year		
Trade creditors and accruals	1,486	
Bank overdrafts	1,217	
	2,703	
Net current assets		1,348
Total assets less current liabilities		2,549
Creditors due after one year – loans		1,700
Capital and reserves		
Share capital	500	
Profit and loss account	348	849
		2,549

(7) *Shares in subsidiaries – CE*

Per B/S	1,550
Rex	(500)
	1,050

(8) *Loans to subsidiaries – CE*

Per B/S	2,000
Rex (fully repaid)	1,000
	1,000

(9) *Overdrafts – CE*	£'000	£'000
Per B/S		17,483
Redundancy (2)		450
Sale of Rex		
Per draft B/S (500 + 499)	999	
Adjustments (250 – 100 – 300) (150)		(849)
(working (6))		
Repayment of loan		(1,000)
		16,084

(10) *P/L reserves – CE*		£'000
Per B/S		2,830
Redundancy (2)		(450)
Profit on sale on Rex (849 – 500)		349
Adjusted		2,729

SOLUTION

Pro-forma B/S of Combined Engineering as at 31 July 19X2

	£'000	£'000
Tangible fixed assets		
Property		3,646
Plant and machinery		4,201
Vehicles		2,948
		10,795
Investments		
Shares in subsidiaries	1,050	
Loans to subsidiaries	1,000	2,050
		12,845
Current assets		
Stock	12,529	
Debtors and prepayments	11,620	
Cash	25	
	24,174	
Creditors due within one year		
Trade creditors and accruals	11,206	
Bank overdrafts	16,084	
Net current liabilities	27,290	(3,116)
		9,729
Creditors due after one year – loans		5,000
Capital and reserves		
Share capital	2,000	
Profit and loss account	2,729	4,729
		9,729

ANSWER 26.1 (ADVANCED)

Norfolk

SOLUTION

(a) Dealing with each matter in turn (reference – Auditing guideline on prospectuses, and the reporting accountant, Appendix 2).

  (1) *Essex*
    Essex was acquired by means of a share-for-share exchange with no resources leaving the

group. For meaningful comparison over a 5-year period it is necessary to include the results of Essex for 19X1 and 19X2. (Had the group chosen to merger account for the combination, the 19X1 and 19X2 figures for Essex would have been included anyway.)

(2) *Kent*

The shares in the associated (related) company were bought for cash. For 19X4 onwards group results included the appropriate share of the results of Kent as opposed to the earnings which the cash used for the purchase would otherwise have earned. It is not therefore appropriate to include the results of Kent for 19X1, 19X2 or 19X3 although there is nothing to prevent them from being referred to in memorandum note.

(3) *Goodwill policy*

The 5-year summary should reflect the new group policy regarding all types of goodwill. The profits of the group for 19X1 and 19X2 should therefore be adjusted.

(4) *Exceptional item*

The £50,000 recovery in 19X4 should also be classified as exceptional.

(5) *Extraordinary items*

The items could all be regarded as extraordinary although it could be argued that the damages of £25,000 in 19X4 were not material in amount and could thus be regarded as normal trading items. However no adjustment of this kind has been reflected in the solution in view of the size in relation to other amounts adjusted.

(6) *Disposal of subsidiary for cash*

As the disposal was for cash, the result of later years reflect earnings from the cash and so no adjustment to group figures is required. It may however be useful to disclose the 19X1 and 19X2 figures by way of memorandum note simply to provide useful information.

(7) *Related company*

Prior to liquidation the results of this company were included in group results in the normal way. The event of liquidation provides no reason for adjusting these figures.

(b) Tabulation of group results for items specifically mentioned:

	19X1 £'000	19X2 £'000	19X3 £'000	19X4 £'000	19X5 £'000
Turnover					
As published	3,000	4,500	5,800	7,200	8,000
Adjustment Essex	800	1,000	—	—	—
Per circular	3,800	5,500	5,800	7,200	8,000
Exceptional items					
As published	—	(200)	—	—	—
Adjustment	—	—	—	50	—
Per circular	—	(200)	—	50	—
Share of profits (losses)					
of related companies	70	(20)	—	210	228
Profit on ordinary activities before tax					
As published	253	352	450	600	650
Adjustment Essex	40	50	—	—	—
Adjustment goodwill	12	10	—	—	—
Per circular	305	412	450	600	650
Profit on ordinary activities after tax					
As published	128	172	225	290	320
Adjustment Essex	20	25	—	—	—
Adjustment goodwill	12	10	—	—	—
Per circular	160	207	225	290	320

Extraordinary items					
As published	(400)	120	(290)	25	90
Adjustment Essex	—	15	—	—	—
Per circular	(400)	135	(290)	25	90
Tax on extraordinary items	200	(60)	145	—	(45)

ANSWER 26.2 (ADVANCED)

Avaricious

SOLUTION

(a) *Investors' ratios in Parochial Ltd*

	Dividend £'000 (1)	Number of shares ('000) (2)	Dividend per share pence (1)÷(2)	Profits available to pay ordinary dividend (£'000) (3)	Dividend cover Times (3)÷(1)
19X4	27	400	6.7	89	3.3
19X5	17	400	4.2	95	5.6
19X6	22	400	5.5	157	7.1
19X7	15	400	3.7	185	12.3
19X8	20	400	5.0	294	14.7

(b) *Value of Parochial Ltd*

The most appropriate basis for the valuation of an entire company is the earnings basis. Net assets per share would provide an additional figure which might be useful for cross-checking. Dividend basis would not usually be relevant as future dividend policy could well differ from past policy.

(1) Earnings basis:

Growth in earnings year-by-year is as follows:

19X5	6.7%	(compared with 19X4)
19X6	65.3%	
19X7	17.8%	
19X8	58.9%	

With this record of growth and in the absence of reliable profit forecasts it would seem more appropriate to consider 19X8 earnings of £294,000 rather than to take a weighted average.

As regards an appropriate price earnings ratio, it is necessary to consider companies K and L. Both companies have dividend cover somewhat below that of Parochial. However, the P/E ratio of L is more than double that of K. The reasons for this are not given but it could be that L has a more impressive track record and superior quality of earnings. In the absence of further information, an average P/E ratio of 11.6 is considered appropriate for the purposes of valuing the earnings of Parochial.

On an earnings basis, Parochial would be valued at 11.6 × £294,000 = £3.4 million (or £8.50 per share).

(2) Asset basis:

This basis may be unsatisfactory for several reasons—
  (i) goodwill does not appear in the balance sheet
  (ii) there is no indication of current values of properties.

Other assets are assumed to be included on a prudent basis.

Subject to the above, net assets per share based on the most recent asset statement amount to £3.24 per share (£1,297 − 400,000). This clearly understates significantly the true share valuation.

Conclusions: A valuation for the entire company might lie around £3.5 million dependent on additional factors such as likely future earnings, effect on existing business and market reputation and so on.

(c) Additional topics to be dealt with in accountants' reports include:

(1) Statement of accounting policies on key areas
(2) Summarised balance sheets
(3) Source and application of funds statements.

Comparability between the five years is crucial. The above information should assist in evaluating trends and progress over the period. Where necessary figures of earlier years may need to be restated to ensure comparability with the latest period reported upon.